D0839796

THE TWICE BORN FICTION

To a former teacher

The Twice Born Fiction

Themes and Techniques of the
Indian Novel in English

MEENAKSHI MUKHERJEE

ARNOLD-HEINEMANN PUBLISHERS
(INDIA) PRIVATE LIMITED

PR
9737
M8
1974

Published by Gulab Vazirani for Arnold-Heinemann Publishers (India) Private
Limited, AB/9, Safdarjang Enclave, New Delhi 110016, and printed in India
by Dhawan Printing Works, 26-A, Mayapuri, Phase-I, New Delhi 110027

PREFACE TO THE SECOND EDITION

Less than three years have passed since the first edition of this book appeared—a period hardly long enough for new trends to be discerned or for perspectives to alter. Hence no major revision or addition was required. Further, since this book is not a chronological survey, there was no question of updating it to include novels published after 1971. However, a few important novels published after 1971 which have a bearing on the themes and techniques discussed in this study have been mentioned in the concluding chapter. Similarly, a few book-length critical works that have appeared recently have now been added to the select bibliography.

New Delhi 1974   Meenakshi Mukherjee

PREFACE TO THE FIRST EDITION

Indian writing in English is the only form of modern Indian literature that is accessible to critical examination all over the country and even abroad. Creative writing in our regional languages remains confined to critical discussion in their respective regions—except perhaps in the case of Hindi, which reaches beyond regions—and it is difficult to sustain any real exchange between critics of different literatures in the country. The critic of Indo-Anglian literature is thus exposed to the larger world of literary criticism and runs the risk as well as enjoys the challenge of such exposure.

I have chosen to write on Indian novels in English both because the Indian novel is my special interest and because the bulk of Indo-Anglian literature is in the novel form. By designating the Indo-Anglian novel as 'twice born' I have not tried to promote it to a superior caste. I find it the product of two parent traditions, and suggest that a recognition of this fact is the first step towards granting the Indo-Anglian novel its proper place in modern Indian literature.

A research fellowship from the University Grants Commission made it possible for me to rest from teaching and begin this work. Professor S. Nagarajan of the University of Poona helped me to complete it, through long hours of patient discussion and invaluable counsel. Nothing that I can say in words will equal what this study owes to him. While the work was in progress, my husband Dr. Sujit Mukherjee acted as the sounding board for most of the ideas contained here and cheerfully suffered this responsibility. Finally, when these pages got to the stage of printing, my daughter Rukmini helped me a great deal in preparing the index.

New Delhi 1971 M. M.

CONTENTS

1. Preamble   9
2. The Literary Landscape   17
3. The Making of a Nation   34
4. East-West Encounter   64
5. Renunciation as an Ideal   96
6. Myth as Technique   128
7. The Problem of Style   165
8. The Prospect   198
   Note on Indian Novels in English Translation   211
   Select Bibliography   213
   Index   227

1

Preamble

INDIANS have been using the English language for creative purposes for more than a century now, but not until the third or fourth decade of this century was there a serious and systematic attempt to place such writing in its proper historical and cultural context and to evaluate it as literature. The reason for this delay could either be the paucity of material worthy of critical examination or the absence of an appropriate frame of critical reference. An early essay like Edward Farley Oaten's *A Sketch of Anglo-Indian Literature* (1908), for example, uses the term 'Anglo-Indian' to cover all writing in English about India without making any distinction between Indians writing in English and Englishmen using India as material. Even as late as 1934, we find Bhupal Singh using the term in the same inclusive connotation in his *A Survey of Anglo-Indian Fiction*. It was not until K.R. Srinivasa Iyengar published his two early books on the subject, *Indo-Anglian Literature* (1943) and *The Indian Contribution to English Literature* (1945) that Indian writing in English by Indians began slowly to be recognised as a distinct entity, different in nature from the writings of Flora Annie Steele or Meadows Taylor or Rudyard Kipling. A similar claim on behalf of Indian writing in English was made by V.N. Bhushan when he compiled and edited *The Moving Finger* (1945), a collection of critical essays on literature by Indians, and *The Peacock Flute* (1945), an anthology of English verse written by Indians. By the time Professor Iyengar's large and detailed survey *Indian Writing in English* came out in 1962, it was no longer necessary to argue that there *is* an 'Indo-Anglian' literature. A general awareness of the identity of Indo-Anglian writing has now spread in Indian literary circles largely owing to the pioneering efforts of Professor Iyengar. A well-organised group like the Writers Workshop of Calcutta—"a small group which believes that English has proved its ability to play a creative role in Indian literature..."[1]—has done a great deal to place such writing before the reading public in India and abroad through its journal *Writers Workshop Miscellany* (1960) as well as through more than a hundred slender volumes published under its auspices.

In the last thirty years, the number of Indians writing in English has gone up considerably, and the need for critical evaluation has become more urgent than ever before. Existing criticism and scholarship have so far been largely historical or sociological in approach—which are valid in their own ways and perhaps necessary at the initial stages of the critical discovery of a literature—but other modes of scrutiny remain unattempted. The Indo-Anglian novel, which is the special subject of this study, has in the last decade or two been frequently discussed in reviews and articles in periodicals, both in India and abroad. But usually these commentators seem to labour under certain pre-conceptions about the unsuitability of the English language as a medium of literary expression for Indian writers, and instead of specific analysis of the book in hand, they use the book as a substantiation of their own existing point of view. Thus a review of R.K. Narayan's *The Guide* begins with the remark : "A creative work of first order can be produced by an author in his mother tongue alone. Consequently, it follows only in works executed in such a language can a true picture of a nation or a people be discovered."[2] A reviewer who begins with this hypothesis can hardly bring an objective mind to the evaluation of a literary work which happens to have been written in a language other than the mother tongue of the writer. On the other hand, there is the tendency among some enthusiastic commentators especially in England and America to admire the very existence of Indian writing in English without paying much attention to the specific work. A review of Kamala Markandaya's *Possession* begins by describing the 'strange and beautiful' qualities of Indian

English : "There is a lilt in it, and it seems inevitably to gather
to itself a richness of colour and texture that is foreign to our
more tepid skies. The important thing is that it is a language
of its own, with its own history, its own way of looking at things."[3]
Neither of these two fairly typical instances of views unsubstantiated by analysis is of any help in understanding Indo-Anglian
fiction, much less in evaluating it. Objective and responsible
reviewing is rare, though not entirely absent, but on the whole
Indo-Anglian novels have not been well served by criticism.

Another variety of opinion about Indo-Anglian fiction is contained
in the prefaces and forewords that are sometimes attached to the
novels and later perpetuated as critical axioms. At one time these
prefaces served a useful purpose as in the case of Mulk Raj
Anand whose first novel *Untouchable* was turned down by nineteen
British publishers until E.M. Forster wrote a preface for it.[4] Now
that the Indo-Anglian novel is being accepted in publishing circles
without such support, commendatory appendages are on the decline. But the practice dies hard, and ever since Graham Greene compared R.K. Narayan to Chekov in his foreword to Narayan's *The
Bachelor of Arts*, it has been customary to suggest such comparisons with the compliments, as it were, of the writer of the
foreword. Thus Iqbalunnisa Hussain was hailed as 'the Jane
Austen of India, by C.R. Reddy,[5] G.V. Desani as the Indian
Joyce, and Hilton Brown in a foreword to K. Nagarajan's *Chronicles
of Kedaram* clutched at several comparisons and ended up by
likening Nagarajan to the author of *Main Street* or of *Cranford* or
at least of *Annals of the Parish*.

Apart from Professor Iyengar's comprehensive historical survey
which will remain for long an invaluable source of information on
the subject, two studies of Indo-Anglian fiction have appeared
during the last decade. Dorothy M. Spencer's *Indian Fiction
in English* (1960) is actually an annotated bibliography, but its long
introductory essay contains several observations of critical interest.
Miss Spencer isolates certain stereotypes of Indian fiction in general,
like the peasant or the ideal woman, and speculates on the author's
attitudes and values as revealed through these stock characters.
She is, however, more concerned with ethnographic depiction in
literature than with literary criticism, and for this reason she treats

together all Indian novels available in English without making any distinction between original English works and those translated from the Indian languages. She denies the existence of 'any marked difference' between the two kinds, that is, of the possibility of the separate existence of Indo-Anglian fiction.

More recently, M.E. Derret's M.A. thesis submitted to the London University in 1964 has been published by the Institut de Sociologie of the Universite Libre de Bruxelles as the third publication in the series 'Collection du centre d'etudes du Sud-Est Asiatique' and is entitled *The Modern Indian Novel in English : A Comparative Approach* (1966). As the auspices of publication indicate, the work combines sociological and historical elements with literary study. The author deals mostly with novels published after 1947, and her sources of reference include a large number of personal letters from the novelists she has discussed. Only four (out of the eight) chapters deal with the Indo-Anglian novel proper; one of the three appendices is "Some observations from the novels on the Background of Life for British People in India." Literary assessment as such is absent from this rather heterogeneous study, and it is not surprising that she should conclude : "the aims of the authors, their real necessity is to express their mixed and sensitive feelings to a potentially, and very recently interested outside world... to widen understanding within India and abroad." (p. 147) She even suggests that applying strict international standards of literary criticism to these works is "not entirely just".

So many western critics and reviewers have tacitly agreed on such a double standard of criticism while dealing with Indo-Anglian literature that William Walsh's rigorous and uncondescending evaluation of R.K. Narayan in *The Human Idiom* (1964) comes as a refreshing change. Professor Walsh's essay[6] is important because, instead of the lumping together of all Indo-Anglian novelists for the purpose of faint praise or safe censure, he makes a serious analytical study of one particular novelist—even more unusual, of one particular novel. This kind of patient and informed practical criticism of single works is still quite rare except occasionally in the pages of Indian journals like the *Writers Workshop Miscellany* (Calcutta) and *The Literary Criterion* (Mysore), both of which

have contributed significantly to the general awareness of the possibilities of Indo-Anglian writing.[7] Among studies of specific
novels, David McCutchion's review articles on Raja Rao and B.
Rajan in the *Miscellany*[8] and S. Nagarajan's essay in the *Sewanee
Review* (Summer 1964) on Raja Rao's *The Serpent and the Rope*
deserve special mention. The same novel of Raja Rao has been
discussed more elaborately in a study done jointly by B.M. Razdan
and S.P. Ranchan and serialised in *The Illustrated Weekly of India*.[9]
C.D. Narasimhaiah has published several detailed analyses
of important Indo-Anglian novels in *The Literary Criterion,* and
his recent book *The Swan and the Eagle* (1969) contains long essays
on Mulk Raj Anand, R.K. Narayan and Raja Rao. Critical
studies of this nature, by Indian as well as foreign authors, are
beginning to appear regularly in journals abroad like *Literature East
and West* in America and *The Journal of Commonwealth Literature* in
England. Incidental comment on Indo-Anglian literature also
occur more frequently nowadays in books in English about
Indians and by Indians. For example, in his *Area of Darkness*
(1964) V.S. Naipaul devotes several pages to a discussion of Manohar Malgonkar's *The Princes,* and Dom Moraes refers to several
Indo-Anglian novels and novelists in his travelogue *Gone Away*
(1960). In general, the views of a practising novelist on a contemporary work would be interesting, but as it happens Naipaul
uses *The Princes* to illustrate his thesis that the educated Indian is
insensitive to the realities of Indian life. The characteristics of a
single work of fiction are employed to make an illicit generalisation when Naipaul says, "This is the Indian withdrawal and
denial; this is part of the confusion of Indian Anglo India." (p. 71)
    The general problems of Indo-Anglian writing have received
much more attention than individual books or authors. Such
general discussion has, on occasion, generated a great deal of heat
as one can see in the controversies which appeared on the pages of
Quest (28: Winter 1960, 29: Spring 1961), *The Statesman* (December 3, 4 and 17, 1961), *The Times Literary Supplement* (September 17
and 24, 1964), and *The Times of India* (July 3 and 10, 1966).[10]
In 1968, an 'All-India' seminar on 'Indian Writing in English'
—perhaps the first of its kind—was held in the University of Mysore
in January; later that year, Karnatak University (Dharwar) pub-

lished their *Critical Essays on Indian Writing in English* (edited by M.K. Naik, S.K. Desai and G.S Amur), the first such collection in book-form, containing twenty-four analytical essays on various aspects and texts of Indo-Anglian literature.

A note on the term *Indo-Anglian* may not be irrelevant here. Prevalent in common use for more than ten years now, this label for original creative writing in English by Indians has not yet gained unanimous approval within India. Professor Iyengar, who made the term current, has justified its use on the following grounds : that of all the possible combinations of the two words *English* and *India*, *Anglo-Indian* has an obvious ethnic connotation in Indian life and cannot therefore be used in another context like literature; *Indo-English* is suitable, but cannot be used conveniently both as an adjective as well as a substantive; *Indo-Anglian* is, there-fore, the only remaining possibility.[11]   A year later Professor V.K. Gokak re-defined the term, distinguishing it from *Indo-English*, a term which he proposes to describe translations from Indian literatures into English.[12] Professor Iyengar, it may be noted, does not always maintain this distinction, and the bibliography appended to *Indian Writing in English* does not discriminate bet-ween the works written originally in English and those translated into English.   Both Professor Iyengar and Professor A.R. Wadia—author of an earlier work, *The Future of English in India* (1954)—have regarded Rabindranath Tagore as an Indo-Anglian, and even today the distinction between an original work in English and a translation is not always regarded as important.

In the Mysore University seminar referred to above, an attempt was made to eschew the term *Indo-Anglian*.   There is a persistent feeling that it is infelicitous even though it has been in circulation for some time and may be on the point of being confirmed for future use.   Alternatives like *Indian-English* Literature or even *India-English* Literature have been suggested.   Whatever term is finally chosen to refer to Indian writing in English, either by fiat or by usage, it will take some time for it to gain currency.   Therefore, the term current at the moment has been accepted for use in this study.

I have, however, restricted my use of the term *Indo-Anglian* to include only the writings of those who are Indian *and* who have

written in English.[13]   I exclude all novels translated into English
from the regional languages even when the translation is done by
the author himself.   This has been done because the technical,
linguistic and artistic problems of a translated novel, and even its
choice of theme, are totally different from those of a novel conceived and created in English.

Within these limits I have chosen a period of about thirty-four
years from 1930 to 1964 in order to arrive at an assessment of the
problems, achievements, and further possibilities of the Indo-
Anglian novel.   The chosen period seems to me a comparatively
productive period of Indo-Anglian fiction, and just enough time
has elapsed for the writings to get into the kind of steady perspective in which one ought to examine literature.   More recent works
or novelists whose careers begin after 1964 would not submit easily
to this kind of scrutiny.

I have not attempted an exhaustive study of all the Indo-Anglian
novels which appeared in this period but have selected only those
novels which seemed to me open to and deserving of critical consideration.   Of the two hundred odd titles published during this
period, some need never have been written, many are competent
and readable works, and a few are genuine achievements.   I have
undertaken in these following pages to analyse and evaluate the
selected novels against the background of the Indian literary scene
and to investigate the conditions which are responsible for certain
marked trends in the themes and techniques of these novels.

NOTES

1. Published on the back cover of their magazine, in every issue.
2. C.L. Nahal, in *Quest*, 21 (April-June, 1959), p. 98.
3. Robert Payne, *Saturday Review*, (May 23, 1963), p. 34.
4. Mulk Raj Anand, "The Story of My Experiment with a White Lie",
   Indian Literature, (July-September, 1967), p. 40.
5. In foreword to *Purdah and Polygamy* (1944). She has now had to yield this
   pride of place to R. Prawer Jhabvala.
6. A general and thus much less satisfactory survey of Indo-Anglian novelists by Walsh was reproduced from *Encounter* in *The Times of India*
   (October 1 and 2, 1964).
7. Special issues on this subject have now been published by *The Banasthali Patrika* (January, 1969 and July, 1969), *Indian Writing Today*

(January-March, 1970), *Indian Literature* (March, 1970), and *Osmania Journal of Fnglish Studies*, 1971.

8. Nos. 6 and 8, 1961. No. 29 (1968) contains eight essays by McCutchion on Indian writing in English.

9. March 13, April 3 and 10, 1966.

10. *Ten Years of Quest*, (eds. Abu Sayeed Ayyub and Amalan Dutta, Bombay, 1966) reproduces two important contributions to this controversy. A review of the general attitudes to the subject is to be found in the *Writers Workshop Miscellany*, No. 11, (May-August, 1962).

11. Professor Iyengar accepts the responsibilities for giving the term currency but denies having invented it, because it was first used as early as 1883 to describe a volume printed in Calcutta containing 'Specimen Compositions from Native Students'. However, Chalapati Rao has claimed (in *The Illustrated Weekly of India*, May 26, 1963) that it was James Cousins who gave this name to Indian writing in English.

12. *English in India* (Bombay, 1964), Chapter VI, pp. 160-166.

13. Thus I have left out writers like Ruth Prawer Jhabvala and V.S. Naipaul.

2

The Literary Landscape

HISTORICAL and political circumstances combined to give the educated nineteenth century Indian a certain proficiency in the use of the English language—in fact, as the century wore on, being educated came to mean knowing English. By the simple law of casuality a few of them came to try their hands at creative writing. Isolated instances stand out in the nineteenth century as literary curiosities. A Toru Dutt here and a Manmohan Ghosh there are chance products of an accidental concurrence of unusual environment, exceptional opportunities, and, of course, an inherent creative urge. The Dutt family (which apart from Toru and her cousin Romesh Chunder also produced four other poets who contributed to a collection of verse entitled *The Dutt Family Album* in 1870) and the Ghosh family (Manmohan and his celebrated brother Aurobindo) were not representative of the Bengali society of the time. These were unusually talented and highly westernised families which sent their children to England for education quite early in life so that England and English became a natural part of their mental make-up. These writers could not constitute a trend. They were not natural products of the general social and cultural conditions of their time, hence they cannot be evaluated against, nor related to, the history and geography of the India of their time.

45-94/71 (2)

Most of the early Indo-Anglian experiments in literature were done in verse. Prose of a non-fictional variety existed in abundance, but it was motivated mostly by extra-literary impulses like political protest or social reform. The novel, the genre of imaginative lite- rature which gives artistic form to the relationship of man and society, was conspicuously absent until the nineteen-twenties. One reason for this absence may be found in the fact that the novel as an art form came to India with the British and it was new in every Indian literature even though it must be said that the Indo-Anglian novel came into existence long after the novel had become an estab- lished genre in other Indian languages. The delay in the develop- ment of prose fiction in Indian literature has often been related to the late emergence of the historical sense among Indians. The novel as it developed in the western world is particularly concerned with time and space and their effects on man. The novelist has been increasingly less concerned with the unchanging moral verities and their presentation in a timeless setting and more with the precise location of historical man in the flux and flow of society. The modern novelist, especially, views time not only as a dimension of the physical world but also as a shaping force of man's individual and collective history. Place has assumed an equal importance, because every human experience is rooted to its particular point in space. In the medieval age, different countries could borrow stories from each other. The prototypes of some of the Canter- bury tales have been traced back to the *Panchatantra*. But the modern novel is the organic product of a particular environment in a particular society in a given time. It is thus impossible to write a good novel today that remains suspended out of time and space; it must have a definite location in temporal and spatial reality.

Therefore, even if Indo-Anglian poetry could be written by Indians in the Victorian idiom, fashioned by a sensibility moulded by a culture seven thousand miles away, the emergence of a genuine Indo-Anglian novel presupposed historical and geographical aware- ness of the Indian situation. Since the novelist's subject is man- in-society, his subject-matter must also be the texture of manners and conventions by which social man defines his own identity. The fact that the language of this definition was English did not auto- matically secure any guidance of unearned benefit. Indo-Anglian

literature may have begun as a colonial venture vaguely aspiring
to continue the great English tradition,[1] but where the Indo-
Anglian novel was concerned, more was needed than great models.
Whatever be the language in which it is written, a novel by an
Indian writer demands direct involvement in values and experiences
which are valid in the Indian context. There was a certain lack
of such direct involvement in the early generations of English-
educated Indians who hoped to create literature in English; those
in whom the involvement was direct and decisive took either to
creative activity in their own language, or to constructive work in
other areas like social reform and political organisation.

The Indo-Anglian novel made a diffident appearance in the
nineteen-twenties,[2] then gradually gathered confidence, and established itself in the next two decades. The momentum has yet to
subside, and more novels have been published in the 'sixties than
ever before. This increase in output is difficult to account for,
especially when there were hardly half a dozen Indo-Anglian novels
until the year 1920. Perhaps one of the reasons is that the flower-
ing of Indo-Anglian fiction coincided with the novel's coming of age
in the regional languages of India.[3]

Since Bengal was the first region to come in close contact with
the British, the earliest Indian novels came to be written in Bengali.
The first few attempts consist of sketches of contemporary Bengali
society, but the new genre really became established with the
historical novel form. It is interesting to note that the novel
emerged at different times in different regions of India, but almost
everywhere the first crop showed a preoccupation with historical
romance. In fact, the full development of the Indian novel as a
whole, allowing for certain oversimplification of details, may be
divided into three large stages : (1) historical romance, (2) social
or political realism, (3) psychological novels showing an introspective concern with the individual. In most Indian languages—
especially in Bengali, Hindi, Marathi, Kannada and Malayalam—
the developments occurred in this order, although not
simultaneously.

In Bengali, Bhudeva Chandra Mukherjee's *Anguriya Binimoy*
(1857) was a best-seller by the standard of the day but was soon
surpassed in the next decade by the novels of Bankim Chandra

Chatterjee. Bankim Chandra really wrote only one historical novel, *Raj Singha* (1881). The rest were romances based on history, unlike Romesh Chunder Dutta's novels, like *Maharashtra Jeevan Prabhat* (1878), which adhered more closely to historical reality. Bankim Chandra's influence—and through him the impact of Sir Walter Scott—was evident in the early historical novels of Hindi in which Kishorilal Goswami led the field for a long time. The first of his long series of historical novels, *Labangalata* (1891), appeared almost at the same time as Devaki Nandan Khatri's *Chandrakanta*, and together they launched this particular phase of the Hindi novel which continued well into the twentieth century. In Marathi, Hari Narayan Apte was the first to establish himself as a widely read novelist. His first novel, *Maisorcha Wagh* (1890), was a translation of Meadows Taylor's *Tippoo Sultan*, but later on he found his themes in Shivaji's life and times in novels like *Gadh Ala Pan Simha Gela* (1906). Almost contemporary with Goswami in Hindi and Apte in Marathi was Raman Pillai, the Malayali novelist, whose *Martanda Varma* (1891) and subsequent works are based on Travancore history. In Kannada, the novels of Bankim Chandra and Apte were translated and widely read until 1913 when the first modern historical novel in Kannada, *Kumudini* by Galagnath, was published.

Indo-Anglian fiction, the last to be born and to grow up among various branches of Indian fiction, also began with a variety of historical fiction in such novels as S.K. Ghose's *The Prince of Destiny* and S.K. Mitra's *Hindupur*, both of which were published in 1909. The 'history' in these novels, however, is entirely romantic with no basis in actual facts. After a long gap during which practically no Indo-Anglian novels appeared, around 1930 we find a series of historical novels by A.S. Panchapakesa Ayyar beginning with *Baladitya* (1930). Three years later, Umrao Bahadur's *The Unveiled Court* (1933) emulated the lead given by Mitra's *Hindupur* in presenting the story of a native prince's court—which may not be historical fiction proper, but exploits the same glamour of a past time as in the genuine historical novel. It is a subject to which Indo-Anglian novelists have returned more often than novelists in the Indian languages. It may be noted that while in most Indian languages the novel form may now boast of nearly a hundred years of development, in the case of Indo-Anglian fiction the entire development has been telescoped into a span of less than forty years. The result is that the various phases overlap. Interest in historical material sometimes co-existed with the more recent social and political awareness which swept over other Indian literatures of the time.

Social realism was ushered in some time during the 'twenties by Munshi Prem Chand in Hindi and Sarat Chandra Chatterjee in Bengali. They dealt with everyday problems of the rural community, and their immense popularity marks the next phase of development in the Indian novel. Contemporary public issues, whether social or political, began to interest the writers, and the national movement for independence offered them rich and ready material. In Bengali, novelists as different as Rabindranath and Sarat Chandra dealt with different aspects of the upheaval—Rabindranath in *Ghare Baire* (1916) and *Char Adhyay* (1934), Sarat Chandra in *Pather Dabi* (1926), a novel which earned the distinction of being banned on political grounds by the British Raj—though their levels of artistic achievement were not the same. In other novels like *Palli Samaj* (1916) and *Arakshaniya* (1916) Sarat Chandra dealt with superstitions and orthodoxy in village life. Prem Chand dealt with the problem of prostitution in *Sevasadan* (1916), while later in *Karmabhumi* (1932) his theme was the Gandhian ideology. Social problems and politics have always been difficult to separate in India and in Bhagavati Charan Verma's more recent Hindi novel *Bhule Bisre Chitra* (1959) which deals with the thirties we find a portrait of society chequered by the conflict of political beliefs and social ideals. The Marathi novelist Khandekar appeared on the literary scene around 1930 with his strong idealism for social and political service; his novels, like *Kanchan Mruga* (1931), *Hirwa Chapha* (1937), *Don Mane* (1937), tell the same story in another Indian language. Even N.S. Phadke, who had already found his audience in Maharashtra with dainty novels woven round love interests, began to introduce a political element into his love-stories to become up-to-date. A Marathi critic has recently summed up the literary trend of the 'thirties in these words : "If past history was romanticized by the previous generation of writers, the history of the present was romanticized by some of these novelists, and most readers lapped it up as realism and politics."

The initial vogue of the historical romance was obviously associated with the awakening of Indian nationalism. During the height of British rule, the safest form of patriotism open to Indians was the celebration of past glory. As nationalist feeling came to the forefront of Indian life in the 'twenties and the 'thirties, it was no longer necessary for novelists to make their heroes sufficiently removed in time; the scene could now be shifted to the contemporary battles and agitations. Even the purely social reform novels were inflamed by politics since any desire to improve the lot of the people was bound to be linked with political independence. The concern for one's motherland was very much in evidence, even if the ardour did not always produce literature of abiding value. This second phase in the development of the Indian novel is seen very clearly in Indo-Anglian fiction as we move from Venkatramani's *Murugan the Tiller* (1927) and *Kandan the Patriot* (1932) to Mulk Raj Anand's passionate progressivism, and the emotional zeal for Gandhian ideals in Raja Rao's early work.

While the vogue of the historical novel and the era of social-reform fiction can be traced quite distinctly in most Indian literatures, the third phase is not so clearly seen because in some languages it is still in the process of emerging. In Bengali fiction, the trend towards introspection starts in the late 'thirties with young writers who belonged to the *Kallol* group.[5] Its first traces can be seen in the early works of Buddhadev Bose, and it had continued in various forms until in the 'sixties we find it has been complicated further by a growing sense of loneliness and drift, derived perhaps from existentialist thinking. In Hindi, Agyeya is the most powerful representative of this shift of emphasis from the public issues of society to the private agonies of the individual, while novels like Ilachandra Joshi's *Jahaz Ka Panchi* (1955) or Naresh Mehta's *Dubte Mastool* (1954) give further evidence of this shift. Similarly, in Marathi the novels of Mardhekar (*Ratricha Divas*, 1942) and Vasant Kanetkar (*Ghar*, 1951) illustrate the changes overtaking Marathi fiction towards probing analyses of the inner life of human beings. Many of the Indo-Anglian novels written in the fifties seem to participate in this all-India trend. The serious Indo-

Anglian novelist no longer seems interested in simply documenting or hopefully improving the country, but in trying to depict the individual's groping towards self-realisation. The present study will attempt to assess how far these intentions have been artistically realised.

If the social and literary conditions which gave rise to the novel in the Indian languages also brought forth the Indian novel in English, and if parallel trends can be observed in the Indo-Anglian novel as well as in the novels of the regional languages, then we must regard Indo-Anglian fiction as a branch of Indian fiction rather than of English fiction. Furthermore, if the Indo-Anglian novel is firmly rooted in the social and cultural ethos of India, then Indo-Anglian fiction has claims to be considered independently of the great tradition of the English novel.

But in spite of the common social and cultural background the problems of the Indo-Anglian novelist are not always the same as those of the novelists writing in the regional languages of India. The Indo-Anglian aspiration in literature faces two large handicaps —first, it endeavours to create literature in a language which in most cases has been acquired rather than spoken from birth; second, it seeks to establish a distinct literature in a language in which great literature already exists. The only comparable case would be that of the Spanish language which is at the disposal of writers in Spain as well as in South American countries like Argentina or Chile. Within the fold of the English language, the case of American literature provides a parallel to some aspects of the difficulties faced by Indo-Anglian literature. There was a time when American critics had to argue for the existence of American fiction as a separate entity from English fiction. They based their argument mainly on the ground that American fiction portrayed the American experience which was so different from the European experience. As the American critic Marius Bewley has pointed out, "The American novel had to find a new experience and discover how to put that experience into art. And the process by which it has been done was one of progressive self-discovery for the nation."[6]

By and large, this finding of a distinctly national experience and its legitimate expression in art is what distinguishes the literature of one nation from that of another. Difference in language is an incidental factor which is becoming less and less important. One notices today the emergence of an Australian literature, a Canadian literature, a West Indian literature, a South African literature, a Nigerian and a West African literature—all written in English, but all as different from each other as American literature is from British. The same argument will justify treating Indo-Anglian literature as a separate entity within the Indian context rather than relating it to British literature.

Of course, an important difference remains. American literature —like, say Australian or English-Canadian literature—is the natural expression of an English-speaking people. This condition does not obtain in India because much of Indo-Anglian fiction is written in a language that in most cases is not the first language of the writer nor is it the language of daily life of the people about whom the novels are written. Thereby a double complication is involved, making Indo-Anglian literature a phenomenon of world literature without a parallel in the world.

Apart from the obvious problem of presenting the nuances of Indian life through a language that is not of Indian origin, the Indo-Anglian novelist is confronted by a number of artistic problems. For example, he has to allow for the heterogeneous nature of his immediate audience. A Marathi or a Tamil or a Bengali novelist stands on a surer ground because he can take for granted certain basic assumptions. The writer and his audience in these cases share a similar background and common experiences, because the cultural units in India tend to be aligned on linguistic lines. The English language cuts across diverse ethnic, religious and cultural backgrounds, and although theoretically this gives the novelist a wider audience in India, it also makes him uncertain of his basic assumptions. Subtle nuances in literature are possible only when the reader and the writer participate in the same process of living. For example, in American fiction of the nineteen-fifties and 'sixties, we find a large number of writers dealing with suburban America, analysing its life with love and malice, irony and despair. The homogenised culture of mid-twentieth century America makes it possible for writers like John Updike or John O'Hara to work in terms of lights and shades of

implications, where a great deal can be suggested by the mere
mention of a detail of dress or manner and even linguistic peculiarities. This kind of suggestiveness is far more difficult in Indo-
Anglian fiction, where, owing to the varied background of the
audience, the writer has constantly to explain rather than imply,
thereby doubling his task.

One way of bypassing the hurdle of diverse backgrounds and
of simplifying the linguistic problem would be to write about
urban and cosmopolitan situations where language is no serious
barrier. In a New Delhi drawing room where north and south
meet, English, albeit a special kind of English, is often the normal
means of communication. But this would be too facile a solution,
though a better solution than that of the Hindi films where
an attempt is made to reach a pan-Indian audience by making
the characters and the situations equally unreal for every section
of the country. Urban culture, specially the more affluent levels
of it, where English is often the language of daily living, does
represent a real slice of Indian life, and, although narrow, it is
varied enough for the novelist to find fictional raw material as
Prawer Jhabvala has done in some of her novels. But in actual
practice very few novelists have restricted themselves to this one
area. In fact, some of the best works in Indo-Anglian fiction deal
with non-metropolitan situations. Nothing could be more pro-
vincial and localised than the life of Malgudi town, yet R. K.
Narayan successfully achieves a universal vision through it.

The Indo-Anglian novelist has sometimes attempted to solve
the problem of heterogeneous audience by choosing themes and
situations that have more or less the same validity all over the
country. These recognisably 'Indian' themes are not many in
number because there is a great deal of regional variation in social
structure, values and customs and problems in different parts of
India, but it is interesting to see how many Indo-Anglian novelists
have chosen subjects where the basic pattern is equally familiar
to all Indians. Take for example the theme of social change : the
disintegration of the old hierarchical and agrarian society or the
breakdown of the large joint family. This is a change that is taking
place all over the country and whether Attia Hosain in *Sunlight
on a Broken Column* writes about a Muslim household in Lucknow

or Menon Marath in *Wounds of Spring* writes about a matriarchal joint family in Kerala or Mulk Raj Anand writes about a peasant family in Punjab (*The Sword and the Sickle*) the underlying situation is real to all Indians, and lies very close to their immediate experience.

Several such 'Indian' themes have emerged to form recurrent patterns in Indo-Anglian fiction, and the patterns are more easily discernible today than they were even ten years ago. The novels laid in the nineteen-thirties and 'forties invariably touch upon the national movement for political independence. This is inevitable because the long years of struggle and sacrifice have shaped and coloured every experience of modern India. A great national experience must surely help in maturing the novel form, because an experience shared by the people at large becomes the matrix of a society and the novel flourishes best in a society that is integrated. The struggle for independence became one such unifying force in the two decades preceding the actual achievement of political freedom, and no novelist living in or dealing with this period could avoid writing about it. This is not a situation unique to Indo-Anglian fiction, because novels in other Indian languages also testify to their intense concern with the national movement. But the phenomenon assumes greater significance in English because this is one of the few pan-Indian experiences of our time and English remains the only pan-Indian language of modern India. Northrop Frye has noted the "alliance of time and the western man" as the defining characteristic of the novel as distinct from other genres of literature. The very genre is western, and it is perhaps a sign of maturity that Indo-Anglian fiction reflects this characteristic orientation of modern thought. E.M. Forster sees the portrayal of "life by time" as the special role which the novel has added to literature's more ancient preoccupation with portraying "life by values." The concern of the Indo-Anglian novel today is the "ultra-historical" modern man whose individuality and personal life are shaped by factors of history.

The awareness of historical forces manifests itself in another preoccupation of the Indo-Anglian novelists. A large number of their novels tend to concentrate on the so-called encounter between East and West, not only at the level of people but also at the level of ideas. This is an area of concern neither limited in scope nor marginal in impact. As a matter of fact, this is one of the most significant layers of Indian experience today and therefore valid material for the Indian novelist. The impact of the West has created certain cultural problems and crises in values in all parts of India, though not at all levels of society, and as such is a theme of all-India significance. The successful writer can exploit the dramatic as well as the symbolic potential of the theme holding the two sides in a poised suspension in an international dialectic. And as Henry James has shown, this inter-cultural theme can often provide the writer with a double-edged instrument with which to carve out a more subtle version of reality than the unicultural essay can.

E.M. Forster was the first English novelist to pit India against England as protagonists. Since *A Passage to India*, no novelist writing in English, Indian or British, dealing with an Indian background, has been able to evade the shadow of Forster. The Indo-Anglians have explored the metaphysical, spiritual, and romantic aspects of the confrontation each in his or her own way. Even when the novel does not deal directly with the Forsterian theme, the personal crisis in the life of each western-educated hero or heroine becomes inter-cultural in nature. The connotation of 'east' and 'west' varies in these novels as do the levels of their artistic achievement. But the absorption of more cultures than one contributes, in many of these cases, to a heightened receptivity to experience. Also, it confirms and asserts the traditionally multicultural make-up of the Indian ethos.

There are, of course, vast areas of Indian life and living where the West has had no abiding impact, and we find some of the Indo-Anglian novelists dealing successfully with these non-urban, indigenous and inward-looking situations and characters. R.K. Narayan once pointed out in an article[7] that western society is based on a "totally different conception of man-woman relationship from ours," and it can certainly be demonstrated that marital bliss is a more frequent subject in Indian novels than romantic love. There are some novelists who deal with the unchanging values of an Indian small town or village, and find their material in the excitement, strain and the clash of temperaments involved in living under the same roof in a joint family. The joint family has always provided rich fictional material because of the variety and complexity of human relationships that it offers. In some recent Indo-Anglian novels, one notices a sense of nostalgia in treating of the joint family, because, along with its spacious group living marked by un-selfconscious give and take, it also represents a way of life that is gradually being lost. The nostalgia, however, does not always descend to sentimentality, and often the central figures in order to seek their own identities consciously try to break away from the kind of life they are nostalgic for.

And often the motivation of rebellion against the family comes from romantic love. In the article mentioned earlier, R.K. Narayan maintains that the theme of the eternal triangle, that perennial peg of western story-tellers to hang their novels upon, is useless for an Indian writer, our social condition not providing adequate facilities for such triangles. Yet a study of recent Indo-Anglian fiction will reveal that even in the Indian context a triangle is very much present; only, the third side of the triangle is often provided not by an individual but by a more powerful and less defined social force represented by the joint family. Thus this familiar Indian institution serves several purposes in Indo-Anglian fiction : it gives opportunity for the study of human group behaviour, it symbolises an expansive pre-industrial way of life, and it represents a deeply entrenched force of orthodoxy against which the individual may find himself helpless. The last-named can perhaps be read in generalised terms as the conflict between two sets of values : supremacy of social hierarchy, and emergence of the individual. Here again the Indo-Anglian novelist who dwells upon this conflict portrays a slice of life that is pan-Indian in its relevance.

Sometimes the conflict resolves itself neatly into two issues : duty to the family, and personal fulfilment. The fulfilment of oneself, however desirable a goal according to the individualistic ideals of Western society, has always been alien to Indian tradition, especially when it is achieved at the cost of duty to the family. The Indo-Anglian novelist thus faces a curious predicament. He is using the language and form of the English novelist, but he has to operate within a totally different frame of reference. Sexual love and personal happiness, those two prime concerns of the Western novelist, do not have such central importance in the

Indian context. The classic ideals of the god-like hero and the patient heroine extol the virtues of the extinction of the ego whereas the novel in the western world often focuses upon the achievement of selfhood or personality. One might argue that classical ideals no longer obtain in the Indian context. But in actual literary practice, numerous characters are found to adhere to classic proto-types—especially the women of fiction who persistently re-enact the suffering, sacrificing role of Sita or Savitri.

Another theme that seems to have fascinated many Indo-Anglian novelists is the place of faith in the socio-cultural life of India. Adherence to rituals, and a simple faith in the superior wisdom of a Guru, shape the action and conduct of many people in all parts of the country. The ascetic or the *sannyasi* has always been held in reverence in India, because renunciation is an ideal not many can achieve, and this partially explains the cult of the Guru very much prevalent all over India. But quite often pseudo-mystic Gurus arise to meet the demands of blind faith, and this process has attracted novelists as different from each other as G.V. Desani, Bhabani Bhattacharya and R.K. Narayan. The imposture is not always pre-planned, and what really matters is not the real or imaginary powers of the Guru, but the phenomenon of faith and attitude of mind implied in such situations. The imposter gains some material benefit, no doubt, but he also fulfils a social need. Hence the ambivalent quality of the novels that deal with this theme : while the blind faith of the people represents an essential moral weakness as well as a very elemental strength, the people who make a business of spiritualism certainly present an aspect of sin or evil. Sometimes the two issues impinge upon one another and the sheer force of simple trust transforms the evil in man's mind into a reservoir of goodness.

Exposing the religious imposter has an aspect of social reform also, and one must remember that in the nineteen-twenties and 'thirties there was a strong wave of protest and reform in the literature of every Indian language. While Sarat Chandra Chatterjee exposed the corruptions inherent in the idealised village life of Bengal, his elder contemporary in Hindi, Prem Chand, fought against the plight of young widows and denounced the evils of dowry and prostitution. It is not mere coincidence that Mulk Raj

Anand wrote his early tracts about the socially depressed more or less in the same period. These broad ideals of progressive liberalism became intensified into a definite literary movement which in Hindi came to be called 'pragativad.' While Yashpal and Nagarjun were its leading exponents in Hindi, Krishan Chander and Khwaja Ahmed Abbas were treading similar paths in Urdu. The inter-lingual character of the movement is seen clearly in the writings of Abbas who is equally prolific in Urdu and English.

These were writers fired with a mission and burdened with a purpose outside the merely aesthetic scope of literature. They were writing in order to promote the betterment of their fellow beings. If some of these novels seem dated today, this is not because the themes have lost their topical relevance, but because the quality of writing in many cases has been unable to survive the test of time. Commenting on the Negro novelist Richard Wright's well-known book, *Native Son*, R.P. Blackmur once said that it was "one of those books in which everything is undertaken with seriousness except the writing." One is tempted to apply this remark to some of the progressive writers in Indo-Anglian fiction.

As the novel developed in the West, the problem of what to say has sometimes been outstripped by the problem of how to say it. Especially in the early years of the twentieth century, the technique of the modern novel was the primary concern of writer as well as of critic. This concern with technique has been slow to evolve in Indo-Anglian fiction, but as early as 1938 we find Raja Rao asserting that the epic method is the most suitable for the Indian temperament : "And our paths are paths interminable... Episode follows episode, and when our thoughts stop, our breath stops, and we move on to another thought. This was, and still is, the ordinary style of our story-telling." How far this method is employed by Raja Rao himself will be discussed in its proper place, but this very attention to technique is a sign of the maturity of Indo-Anglian fiction.

The most recurrent technique in Indo-Anglian fiction has been that of the first person narrative. Moreover, a large number of recent novels are autobiographical in method, if not in substance. Choosing the central character as the narrator solves the problem of "the point of view," a problem which Henry James discussed variously in terms of the "large lucid reflector" and the "central consciousness." Since the theme of some of the best works is the quest for self, this technique is often the most suitable and has been applied in widely diverse situations by Indo-Anglian novelists.

The conscious use of myth for enhancing the effect of a contemporary situation is a device that the Indian novelist has emulated from the West but has naturalised it to the Indian soil. A world-view is required to make literature meaningful in terms of shared human experience, and the Indian epics offer the basis of such a common background which permeates the collective unconscious of the whole nation. As such the Indian writer gains greatly by basing his symbology on this rich mythic material. Also, since most of these myths are part of the heritage of all Indians regardless of their language, using myth as symbol for the Indo-Anglian novelist is an excellent artistic solution of the problems arising out of the heterogeneity of his audience. The contemporary novelist is preoccupied with the idea of expressing the "whole of modern life." In undertaking such a feat, James Joyce turned to the traditional framework of the *Odyssey* in which he could work and achieve a "vital connection" between the demands of the individual creative personality and the influence of the total European literary tradition. For Indian writers, a preoccupation with the Radha-Krishna legend or an allegory based on Draupadi's choice of husbands would provide a similar vital connection. The violence before and after partition becomes a re-enacting of the Kurukshetra fratricide. This is one of the aspects of Indo-Anglian fiction worth study and analysis.

As a new branch of Indian literature, Indo-Anglian fiction is still exploratory in form. But the awareness of its possibilities has made the quest itself vigorous and self-sustaining. Ever since the appearance of the first significant Indo-Anglian novel in 1927, *Murugan the Tiller* By K. S. Venkatramani, the number of novels published every year has constantly been on the increase. Even if the creative experiments in this form had not taken the varied directions they have, the sheer numerical abundance would by now have been enough to demand investigation as a cultural phenomenon. In a country where literatures in fourteen different

languages exist side by side—often quite oblivious of the experiments and achievements of one another—critical discussion of
literary works in English has a special significance. Because
English is a language which even today reaches across regional
barriers—if not at all levels of society, at least at a certain level of
education—it is here that the Indian critics can stand on common
ground and employ critical criteria that are accessible to all. It
is possible here to analyse the experiences that have gone into the
making of Indian literature, and grapple with the problem of how a
successful writer can transform an experience very narrowly
regional in its validity into literature that is universal in its artistic
appeal. It is often said that the achievement of the Indo-Anglian
novelist falls far short of the achievement of the novelist in some
of the regional languages. This may be true, especially in view of
the late development and quantitative disadvantage of Indo-
Anglian writing; but a thorough analysis of the existing material
must precede any such comparative evaluation.[8]

NOTES

1. Thus when Edmund Gosse said that Toru Dutt would have a page
   dedicated to her in the history of English literature, or when George
   Sampson thought that Manmohun Ghose's poems could be read as the
   work of an English poet, both critics regarded such writing as part of
   British rather than of Indian literature.

2. Only a few stray novels were written before that. Those are :
   (1) *Raj Mohan's Wife* by Bankim Chandra Chatterjee. Serialised in
       Indian Field in 1864.
   (2) *Kamala, a Story of Hindu Life* by Krupabai Satthinandhan, 1894.
   (3) *The Prince of Destiny* by Sarath Kumar Ghosh, 1909.
   (4) *Hindupore, A Peep behind the Indian Unrest : An Anglo-Indian
       Romance* by S.N. Mitra, 1909.
   (5) *The Love of Kusuma, An Eastern Love Story* by Bal Krishna, 1910.
   (6) *The Dive for Death : an Indian Romance* by T. Ramakrishnan, 1911.

3. Most of the regional language novels mentioned in this chapter are not
   available in English translation. See note in appendix.

4. M. V. Rajadhyaksha, "Marathi Literature," in *Contemporary Indian
   Literature* (New Delhi, 1959, 2nd edn.), p. 163.

5. *Kallol* : A Bengali magazine which appeared in the early 'thirties, and
   became the nucleus of a rebel group that attempted to move away from
   the influence of Tagore. Many of the older writers of Bengali today

began their career in the pages of *Kallol*.

6. *The Eccentric Design* (New York, 1959), p. 17.
7. "English in India," *The Times of India*, December 2, 1964.
8. All quotations used for illustration from the texts of novels are from editions mentioned in the first section of the bibliography which appears in an appendix.

3

The Making of a Nation

JUST AS the essential predicament of the nineteenth century American novelist was a sense of isolation, the essential condition of the twentieth century Indian novelist, until recent years, was his involvement and concern—involvement with the changing national scene, concern for the destiny of the countny. The independence movement in India was not merely a political struggle, but an all-pervasive emotional experience for all Indians in the nineteen-twenties and 'thirties. No Indian writer, writing in those decades or writing about them, could avoid reflecting this upsurge in his work. Thus many of the English novels written in India in the present century also deal with this national experience, either directly as theme or indirectly as significant public background to a personal narrative. This was an experience that was national in nature. It traversed boundaries of language and community and, since Indo-Anglian novels aim at a pan-Indian readership, this unifying experience has served to establish Indo-Anglian writing as an integral part of Indian literature.

It can be seen from the literature of other countries that a great national experience generally serves as a grand reservoir of literary material which can assume a significance beyond mere historical reality. The French Revolution and its Napoleonic aftermath, the American Civil War and the subsequent reorganisation of the country, the Third Reich in Germany and its repercussions, have all provided novelists with rich material for fiction.[1] Perhaps a comparison between these historical events and the Indian story of independence is not entirely valid. This was neither a bloody revolution nor an armed struggle for power. But it certainly demanded of all Indians a radically new approach to life. It was an emotional as well as an ideological experience spread over a much longer period of time than any other nationalist revolution in world history. And the nationalist movement itself was not a single movement but a combination of many forces sometimes working together and sometimes in contrary directions. The Gandhian ideology may have been the prime mover, but along with it there were the leftist, the terrorist, and the revolutionary parties, working towards the same end through different means. The Gandhian way itself had different implications for different kinds of people. For some, it was a philosophy of life; for others, an expedient strategy in achieving freedom. Some people turned Gandhi into a saint and his teachings into quasi-religious dogma. The ideals of different parties often came into conflict, and the men who matured during these eventful decades felt the pull of different ideologies and sometimes shifted their loyalties from one to the other. Those were years of heady action, and the simultaneous happening of a wide variety of events blurred and confused the basic issues. Any novelist dealing with these turbulent years had to impose an order upon the splendid chaos and thus discern a pattern in it to illuminate the human situation.

The critic's concern is not with the raw material of art, but with the finished product and with the process by which the material becomes transformed into art. To say that the Indian novels written in the first half of this century deal very largely with the independence movement is to say nothing about their value as novels. There are scores of Indian novels which deal with the actions, beliefs and experiences of people who were involved in this movement. A number of them are sincere attempts at recording and interpreting a period of Indian history. But how many of them rise above the level of the documentary by observing the so-called 'figure in the carpet'—namely, the pattern behind the events which illuminates the essential human condition of Indians at this period of their history ?

I

The novels to be discussed in this chapter derive their material
largely from the national and political scene of India between 1920
and 1950. We could classify them in various ways but before choosing any one such principle of classification it would be better to
examine the possibilities of each principle. First of all, among
these writers there are some who carry a burden of commitment
which they hardly ever lay down, while there are others who write
as observers and chroniclers. The difference here is not the comparatively simple one that we can make between propaganda and
art. Among the writers who are ardent believers in the ideology
they are writing about, we find names as diametrically opposed as
Raja Rao and Mulk Raj Anand. Anand's ardour for social revolution, his conviction in salvation through socialistic doctrine, are
undisguised in his novels. His strength as well as his weakness
stems from this fervent belief. Raja Rao in *Kanthapura* appears
to feel an affinity with the Gandhian movement that sweeps over
the village he describes. It is true that the story is narrated by an
old woman who is an active participator in the movement, and the
personality of the author never intervenes directly, yet the commitment of the author to his cause is not difficult to perceive. Among
the non-committed writers again, the degree of detachment differs
greatly. There is R.K. Narayan whose whole achievement depends
on his capacity to remain uninvolved. But there is also Manohar
Malgonkar, who, in a novel like *A Bend in the Ganges*, tries to
stand resolutely outside his subject in order to exploit its potentiality
to the maximum but what he achieves is not very different from
skilful reportage. This is also partly true of K.A. Abbas' *Inquilab*
where the novelist refuses to get involved because he intends to
present the total picture as impartially as he can. The distinction
between committed and uncommitted writers becomes meaningful
only when we examine particular novels.

Another possible way of classification would be to distinguish
between novels that deal directly with the national experience as the
central theme, and novels that use this experience as the background to a personal narrative. Here the difficulty consists in
finding the line that divides the one from the other. While there

are a few novels like *Kanthapura, Kandan the Patriot* and *Inquilab* which deal primarily with the movement, there are others that are clearly concerned with an individual's coming to terms with himself, where national events are important only as far as they touch and affect the protagonist.   There are even a larger number of novels where the historical and the individual strands run side by side and are interwoven in such a way that they cannot be recognised separately.   Also such discrimination would be merely arbitrary, and will not throw any light on the problem of why some novelists have succeeded and others have failed in handling the same material.

There is a third possible way of classifying the novels.   Certain recurrent motifs are discernible in the fiction of this period : the picaresque method in Anand's *The Sword and the Sickle* or in Abbas' *Inquilab*; the theme of growth and maturity as in *Sunlight on a Broken Column* or *A Time to be Happy;* the saga of a family or a community or a village seen against the changing pattern of history, as in Venu Chitale's *In Transit* or K. Nagarajan's *Chronicles of Kedaram*.   But those themes are by no means exhaustive, and they pertain more or less to the content of the novels, whereas a critic's more legitimate concern is with what Mark Schorer calls the 'achieved content.'   The difference between 'content' and 'achiev-ed content' or between experience and art is technique.   Schorer defines the vague and general term 'technique' as "any selection, elimination or distortion, any form of rhythm imposed upon the world of action by means of which our apprehension of the world of action is enriched or renewed."[2]   In this sense theme is not something that can be examined separately from the technique of a novel because the theme is determined by the novelist's choice of point of view.   In recent years critics of the novel have been putting more and more emphasis on the importance of "the point of view" as a means towards the positive definition of theme rather than as the Henry James-device for narrowing or broadening of perspective.[3]

The theme of Raja Rao's *Kanthapura*, for example, is essentially determined by the author's choice of the old woman as narrator. Had Moorthy instead of the old woman been the narrator, the novel would not have had the essential simplicity and directness that it has now, and the complex realities of the *Satyagraha* movement would not have crystallised into living folk-lore. In Nayantara Sahgal's *A Time to be Happy* the theme is defined by the point of view of the aging bachelor who narrates the story; his serenity and his wisdom act as filters through which the agonies and trials of youth are perceived at a distance. In Attia Hosain's *Sunlight on a Broken Column* the troubled years before and after the partition of India are viewed through the consciousness of a young Muslim girl who has led a sheltered affluent life—and this not only determines the tenor of the novel but also the selection of material. It is futile to discuss situation, theme, plot or character as separable elements, because these are all defined and determined by the author's point of view. Any novel is best read as the novelist's reaction to his material.

Thus a more comprehensive and profitable way of grouping these novels for the purpose of analysis would be to classify them according to technique. A comparative study of R.K. Narayan's *Waiting for the Mahatma* and Raja Rao's *Kanthapura* may serve as a useful starting point because these two novels deal basically with the same theme : the impact of Gandhian thought on an ordinary Indian. In Narayan's book this impact is felt by an individual; in Raja Rao's, by a community. But in effect these novels have nothing in common and the difference is the result of the choice of two totally different techniques. *Kanthapura* is narrated by an old woman to a hypothetical listener. The listener, apparently a stranger to the village does not figure anywhere, but his (her ?) presence is indicated throughout by the use of the second person by the speaker. The simple, unlettered narrator's personality is intended to colour the whole movement of non co-operation with the government. The police firing and the exodus from the village are all recollected with a naivete which is not the author's but the narrator's. Raja Rao's choice of this narrator serves several purposes at once. Making this old woman the narrator enables Raja Rao to mingle fact and myth in an effective manner. For the old woman, Jawaharlal is a Bharata to the Mahatma—the Mahatma who, she believes, will slay Ravana so that Sita may be freed. For her Gandhi has attained the status of God, and Moorthy is regarded as his *avatar* in Kanthapura. The characteristically concrete imagination of the uneducated mind pictures the Mahatma as large and blue like the Sahyadri mountains on whose slopes the pilgrims climb to the top, while Moorthy is seen as the small mountain. To her the *Satyagraha* becomes a religious ceremony to which she devotes her sacred ardour.

The second advantage derived by this choice of narrator is that the language used by her is of an elemental quality. Her reaction to things is direct and vivid, not literary and second-hand. She talks of the "pumpkin moon" (p. 236), the streets "milk splashed" on a moonlit night (p. 240), young boys "bright as banana trunks" (p. 245), and of "hearts tied up in sari fringes" (p. 235). The metaphors are taken from familiar phenomena which would come naturally to a village woman.[4] The character also enables Raja Rao to achieve his professed aim of reproducing the rhythm of Indian speech in English as well as of coming closest to the oral tradition of story-telling. In the now well-known preface to *Kanthapura* Raja Rao has stated that the meandering, repetitive manner of story-telling is not only an oral tradition but is also part of the literary tradition in India. He refers to the 2,14,778 verses of the *Mahabharata* and the 48,000 verses of the *Ramayana* to substantiate his view. In *Kanthapura* the constant shuttling back and forth in time is easily justified as an old woman's leisurely manner of story-telling. The narrator thus provides a convenient point of view though she is never sharply individualised. We know nothing about her beyond the fact that she is a widow who has now no one except Seemu (who may be her son or grandson) and has seven acres of wet land and twelve acres of dry land. This numerical precision is again meant to convey the simplicity of the way of life where a man's property is measured not in terms of money but in terms of cattle and land. Her function is representative and her strength lies in being anonymous. She is just one of the many women of Kanthapura who responded to the call of the Mahatma conveyed through Moorthy. Her faith in the Goddess Kenchamma, her respect for the local scholar Rangamma, her unquestioned affection for Moorthy and her trust in him, all these feelings she shares with other women of the village. No quality is given to her that detracts from her representative nature. In this sense she has a choric function.

Waiting for the Mahatma has no narrator as such and the story is related in straightforward third person, seemingly through the point of view of Sriram who, at the beginning, is a shiftless youth spoilt by a huge sum of unearned money and his grandmother's care. Hardly a lovable person, Sriram is conceived in gentle irony. The author keeps an ironic distance between himself and his central figure through whose consciousness all the events are presented. Maintaining this distance is a difficult and precarious task because Narayan never indulges in any direct comment on Sriram.

In the familiar setting of Malgudi Sriram sleeps and eats, sits in his arm-chair, and walks smugly in his circumscribed universe, until suddenly he wakes up in a different world when the Mahatma and his followers come to his town. At first it is not Gandhi but a pretty girl who attracts Sriram towards a new set of values, and to the end Bharati remains the goal towards which Sriram's life moves. There is no mistaking the fact that at the root of Sriram's nationalistic zeal there is no ideological conviction but an infatuation with a girl who believes in Gandhi's way. Yet slowly Sriram too comes under the spell of the Mahatma and begins to identify himself with the cause without really knowing its full implications. That the girl he has set his heart upon should be called Bharati—that is, the spirit of India—may be regarded as symbolic. But the whole tone of the novel is down-to-earth, comical, quite the opposite of the serious, idealistic tone of *Kanthapura*.

The proliferation of the Gandhian ideal in the deep interiors of South India is seen through amusing little incidents that happen to Sriram. Because it is viewed through the consciousness of a rather limited person who cannot see beyond the immediate present, who can think not in terms of abstract ideals but only of concrete facts, the nationalist movement is seen entirely in terms of small events and particular situations. There is no attempt at generalisation. This is a novel of the highly particular. The apathy of the village people is seen through the incident of the picketing of a shop which sells foreign biscuits. The situation becomes uproariously funny as Sriram tries to explain his view to a rapidly increasing crowd. Yet there is a touch of pathos in it because the villagers enjoy the situation as a huge joke, and even

simple Sriram is frustrated by the wall of incomprehension which
seems to separate him from the simpler men of his land. He even
wonders if all his sacrifice is worth the trouble. The enthusiasm
for the freedom of the country is condensed into the shortened tail
of the 'Q' in the slogan 'Quit India' written on the wall :

Sriram dipped the brush in paint and fashioned carefully "Quit
India" on the wall. He wished that he didn't have to write the
letter Q which consumed a lot of black paint... It also seemed
to him possible that Britain had imported the letter Q into India
so that there may be a national drain of black paint. He was so
much obsessed with the thought that he began to write a
modified Q... so that it read, until one scrutinized it closely
"Ouit India". (p. 95)

It is such matters that worry Sriram and not the larger issues of
ideal and principle. He knows his limitations and knows that
although his service is as humble as of the squirrel in building the
bridge to Lanka, even this trivial service will please Bharati. Therefore he overturns trains, sets fire to buildings and performs other
acts of destruction with as much indiscriminate enthusiasm as he
had shown for spinning, for non-violent picketing and for writing
slogans on the wall, unable to see any qualitative difference between
these two kinds of activities.

Sriram's sincere love for Bharati, his transferred loyalty towards
Mahatma Gandhi, and his sense of guilt at neglecting his grandmother—all these combine to give his point of view a peculiar
honesty and authenticity. The impact of Gandhi transmitted
through Bharati changes his whole life, bringing him out of the smug
somnolence of pampered adolescence, just as in *Kanthapura* Gandhi's
impact, conveyed through Moorthy, transforms the life of an entire
community, from the bondage of hidebound orthodoxy to struggle
and sacrifice for an ideal. Both novels have somewhat similar
techniques : seeing a great mass movement through the eyes of an
individual quite limited in his perception. But *Waiting for the
Mahatma* is a novel about that limited individual's growth and
maturity, while *Kanthapura* is the history of a revolution where the
different characters are not important as individuals but as parts

of a greater whole. The movement destroys their homes and ultimately lands the people of Kanthapura, uprooted and impoverished,
in an alien village. There is sadness at the end, a vague nostalgia
when they leave behind their land and their cattle, when Moorthy
departs from the Mahatma's path to become a socialist. Yet, as
the narrator said, there is very little lasting regret because some
abundance has entered their hearts and they look forward to Ram
Rajya. The hope is collective while the loss has been individual.
On the other hand, at the end of *Waiting for the Mahatma*
there is a loss at the national level in the death of Gandhi, but
there is a sense of fulfilment in Sriram's personal life.

Raja Rao has used another variation of the same technique—
namely, of seeing a large movement through a narrowed vision—in
his short story 'Narsiga' in the volume of short stories *The Cow
of the Barricades*. Narsiga is a pariah shepherd boy who hears of
Gandhiji through the master of his *ashram* and prays to Gandhiji
at night : " 'Saint, saint, I fall at thy feet and kiss them. O saint...'
And Narsiga burst into such a flood of tears that it gently floated
him down into softer sleep." (p. 116) Like many characters in
Raja Rao's novels (including Ramaswamy of *The Serpent and the
Rope*) Narsiga sheds unprovoked tears, and the author seems to
weep with him. This is in sharp contrast to Narayan where the
author stands at an amused distance away from the tantrums of
his characters. Like the village folk of Kanthapura, Narsiga the
shepherd boy mingles legend with history and equates the release
of Gandhi from prison with Rama's return from Lanka: "He is
going to fly in the air in a chariot of flowers drawn by four horses,
four white horses." (p. 116) This is repeated three times at regular
intervals, giving the language a deliberately stylised and archaic
effect. This short story is, in fact, a piece of poetic fantasy shot
through with political mythology, consciously kept at the level of
non-realism. Narsiga can romanticise the independence movement and the person responsible for it mainly because he is not
directly involved in it. The extent of his involvement is confined
to throwing stones at 'the redman's railway train.'

Narsiga, Sriram and the woman narrator of *Kanthapura* are all
simple beings, limited in education and sophistication. But
whereas Raja Rao seems to obliterate any implied intellectual differ-

ence between creator and created, Narayan stands apart from Sriram in mildly ironic detachment. Irony, however, is a double-edged instrument—while it lends Narayan an objective stance, it also limits his scope. Raja Rao's strength lies in the strength of his conviction; he aims at rendering his conviction about Gandhian ideology into art. Narayan has no such ambition; he merely studies an ordinary young man's reactions to an issue much larger than the young man's comprehension. There is no attempt at idealising Sriram's interest in the national issue; it invariably remains subsidiary to his interest in a pretty girl. Thus to condemn *Waiting for the Mahatma* as an inadequate presentation of the Gandhian movement is to condemn it for not doing something Narayan never set out to do.

II

Lalu, the central character of Mulk Raj Anand's trilogy, in the third volume *The Sword and the Sickle* is in some ways comparable to Sriram. This is the only part of the trilogy that is related to the national movement towards independence. Lalu has Sriram's ardour for serving the country and the same lack of judgment and discrimination. Here is an excerpt from Lalu's conversation with Mahatma Gandhi, where Lalu proudly describes his part in the peasant's scuffle with the landlord's men :

When we were intercepted in our march on the outskirts of Nasira-bad I called on them to hit back and that had the proper effect... "Your advice to them was utterly wrong in my opinion," the Mahatma said, his face lined with a painful impatience. (p. 205)

This is similar to Sriram's answer to Gandhi when he was asked about his political activities.

He said "For some time I preached 'Quit India', but later I was overturning trains and—" Mahatma looked grave. "You have done many wrong things..." (p. 238)

The similarity however is entirely superficial, because the two

novels differ almost totally in technique. *Waiting for the Mahatma*
is sustained by a single point of view, that of Sriram's, and the
author's ironic distance from Sriram provides situations like the
one quoted above with their comic undertones. In *The Sword
and the Sickle* there is no consistent point of view. For the most
part Lalu is the central figure as well as the 'large lucid reflector'
through whose consciousness events and situations are presented to
the reader. But in many places the author intervenes and narrates
directly, making Lalu a mouthpiece for his own observations and
ideas. It is this confusion of point of view that prevents Lalu
from becoming a sharply defined objective character. Lalu, like
Sriram, has had only a limited education, but his actions, thoughts
and conversation hardly ever betray this. He thinks in terms of
lofty ideals, and his speech often has literary allusions. In one
place Lalu talks of "One crowded hour of glorious life" (p. 355);
elsewhere he refers to "Mahatma's experiments with truth"
(p. 216).

Not only is there a confusion between Lalu's point of view and
the author's point of view, but there is a similar confusion in the
author's attitude towards his material. Irony and seriousness of
purpose mingle in a manner baffling to the reader, and one does
not know if the fantastic 'Count' and his comic aspirations are to
be taken seriously. Is there, or is there not a touch of satire in
passage like this ?

And they immediately began to plan the revolution : Verma
Sahib was to go to Allahabad to arrange for the publication of
Naya Hind; Ram Din was to explore the possibilities of finance
while Lal Singh was to arrange a meeting of peasants...
(p. 130)

In certain situations—e.g., where Lalu leads the procession taking
the dead body of a peasant boy to Allahabad as a protest against
the landlord's oppression—there is no doubt of the author's earnest-
ness. Yet the fiasco that ensues is pervaded with an air of comic
extravagance, almost in the same way as the farcical tea-party
described earlier in the book at the palace of the Nabab of
Nasirabad where the tea gets cold, there is no sugar, the bearer's

fingers are dirty and the milk has skins floating on it. Except
the long speeches of Comrade Sharshar, one is never sure where
satire ends and ordinary seriousness begins.

Anand's main intention however is to get his message across.
"The alleviation of pain and its expiation are the only values given
to our intelligentsia at the present time," he wrote in a letter,[5]
and he cannot be expected to concern himself with subtleties of
technique in a novel. And yet the message loses its effectiveness
because of the uncertainty of technique. Technique is not an
embellishment, but an essential structural element, and a more
vigorous adherence to a definite point of view would have made
The Sword and the Sickle less diffuse and ineffectual as a novel
and perhaps would have got the message across more successfully.

The first two parts of the trilogy, *The Village* and *Across Black
Waters*, dealt with Lal Singh's adolescence in Punjab, and later his
youth as a soldier and prisoner of war in France and Germany.
In *The Sword and the Sickle* Lal Singh comes back to India in 1918
where there is change and restlessness everywhere, and an awareness
of political rights. Lalu meets different kinds of political workers—
the non-violent Satyagrahi, the arm-chair revolutionary and the
communist. He meets Gandhi, but does not agree with his policy.
The novel thus presents a cross-section of the political thought of
the early years of the independence struggle and the theme is
supposed to be Lalu's journey through these conflicting ideologies
until he finds his true mission. But in effect it turns out to be Mulk
Raj Anand's commentary on various people and ideas. The
limited vision of Lalu and the omniscient vision of Anand come
into conflict with each other in the novel and this results in a dissipa-
tion of effect. The intention of the writer is clear, but it does not
always become artistically realised.

The American critic, Wayne C. Booth, has made a distinction
between "self-conscious narrators, aware of themselves as writers,
and narrators or observers who rarely, if ever, discuss their writing-
chores or who seem unaware that they are writing, thinking, speaking or reflecting a literary work."[6] It is a useful distincion because the conscious narrator acts as a chronicler who is concerned with the technical problems of recording events in their
proper perspective, while the unconscious narrator does not

distinguish between events and their literary rendering. In effect the
narration becomes the autobiography of the narrator attempting
to catch as much of the fleeting impressions as possible.

In K. Nagarajan's *The Chronicles of Kedaram* and in Nayantara
Sahgal's *A Time to be Happy* we meet self-conscious narrators who
take the reader into confidence about the difficulties of their task.
The history of the town of Kedaram is related not by the author
but by a sharply delineated dramatised character called Gokarnam
Shastri, an orthodox Brahmin, steeped in tradition and opposed to
change. On no account can Gokarnam Shastri be mistaken for
the voice of the author himself, because one can clearly see the fun
that the author derives at the expense of Gokarna, the conformist, the man without a sense of humour, who thinks Brahmins
are God's chosen people, has a child every year and some years
twins, who is a butt of ridicule for his quick-witted friends and who
speaks in an outdated cliche-ridden style. Pompous and self-
righteous, Gokarna is yet a character with whom the reader can
easily sympathise. The mediocre quality of the narrator's mind is
aptly brought out in the manner of narration as well as in his reflection and 'asides' to the reader. For example, the narrator justifies
the conventional beginning of the story by a rather pedestrian
excuse in the opening paragraph :

> When I set about recording these chronicles, I was faced with
> an initial difficulty, and that was about taking off. There were
> at least half a dozen different openings possible, and I wished.
> if there was no objection to such a course, to go bald-headed
> right into the middle of it and work backwards and forwards.
> But my venerable friend and neighbour, Gangadhar Suri...
> suggested that I had better begin at the very beginning. (p. 3)

This heavy pompous style fits in very well with the character of
the narrator.

The Chronicles of Kedaram does not deal directly with the nationalist movement but with the effects of the movement on a small
town seen through the consciousness of an old-fashioned young man
who, surprisingly, is also an alter ego of his westernised sophisticated friend Vasu. Gokarna disapproves of Vasu's ideas and ways.

He is shocked when Vasu employs an untouchable as a servant, or when he decides to spend a holiday abroad : " . . . sheer madness, I called it. Holidays were best taken at home or at places of pilgrimage." (p. 246) Yet he is constantly echoing Vasu's words:

Kedareshwar, as I have said, was a kindly God—very dependable, as *Vasu used to say.* (p. 41)

It was not as clear as all that when the row began. It was all a confounded jumble, as *Vasu termed it.* (p. 43)

This reference to Vasu's opinions seems to be a device in the characterization of Gokarnam Shastri. He is essentially a second-rate person who needs constant endorsement of his own opinions by his more brilliant friend. There is a great deal of overt irony and humour at the cost of Gokarna : "I am not susceptible to flattery as you can well believe, but his frank reliance on me made me see him in a favourable light." (p. 105) He says this about a shady character in the novel. His words and his actions only convince the reader of his susceptibility to flattery. This ironic gap between what Gokarna says and what the reader perceives, constitutes the real achievement of the novel. If this distance between the author and the narrator is overlooked, *The Chronicles of Kedaram* might appear naive as a novel. But when Gokarnam Shastri is regarded as a consciously created narrator, the novel's technique deserves study.

The narrator is dismayed when after the battle by the Congress for the equality of castes, temples in Travancore were thrown open to every one :

I was unhappy. It was as though saw dust had been mixed with my food. I saw the India of my forefathers crumbling away before my eyes. If this was the prelude to independence what would independence be like ? (pp. 241-42)

Situations and characters are presented to the reader by Gokarna, sometimes with comments, and yet they exist outside him, and the reader is left free to make his own judgment. For example, the barrister P.P.T. Chari is not approved of by Gokarna. Chari is an atheist, he drinks heavily and has western manners; none of these qualities endear him to the narrator—and yet Chari emerges as an upright and likeable character.

Every now and then the reader is reminded of the technical problems of the chronicler when Gokarna makes confessions like this : "I have anticipated a good deal—a chronic defect in these chronicles I am afraid." (p. 95) Or, after a long digression :

> To get back to Vanchinatha Sastri (I am afraid that in these chronicles, I am like one of those engines in big railway junctions, shunting backwards and forward, trying to get a train moving).

By taking the audience into confidence, he gives an immediacy to the events, rather as in the oral tradition of story-telling. The narrator himself is not directly involved in the changes taking place around him. Except for one minor election speech he never actively participates either in the Harijan uplift or in the independence movement ; yet he is not a total outsider, he is an average man, neither rich nor poor, neither brilliant nor politically dumb, one of the many such in Kedaram that make up its population. Thus, in spite of his sharply delineated character, his function is also choric in the manner of the narrator of *Kanthapura*.

The narrator in Nayantara Sahgal's *A Time to be Happy* is a middle-aged bachelor. He too is mainly a chronicler and not a direct participator in the events and his task is made easier by the fact that the central characters confide in him their innermost thoughts. This is an advantage the chronicler of Kedaram did not enjoy; for instance, in *The Chronicles of Kedaram*, the narrator Gokarna is as much in the dark about the actual relationship between Vasu and Nirmala as the reader. In *A Time to be Happy* the narrator is omniscient, and his job is to record the confessions of the hero in a definite order. He digresses here and there and apologises directly to the reader : "The reader will forgive me if here, as in the past, I bring in a little of my own history." (p. 71) "In any case it is difficult to avoid the subject of oneself altogether in any account written in the first person." (p. 72) The narrator is aware of the responsibilities of a writer, his technical difficulties, and Thackeray-like pauses to consult the 'dear reader,' or to confess his shortcomings. We are told repeatedly that he is merely an observer, not an agent in shaping or influencing the course of events, that this is not his own story, but the story of Sanad Shivpal. Yet when this onlooker who is supposed to remain on the fringe gets emotionally involved (as in the incident with Maya), then the point of focus gets blurred. This indicates a definite confusion in technique because the narrator's love for Maya contributes nothing to the total design of the novel and has no relation to Sanad Shivpal's personal crisis, which avowedly is what the novel is about.

Although the central character Sanad Shivpal belongs to a rich westernised family, leading a sheltered life away from the strife of the people, the national movement touches the novel at various points. The narrator himself is an active participator in the Satyagraha movement and spends some years in British jails. This colours his whole view-point and makes it possible for characters like Sohan Bhai and Kunti Behen, Khadi-clad social workers, to appear in a novel dealing mostly with the upper classes of society. Social work also becomes a symbol of a way of life where duty is more important than happiness. An attempt is made to give this personal narrative a larger significance by relating it to events of national importance. Sanad's first posting after joining a British firm happens to be on August 9, 1942, the historic day when the Quit India movement started :

Sanad arrived in Sharanpur in August. As it happened it was August 9, a date that will long be remembered because Gandhi had been arrested the night before, and his arrest was prelude to an avalanche of happenings all over the country which have no place in this account. (p. 108)

In spite of the author's avowal that these historic happenings "have no place in this account," we find the novel is shaped by at least two of those happenings. A clerk in Sanad's office comes to the office wearing a Gandhi cap, and in these troubled days it is enough to provoke the British officer. Sanad later speaks to the

45-94/71 (4)

clerk Raghubir, and it is his first contact with the kind of common
life he knew nothing of, and it is the beginning of his sense of
alienation in his own country. Later, Sanad's marriage with a
college professor's daughter is motivated by his desire to overcome
his alienation from Indian life. The brother of the girl he marries,
a promising young poet, is killed by a British bullet in the August
unrest of 1942, and his shadow lies till the end on Sanad's relationship with his wife.

A Time to be Happy begins with Sanad declaring his decision to
resign from the British firm where he is working. The novel then
moves back in time, and the narrator recalls Sanad's background,
childhood and education. But nowhere in the novel, not even at
the end, do we come back to the initial point. The end, we are
given to believe, is one of happiness and contentment all around.
We find that Sanad has found a sense of belonging by learning
Hindi and by spinning home-made cotton yarn. He also draws
up a more satisfactory contract with his firm. The reader is left
wondering how to relate the beginning with the end. Such flaws
can be attributed to the basic confusion of point of view. A single
method followed consistently would have given the novel a unified
pattern, because the theme would have been defined by the narrator's sensibility, vantage-point and experience. In *A Time to be
Happy* the point of view shifts uneasily between an impersonal
observer, a narrator agent, and an omniscient author, and the
result is not a successful novel, but merely an interesting social
document depicting the educated upper class people who lived in
the period covering the non-cooperation movement, August
disturbances in 1942, the Bengal famine and the great year
1947.

The other technique, that of choosing an 'unself-conscious
narrator' can be seen in Attia Hosain's *Sunlight on a Broken
Column* and Kamala Markandaya's *Some Inner Fury*. In both
cases the method is strictly autobiographical, and in neither case
does the author make any effort to maintain a distance between
herself and the narrator. Both are written in a retrospective manner, both deal with a young woman's personal crisis set against
the larger historical background of the independence movement
of India. Neither avoids the danger of sentimentality inherent in

such reminiscent writing. In *Some Inner Fury* the action takes place in the historical year 1942; yet it is essentially a novel of love. The two individuals who love each other belong to the different races of the ruler and the ruled, and the novel studies the impact of the troubled national spirit of the early 'forties upon their love. *Sunlight on a Broken Column* is a record of the growing up of a young girl in the two decades before and after independence during which India passed through a number of crises, and love is merely one thread in the complex fabric of this ambitious novel. The narrator-heroines of both Attia Hosain and Kamala Markandaya's novels are passive observers as far as political actions are concerned, but central agents of the personal drama which is enacted against the political background.

Laila, the narrator of *Sunlight*, is a young girl when the novel begins, living a sheltered life behind the walls of the zenana in an orthodox aristocratic family. And as Laila changes from the lonely, perplexed introspective girl behind the purdah into a young woman who can think and choose, our perspective on the world changes along with the changes in her vision. Laila's first awareness of the political scene of India is fragmentary, processions seen through the chinks of the terrace wall, the rumour and gossip of servants and later the fractured skull of a cousin in a political demonstration. Since the events are presented through Laila's consciousness, we feel the limited world gradually widening and the circumscribed interests of domesticity giving way to the broader issues of ideals and principles. Her two cousins Saleem and Kamal stand for two different ways, Muslim League and a secular nationalist ideal, and it is not difficult to see with whom the narrator's sympathies lie. Laila may not be a direct participator, but she is not an impartial observer either. Her recording of events carries implicit value judgments.

The novel is divided into four parts and the first three parts are united by Laila's point of view and there is a logical inevitability in their development. In the first part politics hardly touches Laila's life except through rumours of occasional riots : the second and the third parts are full of political activities, agitations, discussions about different party ideals and confrontation between opposing points of view. Elections are fought, and Laila discovers with dismay how little the principles of political theory matter in the practice of actual politics. There is an increasing clarity in Laila's understanding of the situation, which is conveyed through the narration.

The fourth part takes up the narrative fourteen years later. These fourteen years apparently cover a critical period of Indian history. The Second World War, the formation of the Indian National Army, the agitation of 1942, communal violence, independence and partition of the country, the impact of all these events divides the narrator of the fourth part from the earlier idealistic young woman. The novelist's primary concern here seems to consist in bridging the gap in time. The focus is directed on each of the minor characters in turn; the fate of each one of Laila's circle of friends and relatives is brought methodically up-to-date while Laila is seen indulging in an orgy of sentimentality, revisiting her childhood home. While individual case histories certainly have an interest of their own, they do not in this novel contribute to its structural cohesion. Saleem's opting for Pakistan and Kamal's staying back, Zahid's cruel death on the train to Pakistan, Zaira's denial of the country of her birth with the zeal of a convert —all these have dramatic poignancy and some have a certain inevitability, but the documentary elements do not serve the purpose of the central theme. The trouble lies in the confusion of purpose. Does the novelist intend to present from Laila's point of view a picture of men and manners in a particular period of Indian history, or does she intend to present one individual's groping towards self-realisation ? If it is the former, then the case-history method of the last part has some validity; but if the novel is taken as a personal document the last chapter becomes extraneous. As a piece of social documentation *Sunlight on a Broken Column* is competently written, but as a novel it is not satisfactory because of its stock situations, its predictable conflicts between love and loyalty, its over-indulgence in nostalgia and sentimentality, and a general weakness of structure. It is however one of the few novels where the partition of India is presented as the enormous event it was and the narrator (as well as the author) being a Muslim, the issue of loyalty, idealism and expediency are fraught with a special significance.

Some Inner Fury also begins (and ends) on an unabashed tone of sentimental longing, when Mira the narrator opens a dusty silver box in her cupboard to find a torn piece of cloth. The author attempts to forge a link between the beginning and the end by repeating certain words like 'reddish dust,' 'hot,' and 'swirling.' Mira is the central character in the love-narrative while remaining a passive spectator in the political and social upheavals of the times. Apart from Mira's brother Kit who is in the I.C.S. and Richard who is an A.D.C. to the Governor (both, by virtue of their official positions, must stay out of politics), the four remaining characters are all involved directly in social and political action. Hicky the Englishman and Kit's wife Premala devote all their energy to the reconstruction of a village. Roshan Merchant runs a progressive newspaper to agitate for various constructive change while Govind is involved in terrorist activities against the government. Mira remains uncommitted, partly because of her love for Richard. To her an individual is more important than what he stands for, hence Kit the loyal servant of the British *Sarkar* and Govind its arch enemy are both viewed with equal tolerance and understanding. The belief that persons are more important than ideas colours the point of view of the whole novel, and thus a politically neutral attitude is maintained throughout. In the last pages of the novel we are told of the angry mob that separated Richard from Mira. She is asked to leave the place. As she leaves, the crowd turns on Richard to destroy him.

Mira's belief that individuals are more important than their race proves to be naive. The tide of history apparently can sweep aside the aspirations of individual men and women. At the end of the novel Mira accepts defeat and admits that "the forces that pulled us apart were too strong." (p. 285) The tragedy was inherent in the situation, and the romantic nostalgia of the tone made it more or less predictable from the first line of the novel.

It is interesting to note that the vague romanticism of *Some Inner Fury* is further accentuated by the anonymity of its location. In most Indian novels of this period the time and place of action are important factors. The scene of Attia Hosian's novel is Lucknow and its environments, the leisure and grace of the feudal city

being a necessary background. In the novels of Narayan and
Nagarajan discussed earlier, Malgudi and Kedaram play vital roles
in determining the action and development of the story. *Kanthapura* is admittedly a *sthala-purana*: a legend attached to a particular
locality. In Mulk Raj Anand's novel the Punjab and the U.P.
have very distinctive identities. It deals with real places like
Anand Bhavan in Allahabad and some real people. But Kamala
Markandaya consciously avoids naming the location. It is 'the
city' and 'the town' and the characters are vague enough not to give
away any geographical clue. This vagueness fits in with her general
refusal to face life directly. The point is made by Brian Elliot
in a discussion of Australian literature,where he divides Australian
novelists into 'namers and anti-namers,' that "novelists looking for
a cheap universality still pitch their scenes in 'the city'—even 'the
place' or 'the dump' without naming it." He adds, "You could
divide most such writers into two schools. They belong to Snake
Gully or the Dump, namers and anti-namers... It would seem that
the anti-namers are the more incorrigible romantics of the two."[7]
And there is little doubt that the point of view of Mira in
Some Inner Fury and by implication of the author, is in that sense
incorrigibly romantic.

This kind of vague adolescent romanticism is combined with
Gandhian idealism in Zeenat Futehally's *Zohra* (1951). Zohra,
a sensitive girl, brought up in the zenana of an aristocratic Muslim
family of Hyderabad, is married to a practical, efficient, western-
educated young man who does not share her enthusiasm about
poetry and sentimental love. In spite of herself Zohra slowly falls
in love with her husband's younger brother Hamid,who is the stock
romantic hero, melancholy, lonely and forever an outsider. Using
the traditional imagery of Urdu poetry he describes himself : "I
am all out of tune, a kind of broken symphony." (p. 157) The fact
that he is inspired by a selfless love for the country and by the
ideals of Gandhi, only adds to his romantic attraction. The dis-
agreement of the two brothers over the Gandhian method is meant
to indicate a more basic temperamental difference. When Zohra's
husband becomes impatient with the slow pace of progress and
speaks of the need for a quick industrial revolution, Zohra echoes
the words of Hamid : "But is not Mahatma Gandhi doing that ?

Only his is a new way of Revolution.   But it will surely lead to the regeneration of India." (p. 83)

The emphasis of the last line indicates the enthusiasm and simple faith of Zohra.   Zohra is shown as a romantic school girl when she is forced into marriage, her head full of ideas about love picked up from sentimental novels and poetry, just as later her faith in Gandhi's methods is also purely second-hand.   She remains the same naive adolescent till the end, even after three children and many events.   Her idealism is unabated and her feeling for Hamid is exactly the kind described in romantic love poetry—ethereal and dreamy, untouched by physical desire.   But there is no irony in the treatment of Zohra.   The author is not amused at her innocent romanticism, and the reader is expected to have complete empathy with her.[8]

Hamid's interest in the Satyagraha movement becomes a means of sublimating his love for Zohra.   Since he cannot dishonour the family name by declaring his love for his brother's wife, he turns to political work.[9]   Zohra also languishes because of her unrequited love.   Zohra's protracted death-bed scene is the culmination of sentimentality in a novel that can be read as an interesting case of a decadent literacy convention influencing a modern novel.   As in Petranchan sorrets and in the courtly poetry of the Middle Ages, the convention in a certain variety of Urdu love poetry is that the beloved is unattainable : The ashik merely loves her from a distance.   The denouement of Zohra is shaped by that convention.

The heroines of the three novels discussed above are not directly involved in the national movement for freedom.   As a contrast, the hero of K.A. Abbas' Inquilab is shaped directly by the forces of history.   Events of national importance are presented through the point of view of a young man who grows up and comes to maturity in the third decade of the century.   This is not a first person narrative, but Anwar forms the central consciousness of the book and in this respect, the novel is comparable to Attia Hosain's Sunlight on a Broken Column. It is the story of Anwar's development which is determined largely by events of national importance. Every major political incident of the decade between Jallianwala Bagh and the Gandhi-Irwin pact (1919-1931) is recorded in Inquilab, the linking thread being Anwar's involvement in each crisis.

Anwar provides the author with a very convenient point of view, because Anwar sees everything, experiences everything, yet is not committed to any single ideology. Because Anwar is given the capacity (or the essential weakness) to remain uncommitted, of thinking of all sides of an issue and giving every party the benefit of doubt, we can observe the totality of the Indian political scene through his unbiased view. "Being one of the rare ones who were interested in politics but were not fanatically attached to any one party, Anwar was being baited by all the political anglers. Congressmen, Muslim Leaguers, and even the toadies of Government, who called themselves liberal, all seemed to be fighting for the possession of his soul." (p. 218) It is not enough for the author that Anwar should remain non-committed, but he tries to give a symbolic significance to Anwar's neutral position by revealing, rather melodramatically, the secret of his birth. He is discovered to be the son of a Hindu merchant and a prostitute who is casteless by virtue of her profession, and he is brought up in a Muslim family. A comparable situation can be found in Rabindranath Tagore's novel *Gora* where the discovery of his Irish birth becomes a turning point in the Brahmin hero's life. In Abbas' novel the discovery comes at the end and the neutral position of Anwar which was gradually built up in the body of the novel seems totally undermined in the last two pages where his neutrality is given a facile geneological basis and a symbolic meaning is foisted on the circumstances of his birth.

Could it be that he who by birth was neither a Hindu, nor wholly a Muslim, or rather, who was both, an oddly symbolic son of India, was in a peculiarly advantageous position to understand both communities and work for the synthesis that was symbolised in his person. (p. 384)

Anwar's involvement in the destiny of the country, his development and maturity which were traced with confidence till the very end, are rendered trivial by this cheap symbolic trick. What could have been a satisfactory novel depicting the effect of great historic forces on a sensitive individual is finally reduced to a journalistic tract with a conclusion worthy of a Bombay film.

The ending of D.F. Karaka's *We Never Die* (1944) is somewhat similar in nature. Dealing with the upsurge of nationalism in an unnamed Indian village, this novel describes stock situations (a sensitive girl married to a crude husband, the curse of an angry goddess on an Englishman, a local prince collecting women for his harem from the countryside) and ideal relationships (friendship between an Englishman and an Indian, the true love between a sophisticated I.C.S. officer and a village belle, even though they have seen each other only once). Communal riots and terrorist activities are described. But the book ends on a note of easy optimism. A Hindu-Muslim marriage is regarded as symbolic and it is suggested that out of this marriage will be born the true India, heralding a new era. Karaka is bent upon 'connecting' at all costs : connect the Hindu and the Muslim, connect the British and the Indian, connect the village and the city, and all shall be well. The theme is presented not so much through the actions and responses of the characters, but stated plainly in long explanatory speeches given to them. For example, Ram Chandra, an idealistic I.C.S. officer, elaborates on his reaction to the creed of non-violence :

It grips me. I know nothing will come out of it, because as a protest it is feeble; as a challenge it is futile... But it does not try to appeal to my judgment. The appeal as it reaches me is emotional, and that's where it touches me. (p. 95)

Later on he gives his reason for marrying the village girl Ayesha, "Who knows, for she is Muslim and I am Hindu and from us may spring that new India." (p. 166)

This was written some years before 1947, before the violent outbursts of communal hatred rent the country and a theoretical and idealistic approach to Hindu-Muslim amity was not surprising. But the same idealism can be traced in some post-independence novels also. The Indo-Anglian novelist has repeatedly attempted to show that genuine human feelings are beyond artificial barriers of religion and in this his idealism is often evident. Khushwant Singh's *Train to Pakistan* (1956), a novel that is racy, down to earth and ruthless in its graphic description of human atrocities, hinges on the love between Jugga, a Sikh ruffian, and a Muslim girl. Similarly in B. Rajan's *The Dark Dancer* (1959), the idealised character Kamala dies trying to save a Muslim prostitute from the attack of two Hindu hooligans. In both these cases there is a well-meant attempt to invest these deaths with some greater significance through deafening symbolic overtones.

A more satisfactory, if less ambitious treatment of Hindu-Muslim relationship is to be found in one episode of Manohar Malgonkar's first novel *Distant Drum*, where two friends who had served together in the British army meet again across the border in Kashmir—one as a Lt. Colonel in the Indian army, and the other as the C.O. of a Pakistani regiment. The situation is dramatic but the novelist does not attempt to invest it with any symbolic meaning and if there is any sentimentality, it is counteracted by the subsequent realisation of the characters themselves of the folly of displaying emotion in such a situation.

Malgonkar in his first novel worked within his limitations, and succeeded in writing an honest and remarkable novel. Later on he grew more ambitious, and in his latest attempt he has tried to write the Great Indian Novel, an epic presentation of the whole struggle for Indian independence and its aftermath.

A Bend in the Ganges is panoramic in scope and epic in aspiration, crowded with events from modern Indian history, beginning with the Civil Disobedience Movement of the early 'thirties and ending in the post-partition riots in the Punjab. Between these two poles are packed all the excitements of two decades : the boycott of foreign goods, the secret activities of terrorist groups, the outbreak of the Second World War, the Japanese occupation of the Andamans, the British retreat from Rangoon, the long march of evacuees from Burma, the Bombay dock explosion, the dismemberment of India. There was a similar massing of events in Abbas' *Inquilab* also, but the period was limited to one decade only. *A Bend* differs from *Inquilab* not merely in the number of great national events, but there is a fundamental difference of point of view. In *Inquilab* history is important because it makes an impact on individuals, but in *A Bend* the author is more interested in events and episodes for their news value and sensation rather than for their effect on men and women. It is not that the novel is totally devoid of human interest. Instead of the usual central character of most novels, here we find the device of the double hero, chosen from two different layers of society. Gyan Talwar comes from simple peasant stock, Debi Dayal is the son and heir of a business magnate. However, they remain devices only, convenient tools to build up the parallel structure of the novel. The two heroes are not only chosen from different social backgrounds, but they are presented as two different personality types. They go through the same national events and the difference in their re-actions to experience provides the novel with its basic pattern of contrast. Debi Dayal is dedicated, purposeful, and firm in his ideological conviction. Gyan is essentially a self-seeker and an opportunist. The opposition of the two different personalities serves as a device for juxtaposing two different ideologies of non-violence and terrorism. The balance on two sides however is not the same, because while Debi Dayal's belief in violence being the right way to fight the British rule in India is unswerving, Gyan Talwar's commitment to Gandhian ideals is at best troubled with self-doubt : "Was his non-violence merely that of a rabbit refusing to confront the hound ?" (p. 45) Events are put up to show that non-violence for Gyan was not a strongly felt creed but a tempo-rary expedient.

The destinies of both Debi Dayal and Gyan Talwar are shaped by two factors : the forces of history, and the elements of their personalities. Gyan who adapts his policy to suit every circumstance, by cringing, deceiving, humiliating himself, bending with every wind, finally withstands the storm, while Debi Dayal is broken because he refuses to make a compromise with circusmstances.

Malgonkar as the omniscient author has inside knowledge of both the characters, but he does not treat them equally. A delibe-rate distance is kept between the reader and Debi Dayal, while the reader is offered intimate glimpses of the working of Gyan's mind. Debi Dayal remains aloof and superior, not only because of his truly aristocratic background. The dice are definitely loaded in his favour. Even when he marries a prostitute and lives in penury he remains a loftier character than Gyan. The characters, however, remain secondary to the events which carry them along breathlessly, and the action moves so rapidly from one excitement to another that sometimes the reader is oblivious of the vacuum

below the constant motion.   The vacuum, if one pauses to reflect
on it, is the inevitable consequence of the novelist's ambition to
gain in wide coverage what he cannot in depth.   *A Bend in the
Ganges* is not so much a story of men and women as of places and
episodes, not an integrated human drama but an erratic national
calendar.

III

No discussion of Indo-Anglian fiction dealing with the independence movement would be complete without an assessment of the
function of Mahatma Gandhi in these novels.   The most potent
force behind the whole movement, the Mahatma is a recurring
presence in these novels, and he is used in different ways to suit
the   design of each writer.   He has been treated variously as an
idea, a myth, a symbol, a tangible reality, and a benevolent human
being.   In a few novels he appears in person, in most others his
is an invisible presence.   Raja Rao, who among the Indo-Anglian
novelists seems most deeply influenced by Gandhi, prefers to deal
with him through a local figure who appears to be his representative.   This device may be seen in two of his short stories.
"Narsiga" and "The Cow of the Barricades," and on a larger
scale in the novel *Kanthapura*.   In each of these stories, there is a
"master," as noble and compassionate as Gandhi himself.   It may
be noted at this point that there are two symbols which occur
with noticeable frequency in Raja Rao's work, developing and
enlarging two dominant ideals.   These are the symbols of "the
cow"—representing compassion, gentleness, and the ability to
give without any expectation of return—and of "the prince," a
superior being whom the common man may admire and hero-
worship.   In Raja Rao's concept of the Mahatma these two ideas
fuse into one, so that Gandhi attains a mystic and symbolic
significance not attainable by a common man.   Gandhi never
appears in person, but in the two short stories mentioned above
and in, *Kanthapura*, we find his God-like presence, visible nowhere,
but operating behind and above everybody's thoughts and deeds.
     R.K. Narayan, on the other hand, has introduced Gandhi as a
person and not as a symbol in *Waiting for the Mahatma* where the

Mahatma is not a remote and supernatural presence but a warm human being who touches two young lives. While retaining his historical authenticity, Narayan has invested the Mahatma with that characteristic quality of Narayan's world : an amused and tolerant humour. But this treatment has not been accepted by many readers. "It will be universally agreed," writes one critic, "that R.K. Narayan is hardly at his best in *Waiting for the Mahatma* which as a picture of the Gandhian movement fails sadly to be evocative or profound." It is likely however that Narayan intended the novel merely as the study of a rather simple-minded young man's involvement with a girl who happens to be a Gandhian worker. Sriram's participation in the freedom move-ment can be seen then as incidental, an activity whose meaning he himself does not fully understand.

Gandhi appears in person also in Abbas' *Inquilab*, Nagarajan's *The Chronicles of Kedaram*, and Anand's *The Sword and the Sickle*. In *Inquilab* he is a noble being seen through the emotional reve-rence of a young boy overwhelmed by the fact that he has met the great man face to face. In Nagarajan's novel Gandhi comes to Kedaram to heal a long standing quarrel between two Iyengar sects. Here what Gandhi stood for in the public mind is far more important than his actual words or presence, because even if no-body could hear a word of what he said in the temple, the feud was miraculously resolved after his visit. Mulk Raj Anand's treat-ment differs from all the rest because he does not idealise Gandhi. The revolutionary group from whom Anand's hero, Lal Singh, learns his political lessons does not think very highly of Gandhi. One member of the group speaks ironically of the "godhood" achieved by Gandhi, and another answers "but as you know God appeals to the imagination of our peasants and can still be ex-ploited." (p. 200) When Lalu meets Gandhi personally, he is struck by the directness of the man. He agrees when the Mahatma says that fear is the first enemy of the peasants. But he cannot accept Gandhi's insistence on celibacy, hand-spinning, and passive resis-tance. A Punjabi peasant by birth and a soldier by profession, Lal Singh's instincts are in favour of direct, positive action, and he cannot really respond to Gandhian principles :

The Mahatma seemed full of himself, of his spiritual struggles. And Lalu felt himself lapsing into listlessness, as if he were being suffocated by the deliberate simplicity of the egoistic confessional talk of self-perfection. (p. 207)

Whether Gandhi would be treated as an idea or as a human be-ing, as a symbol or as tangible reality, is ultimately determined by the point of view of the novelist, and Gandhi's presence in the novel is justified only if it fits into the internal pattern of events. In lesser novels the aura of emotionalism radiating from the figure of Gandhi sometimes obscures the actual issues of the novel; in some other novels a distant view of the Mahatma is used merely as a device to fix the novel in a particular time of history.

Many more Indo-Anglian novels than the ones discussed here have dealt with the independence movement, but no major novel has as yet emerged on the theme of this great national upsurge. Nearness probably blurs the edge of events and inhibits the detachment necessary for rendering a massive experience into art. If Indo-Anglian literature continues in its vigorous growth, it may yet produce a convincing treatment of this great theme which is potentially rich in human interest as well as powerfully imbued with the larger forces of Indian history. But at the moment what we have is a number of minor essays, some of which are more successful than others because they have greater technical competence.

NOTES

1. Some of the most well-known examples are *A Tale of Two Cities*, *War and Peace*, *All Quiet on the Western Front*, *A Farewell to Arms*, *The Red Badge of Courage*, *From Here to Eternity* and *The Naked and the Dead*.
2. Quoted, *Critiques and Essays on Modern Fiction*, 1920-1951, ed. John A. Aldridge (New York, 1952), p. 68.
3. See Wayne C. Booth, *The Rhetoric of Fiction* (Chicago, 1961), Chapter VI.
4. Some of these expressions, I understand, are direct translations of common Kannada phrases. This element is discussed in detail in Chapter VII.
5. Quoted by Prema Nandakumar, "The Achievement of the Indo-Anglian Novelist," *The Literature Criterion*, V:1 (Winter 1961), 153.

6. *The Rhetoric of Fiction* (Chicago, 1961), p. 155.

7. "Tea on the Piazza with Mrs. Campbell Pread," *Commonwealth Literature*, ed. John Press, London, 1965, p. 75.

8. An interesting contrast can be found in Prawer Jhabvala's *Esmond in India* where irony is the chief tool in the delineation of a similar character. Shakuntala in *Esmond in India* is of the same temperament as Zohra, but she is conceived in an amused detachment. Her passionate love for Esmond and her heartbreak are not meant to be taken seriously, while the characterization of Zohra is totally devoid of irony or humour.

9. Much in the same manner as Devdas turned to drinking in order to drown his unrequited love for Parvati in Sarat Chandra's novel.

4

East-West Encounter

IN THE complex fabric of contemporary Indian civilisation, the two most easily discerned strands are the indigenous Indian traditions and the imported European conceptions. Almost every educated Indian today is the product of the conflicts and reconciliations of two cultures, although the consciousness of this tension varies from individual to individual. What is generally true of the educated Indian is especially true of the Indian writer, because a writer is concerned with the springs of human action and with the motivation behind human behaviour. Thus he is more aware than others of the elements that make up his personality. At the present point of Indian history, a writer's analysis of his self necessarily involves the evaluation of his own attitude towards these two aspects of his being—one inherited from birth, the other imbibed through education.

This cultural conflict—or synthesis, as the case may be—has for some reason always assumed a vital significance for the Indian novelist who writes in English. As early as 1909, Sarath Kumar Ghose wrote a novel called *The Prince of Destiny* dealing with this inter-cultural theme where the hero, the prince of a native Indian state, has to choose between the love of an English girl and marriage with an Indian princess. And as late as 1960, J.M. Ganguly's *When East and West Meet* shows that the East-West motif has not yet exhausted itself. In the intervening half-century a number of novelists have attempted to study this encounter at various depths of meaning. In some novels the West appears as a character, in some others as an attitude or a set of values. In the novels written during the Gandhian era, we find the East-West theme operating as the conflict between pre-industrial modes of life and mechanisation, as in K.S. Venkatramani's *Murugan the Tiller* (1927) and in V.V. Chintamani's *Vedantam, the Clash of Traditions* (1928).[1] In the years following independence, however, a number of novels have appeared where the conflict between the two cultures is not on the social but on the personal level, whose theme in broad terms may be called an individual's search for identity in a changing India. The definition of 'East' as well as of 'West' varies from novel to novel, but each tries in its own way to grapple with the problem that has continued to concern the Indo-Anglian novelist for more than fifty years. One is struck by the unabating interest shown by these novelists in the interaction of the two sets of values that exist side by side, and often coalesce, in twentieth century India.

To a certain extent, this interest is noticeable also in novels of the period written in the Indian languages. S.H. Vatsayan has noted in a survey of modern Hindi literature that "the search for a satisfactory attitude towards the west and of an emotionally and spiritually significant image of the east" marks the Hindi novels after the Second World War.[2] But the Indian novelist in English is more seriously and consistently involved with the East-West theme than his counterparts in the Indian languages, if only because his very choice of language[3] indicates an awareness of and exposure to a culture other than the traditional Indian. We assume that an Indian, when he writes in English, does so only because it comes most naturally to him. As Balachandra Rajan has argued, the real necessity of a writer is the necessity to render his individual vision without compromise into a public language—"If that language happens to be English the creative choice must be respected and one should judge by results rather than by dismal prophecies of what the result must fail to be."[4] The need to realise oneself creatively in English, however, presupposes a familiarity with the language which goes along with a greater degree of exposure to western culture than what the average educated Indian undergoes. The latter, in spite of all his English education, is usually more at home in his regional language. The majority of Indo-Anglian writers today (with one or two notable exceptions), it will be observed, have had at least part of a their education abroad. Because of their intimate experience of a culture other than their own, they are made aware of their Indianness as well as of the difference in the two systems of values: one rather acquired, the other inherited and often taken for granted. Not all Indians educated abroad develop this awareness, but a writer certainly is likely to be more sensitive in his responses than other men. The inter-cultural nature of his own being becomes for such a writer a theme of profound interest. Therefore, the search for one's identity is found to be a common and recurrent theme in Indo-Anglian fiction.

There may be other reasons for the Indo-Anglian writer's concern with the East-West theme. One could argue, that this theme is no more than a manifestation of the Indo-Anglian writer's constant awareness of a western audience. The East has to be deliberately interpreted and defined for this supposed audience, hence the need for this dialectical and contrastive theme. This is a nebulous charge, which has to be examined in specific novels before it can either be accepted or rejected as a worthwhile generalisation. The fact that the Indo-Anglian novelists are generally more closely acquainted with western culture seems to be a more valid reason of this concern. The Indians who have learned the English language merely as part of the educational curriculum, as something not really connected with their daily life, need not be seriously affected by the western values to which this language introduces them. It is as easy for them to discard the acquired values as it is to take off their western clothes at the end of a working day. But for those who have had a more intensive exposure, the confrontation of these two kinds of values becomes a major concern.

There are a few examples among Indo-Anglian writers of those for whom the confrontation has not resulted in any tension, creative or otherwise, who have been able to write as if the acquired values alone can sustain their view of life. D.F. Karaka is an example of this kind of writer. He must be the only Indian novelist to write a novel set in England using only British characters.

Karaka's *Just Flesh* (1941) undoubtedly displays the author's intimate knowledge of English life and culture, but it makes no contribution either to English or to Indian literature because it nowhere comes to grips with reality. His second novel, *There Lay the City* (1942), is set in Bombay, but its narrator admits he "touched the great city only on the fringe, mentally, spiritually and physically," (p. 19) while he dreamt of London streets, the *bois* of Paris, or of "the cobbled streets of a little Spanish town." (p. 72) In his last novel, *We Never Die* (1943), Karaka makes a belated attempt at writing about an Indian village. But it remains a purely theoretical exercise, far removed from the real predicaments of rural India, and the solution that is suggested at the end is too facile to be taken seriously.

Another group comprises novelists for whom the inter-cultural tension exists, but does not seriously affect the course of events in their fictional world. R.K. Narayan and K. Nagarajan are two examples of writers who have been able to write about life as it is known to them, in their particular areas of the earth—Malgudi and Kedaram—without the need to indulge in any generalisations about what is Indian and what is western. Their characters are that curious blend of the East and the West which all Indians are, but they refuse to sift the elements. Their refusal to take sides, to justify, to explain or to condemn, is responsible for a good deal of their success as novelists.

Then there is the curious case of Manohar Malgonkar, for whom the conflict is not between East and West, but between the sense of justice, fair play and integrity (exemplified by the British in India) on the one hand, and on the other, inefficiency and servility, dishonesty and a sense of inferiority, which by Malgonkar's definition are typically Indian. It is true that none of his novels hinges entirely on this conflict, but even a casual reading of his four novels will make the basic pattern of contrasts clear. British public school code of conduct constitutes the norm in Malgonkar's novels and, let it be said to his credit, the norm is maintained consistently.

His choice of theme in the first novel, *Distant Drum* (1960), was lucky, because the Indian Army is a direct inheritance from the British and still adheres fairly closely to the British system of values.

In *Combat of Shadows*, his second novel, Malgonkar bypasses the problem of reconciling British values with Indian characters by making his central figure an Englishman. Henry Winton, the tea-planter is a healthy young man of the hunting and shooting type, and in spite of the difference in race and nationality, he is essentially of the same species as Kiran Garud, the squash-playing, upright military officer of *Distant Drum*. Abhay Raj, the hero of the third novel, *The Princes* (1963), is again another version of Kiran Garud, though a much weaker one. Having been born in a princely family, Abhay Raj is subject to a special princely code of conduct. But this conduct is not very different from Kiran Garud's code of honour or Henry Winton's ideals of masculine life. And the more enduring ideals of Abhay Raj's life, by his own admission, are derived from two Englishmen : his private tutor, Mr. Lawrence, and the principal of his college.

As a contrast to these decent, clean and honourable young men, there is the other type of character, who appears in every Malgonkar novel in various guises. Servile before superiors, arrogant before subordinates, thoroughly untrustworthy and corrupt, these characters all correspond to Gyan Talwar's analytical description of himself in *A Bend in the Ganges* : "Was it part of the Indian character itself ? Did he in some way represent the average Indian, mixed up, shallow and weak ?" (p. 122) The I.N.A. brigadier in the same novel represents the type physically : "He was soft and fat and dripping with perspiration... He was the embodiment of all that was servile in India... How many such creatures did India possess ? Thousands upon thousands." (pp. 256-7) This contrast between the fairness of the British and the pettiness of Indian officials forms a running theme in *A Bend in the Ganges*. If Gyan Talwar was the only person to observe this contrast, it could have been attributed to his personal inferiority complex. But all the characters repeat the observation, until it begins to look like a statement of the author's own point of view. Almost everyone in the novel shudders, like Debi Dayal's father, "to think what the nationalists would make of this country." Not surprisingly, the nationalists in all the novels are invariably like Lala Vishnu Ram of *Distant Drum* who is constantly boasting, "I yam the Chairman aaf the Dishtrict Caangress

Committee"—and just because Malgonkar completely withholds
his sympathy from all the characters who are not "rich and well-
born" or do not share the British public school virtues, these
characters remain either entirely comic or merely unreal. As
characters they never become as fully realised as those the author
favours. In this sense there is no real conflict in the novels of
Malgonkar.

But apart from these three kinds of exceptions (represented
by Karaka, Narayan and Malgonkar), the majority of Indo-Anglian
writers have found a creative challenge in this tension between two
civilisations. A few have confronted it with some measure of
success, while some have reduced the inter-cultural dialectic into
a narrow national commitment. The duality of culture as it exists
in India today can either be a source of a strength to the writer,
providing him with a double-bladed instrument with which to
conquer India's hydra-headed reality; or it may be a serious
handicap, because writing about a society in which different sets
of values are flowing into each other, each at a different level of
internal change, cannot be an easy task.[5] To make out of this flux,
where no single standard exists for all, a coherent social context
for a novel, calls for exceptional qualities of organisation and
selection.

In this chapter I shall attempt to examine how this task has been
tackled, and to trace the different patterns and examine the levels at
which the encounter of cultures has been rendered in the Indo-
Anglian novel. This conflict undoubtedly offers a richer field of study
to the anthropologist or the sociologist, but my concern here will
be strictly limited to studying how this conflict has been put to
use in literature—more specifically, in the Indo-Anglian novel.

I

"We, Russians, have two motherlands—Russia and Europe—
even in cases when we call ourselves Slavophiles," wrote Dostoevsky
in his diary.[6] This statement is applicable to the Indo-Anglian
novelist's situation in the present century, because his loyalties too
are of a dual nature, to India and to Europe—or rather, to India
and to England, because European culture has filtered down to him

largely through contact with the British and with the English
language. In certain ways similar, though by no means identical,
was the relationship between America and Europe in the nineteenth
century. Henry James summed this up when he said, "It's a
complex fate, being an American, and one of the responsibilities it
entails is fighting against a superstitious valuation of Europe."[7]
The parallel with India is not quite exact; unlike American culture
which derives largely from Europe, Indian culture has its own
distinctive past. Yet the same superstitious valuation of England
has now become the burden of the Indo-Anglian writers also,
fighting against which they have sometimes tended to adopt a
defensive attitude towards all traditional Indian values. The
ambiguous yet determining nature of the relationship to Europe
was a recurrent motif of both Russian and American literature
during the nineteenth century. In both cases, the attitude towards
Europe assumed diverse and complex forms, ranging between
acceptance of the old world (Europe) and refusal of it in favour of
new nationalism. Turgenev, Henry James—and later on, Eliot—
offer examples of a basic acceptance of Europe. Melville and
Tolstoy were the great refusers. But almost in all cases, their
feelings were ambivalent but compulsive. Thus James Fenimore
Cooper asserted in *Gleanings in Europe* (1828) "If any man is
excusable for deserting his country it is the American artist."[8]
On this precise point the Russian intelligentsia was fiercely divided.
But whether they welcomed the probability or deplored it, both
Russian and American writers tended to agree that their formative
experiences would entail a necessary part of exile. Often the
European pilgrimage led to a discovery and revaluation of one's
own country. Gogol, for example, rediscovered his Russia while
in Rome. George Steiner in comparing mid-nineteenth century
Russian and American writing says that "in both literatures the
theme of the European voyage was the principal device for self-
definition and the occasion for the normative gesture : Herzen's
coach crossing the Polish frontier. Lambert Strether (the protagonist
of James' *The Ambassadors*) arriving in Chester." Steiner also
quotes the early Slavophil Kirevsky's remark that "to understand
anything as vast and terrible as Russia, on emust look at it from
afar."[9]

Confrontation with the West for the discovery of one's own country, and of one's own self : this is not an infrequent motif of contemporary Indo-Anglian novels. Homecoming after a sojourn abroad and consequent readjustment and revaluation of the terms in which to face life constitute the major issue in a number of these novels. Although the level on which this revaluation takes place varies considerably, the recurrence of the theme itself is significant. In both the novels of B. Rajan, the protagonist's return home after a period spent abroad forms an important incident. Raja Rao's *The Serpent and the Rope* begins with Ramaswamy's coming back to India after spending some years in France, and his metaphysical definition of the rediscovered country. Santha Rama Rao's young heroine Baba Goray has just returned from school in England as *Remember the House* opens. In most of these cases there is an autobiographical element in the apprehension of the predicament of the person who has returned, though in the case of the more successful novels the autobiography does not interfere with the integral design of the work. In each case the protagonist's awareness of two civilisations intensifies his concern with his own identity. They are all in search of their true image, torn between the traditional values they have absorbed from childhood and the new values their education has bestowed upon them. In each case, the novel ends with the resolution of their dilemma through a definite act of will.

Then there is the homecoming in novels where it is not the central incident, nor does it affect the protagonist personally, but incidentally it illustrates the interaction between two cultures. The return of Kitsamy in *Some Inner Fury* and the homecoming of Laila's cousins in *Sunlight on a Broken Column* are examples of this interaction at a rather superficial level, because the impact of the West upon these characters is presented very incidentally. Kitsamy, we are told, submits to the family priest's benediction on his return with ill-concealed annoyance—"his face took on a faint insolent impatience as if he was above all this sort of thing and amazed that we were not" (p. 12)—while for Laila's cousins, Kemal and Saleem, "the ten years of estrangement had no significance. Centuries of kinship swallowed them up in a moment." (p. 174) These two examples indicate the different levels on which the inter-cultural theme can be treated in a novel, ranging from the attitudes of a novelist of manners who is concerned with the shallow stereotypes to those of a more serious analyst; for some, the encounter of two civilisations results in a dilemma that must be solved in order to define the self.

In this distinction between eastern and western values, we tread dangerous grounds. Apart from the fact that after two centuries of proximity it has become increasingly difficult to demarcate precisely between the two traditions as available in India, such patent oppositions tend to prove disastrous in fiction insofar as they oversimplify action and conflict. Nevertheless, in spite of the constant overlapping and interchangeability of values, some kind of basic difference does exist between the two civilisations. Granting that in literature each writer has to make his own definition of what is for him the West and what is East, it would probably not be out of place here if we try to make, as a starting point, a tentative definition of the two value systems.

The American sociologist Clyde Kluckohn has indicated one way of defining this vague term 'values' when he says, "It should be possible to construct in general terms the views of a given group regarding the structure of the universe, the relation of man to the universe... and the relations of man to man. These views will represent the group's own definition of the ultimate meaning of human life."[10] Socioloogists, anthropologists and philosophers have tried many times to define the precise nature of oriental and occidental value systems. Among these definitions, the most comprehensive and least controversial seems to be the one suggested by Cora Du Bois.[11] She sums up the entire issue in three questions, the answers to which—in her opinion—will indicate the value system of a particular culture. These questions are :

(1) What is man's relation to nature ?
(2) What is man's conception of time ?
(3) What is man's relation to man ?

In posing these essentially metaphysical questions, she is raising universal queries for which men in all cultures have sought explicit answers. The answers they have selected from the total range of possibilities, and the consistency among the answers, constitute the basic premises of their varying value systems, their 'way of life.'

With regard to the first question, namely, man and nature, we find man can either accept the forces of nature as invincible or he can strive to master nature through the application of science in the form of technology. As for a concept of time—the second question—man can either look backward to a lost golden age or forward to an even more perfectible world; that is, have belief in progress. As regards the third question, society can either be envisaged as a strict hierarchical order where each man performs duties allotted to him, or man can look upon himself primarily as an isolated individual, charged with cherishing and developing his unique potentialities.

It must be remembered, of course, that each of the questions asked above has more than two alternative answers. In reducing the complex issues involved in these answers to two opposed viewpoints we certainly oversimplify the cultural diversity of the human race. But we may at least tentatively accept these opposed alternatives—as philosophers such as Charles Morris and Ethel Albert, have done—as representative of the mutual opposition of eastern and western values.[12] These alternatives may therefore be treated as a working hypothesis for the examination of a particular aspect of the Indo-Anglian novel, though ultimately, East and West are subjective terms interpreted differently by different writers.[13]

II

The heroes of Mulk Raj Anand are rugged individualists who suffer because they refuse to conform. Munoo the coolie, Bakha the untouchable, Bikhu the chamar, Lal Singh of the trilogy—all are persecuted by society for their non-conformity, but all of them are indomitable in spirit. Anand wrote in *Apology for Heroism* : "I am conscious that much of my insistence of the role of man in the universe derives from European Hellenism. For the traditional attitude of India in this regard is essentially non-human, super-human : 'This atman... is the same in the ant, the same in the gnat, the same in the elephant, the same in the whole universe' so says the Brhadaranyak Upanishad." (p. 95) But for Anand the novelist, the atman in each man is something rare and precious.

It is clear on which side of the East-West dialect Anand takes his stand.

If we take Cora Du Bois' first question in relation to Anand's work, what is man's relation to nature—it is easily answered. Belief in man's power to master nature through a rational technology is evident in every novel of Anand. While others in the village take the filth and drought and misery as inevitable, Anand's non-conformist heroes rebel against the existing conditions because they have faith in the possibility of controlling nature for man's benefit. "The seasons will be changed by man. There will be water from the wells, with electric pumps... and medicines will renew the earth," proclaims Gauri towards the end of *The Old Woman and the Cow*. If the majority of the villagers in Anand's world share the traditional fatalism about nature's cruelty to man, his protagonists stand out as rebels and visionaries who believe in the prospect of improvement. They suffer because they cannot accept and be resigned, yet often find themselves unable to act. Added to the suffering imposed upon them by society is their own helplessness. Lal Singh is from his boyhood fired with a vague idealism and desire to change his village; these ideals find concrete objectives when he sees a French farm for the first time, observes the advanced methods of cultivation, notices the resulting prosperity. Like Bakha, Lalu admires the white man with a naive adulation. Even amid the stress of actual battle in the trenches, he "felt curiously thrilled to be among them, for in spite of their haggard faces the tommies had not lost that look of exalted sahibhood." (*Across the Black Waters*, p. 99) This sahibhood consists in the efficiency of the white man, his ability to act, to use science for changing existing conditions to suit his own convenience. For this reason, the machine is such a dynamic symbol in Anand's work.

The answer to the second question (namely, what is man's concept of time ?) is found in equally unambiguous terms in Anand's work. While the older people sit mourning their fate, speaking nostalgically of the good old days and the debased state of affairs at present, Anand's young people—village adolescents (Bakha, Munno, Lalu, Bikhu) as well as city labour leaders (Anant in *The Big Heart*, Ratan in *Coolie*) and patriotic poets, doctors or wise men (Iqbal Nath Sharshar in *Untouchable*, Puran

Singh Bhagat in *The Big Heart*, Dr. Mahindra in *The Old Woman and the Cow*)—all look towards the future to a more perfectible world. On the second page of *The Village* Lalu is found arguing with his father about the advantages of the goods train over the bullock cart which his father still prefers. From this point onwards Lalu becomes a representative of the forces of modernity or progress. Lalu, along with the other protagonists of Anand, shares the values of his creator, and these values are in sharp opposition to the traditional values of an Indian village.

But the issues raised by the third question—'What is man's relation to man'—are the most important in a discussion of Anand's work, because a crusade against caste with its faith in a hierarchical society has always been the motivating force of Anand's writing. Though he writes mostly of villages where life is strictly compartmentalised, where a man is labelled from birth, his victim-heroes invariably rebel against the social mechanism. Lalu as a gesture of defiance eats in a Muslim cookshop—which is almost the replica of an incident in *Coolie* where Munoo does the same thing for the same reason. Anand believes in the intrinsic merit of each individual quite apart from his caste and profession, and he has never tired of propagating universal brotherhood through his novels.

Thus Anand leaves us in no doubt of his position regarding man's relation to nature, time, and fellow human beings. He is a rational humanist, in the western tradition, believing in the power of science to improve material conditions, in progtress and in the equality oJ all men, and his manifest intention is to propagate his beliefs through his novels. Judging how far he succeeds in the artistic realisation of his intentions is for the literary critic a far more important task than the evaluation of the intentions themselves.

First of all Anand seems to simplify the conflict between tradition and modernity by creating clearly distinguishable sets of characters, withholding his sympathy from some, while deluging others with compassion. His characters fall neatly into three types : the sufferers, the oppressors and the good men. Usually the protagonist is the sufferer-in-chief. All money-lenders, priests, and landlords, i.e., people with a vested interest in resisting change or progress, come under the second category. The Sahukar, Mohant Nandgir and Hardit Singh in the trilogy are examples of this triple figure of evil which appears in every Anand novel under different names. The good men, an assortment of labour leaders, social workers, poets and idealistic doctors, are all advocates of the benefits of the machine and the need for progress and equality. Dr. Mohindra (*The Old Woman and the Cow*) emphasises the use of medicine and soap and the need for cleaning up the village; Iqbal Nath Sharshar (*Untouchable*) speaks of mechanising the mode of the disposal of garbage which will ultimately eradicate caste; and Puran Singh Bhagat (*The Big Heart*) voices Anand's opinion when he says, "But don't let us forget that for all their sins the English at least had the Bible and Browning in their background... Our merchants are descended—let us be honest—from a caste-ridden society with an utter contempt for the lower orders ingrained in them as part of their dharma." (p. 144)

Anand's dice, therefore, are heavily loaded; there is a a too obvious taking of sides, and the patent opposition between two neatly divided groups does not express truth which is often complicated and elusive.

Anand is free from what the Bengali critic and writer Annanda Sankar Roy has called the East-Past complex[14] and there is no nostalgia or sentimentality in his attitude towards Indian traditions. If the rejection of the superstitions and narrowness of traditional life involves the loss of the strength that a continuity of culture provides, it is for Anand a deliberate choice. He substitutes the international doctrine of socialism for the myth of the race, but this is preceded by an exposure to a number of view-points, great deal of soul-searching and a certain intellectual process, the record of which can be found in his *Apology for Heroism*. However, when he imposes his convictions directly upon his heroes, who are usually country-bred or unsophisticated people without the advantage of his wide background, the characterization fails because instead of becoming fully rounded individuals they become mouthpieces of the author's ideas. Anand's characters are lonely misfits— not lonely in the tradition of the modern European protagonist of fiction, whose loneliness is a form of intellectual alienation, but lonely because they do not arise out of the soil they inhabit, because Anand has stuffed them with his own beliefs. They lack the necessary background, are thereby rootless, and appear somewhat unreal.

III

Anand was at the height of his power in the 'thirties and early 'forties, when a sociological approach to literature was very much in vogue both in India as well as outside. It has been shown in Chapter 2 that in almost all the Indian languages, these two decades were predominantly the period of public concern in literature. The independence movement, the uplift of the downtrodden, the reform of social evils : these public preoccupations were followed, in the next decade, by a concern with one's own self that was basically a private search. Trends in literature do not confine themselves to specific dates and years, but the shift of interest from the public to the private sphere may be regarded as a characteristic of the 'fifties and the 'sixties. This private search often constituted a quest for a satisfactory attitude towards the West, and for a realistic image of the East that would at the same time be emotionally valid. This search has taken varied and complex forms. At its lowest, it has often descended into sentimental chauvinism and neurotic rejection, at its highest it has attempted a reintegration of personality, a revaluation of all values.

As examples of this we shall now examine five novels which basically deal with the same theme—a quest for the self—and in doing so necessarily touch upon the East-West conflict at different levels of meaning. The novels are *Remember the House* (1956), *A Time to be Happy* (1957), *Some Inner Fury* (1957), *The Dark Dancer* (1959), and *Sunlight on a Broken Column* (1961). This chronological sequence may be accidental, but one notices that these novels were published in close succession, all towards the end of the 'fifties. It is significant that another major novel to deal with the same theme, Raja Rao's *The Serpent and the Rope*, also appeared during this period.

Remember the House is a first novel and, like many Indo-Anglian first novels, is autobiographical in technique, if not in substance. The central conflict of the adolescent heroine is between two ideals of life. As in B. Rajan's *The Dark Dancer* the West here appears in person, and Alix Nicoll, the narrator's American friend who makes happiness her goal in life, represents one side of the conflict. The other side does not have a similar concrete

personification but the heroine's mother is the closest to an
embodiment of the truly Indian values. The narrator, Baba Goray,
briefly infatuated with the American way of life finds the ideals
of 'enjoyment,' 'success' and 'happiness' supremely desirable.
But all the time she is aware of the basic incompatibility of these
ideals with what she has always been taught. The difference
between the two modes of life is rather obviously pointed out in an
explanatory passage :

> She (Alix) held up the glass. "To happiness," she said
> laughing. I sipped my lemonade and laughed with her. In
> Jalnabad, I thought, no one made a point about happiness.
> We were given, and we accepted almost without thinking, certain
> precepts. The importance of the family, the one we were born
> to or the one we are married into. Our place in a certain struc-
> ture, a pattern of life, of birth, of marriage, children, peace and
> death... Within our framework we would make our happiness...
> It was never suggested that we pursue happiness. We were not
> encouraged to waste our time. (p. 98)

Reiterating the same difference between two ideals of life there
is this brief conversation between mother and daughter much later
in the novel :

> "Now are you happy ?"
> "Is happiness what you want ?" She asked me with infinite
> compassion... "Oh my poor child." (p. 212)

It can be observed in passing that other Indo-Anglian novelists
also have insisted that happiness is not an Indian goal. One
remembers Nalini in Rajan's *Too Long in the West* who, when asked
by Ernest, her American admirer, "Don't tell me you are happy in
this mud-bath" answered "It isn't a question of happiness."
In *Remember the House*, contrasted with the serenity of the
heroine's mother, Alix has an effervescent vitality that is intoxicat-
ing. Baba's friendship with her however does not last long—
but even after their parting Alix's effect does not wear off easily.
Baba stumbles through another infatuation before she reaches

the bed-rock of sensible values. Santha Rama Rao intends to convey that Baba's sudden interest in the South Indian school teacher was merely a fancy based on the western conception of love, and did not have any basis in reality. At the end Baba's marriage with Hari, the steadfast, undemonstrative old friend, approved of by the family, is in fact the triumph of traditional values over a temporary infatuation.

A variation on the same theme, personal fulfilment as opposed to loyalty to the family, is found in Attia Hosain's *Sunlight on a Broken Column*, another first novel by a woman novelist. The conflict here does not resolve neatly along East-West lines, though the heroine's quest for her personal destiny itself is a result of the impact of the West on her. The West, if it appears explicitly at all does so in terms of ideas than of persons. The theme of the novel, until the last part where it badly disintegrates—is Laila's journey from the acceptance of traditional family values to questioning and rebellion. Her search for her own personal fulfilment goes against the expectation of her family. When Laila takes the decision of marrying Ameer against the will of her family she has this unpleasant encounter with a favourite aunt :

I wept the last time I was with her.
"Phuphi Jan, I have done nothing wrong."
She was cold and unyielding and drew away from me.
"You have been defiant and disobedient. You have put yourself above your duty to the family."
...I know that understanding was impossible between us. She was part of a way of thinking that I had rejected. (p. 312)

Unlike the heroine of Santha Rama Rau, Laila chooses to defy tradition. In the conflict between society and the individual, the latter wins. But even in this novel the triumph is temporary. From the disintegrated reminiscence of the last part one gathers that Laila's marriage with Ameer was cut short by Ameer's death, and even during its brief duration the marriage was made uneasy by the disparity in their social and economic situation. At the end Laila comes back to the deserted family house, and in an orgy of sentimentalism, rediscovers her cousin Asad, who, apparently, has been waiting for her all his life. One can see that Attia Hosain's heroine also finally follows the same pattern as the heroine of Santha Rama Rau : rebellion, romantic quest, final submission to traditional values.

There is a very large streak of nostalgia in both these novels as well as in Kamala Markandaya's *Some Inner Fury*. Mira in Markandaya's novel recalls wistfully the laughter and the happiness of her father's home, the gulmohurs and the peace which later she chose to renounce in order to move in a circle she would create for herself. In *Remember the House*, as the very title indicates, the memory of a particular house in distant Jalnabad becomes a senti-mental motif in the structure of the novel. The expensive inclusive-ness and tolerant co-existence in her grandmother's large house-hold where the narrator had spent her childhood remains a fixed focal point to which her thoughts return again and again as if to the roots of her being during the confusing search for identity. As in the case of Jalnabad in Santha Rama Rau, Hasanpur in Attia Hosain's *Sunlight* stands for a deep sense of belonging.

Jalnabad or Hasanpur thus give a local habitation and name to a vague feeling of nostalgia about a way of life that seems to be pass-ing away. This feeling is compulsive and can be seen even when this way of life is deliberately rejected. For Example, in *Sunlight on a Broken Column* as well as in *Some Inner Fury* the protagonists themselves consciously break away from the kind of life they are nostalgic for. They struggle against this way of life to seek their personal fulfilment in another sphere created by themselves. And in both cases, love for a man is the incentive for rebellion. R.K. Narayan has pointed out the absence of the eternal triangle in the Indian social context.[15] But it seems to me that in the Indian context the triangle is very much present in another sense; only the third side of the triangle is provided not by a human being, but by a more powerful and less defined force—the joint family, tradi-tion, orthodoxy. The joint family is a formidable force even when the love interest is absent and in Indo-Anglian fiction it has served a number of functions at the same time. It represents the voice of authority and tradition and serves as a microcosm of the hierarchi-cal society which the individual has to rebel against in order to attain his personal identity. Just as society has various levels based on caste, the joint family has various levels of authority, different roles being allotted to individuals. The hero of B. Rajan's *The Dark Dancer*, speculates on the correctness of his self assertion : "It was blackmail to say... he should not protest simply because his protesting might hurt others. Iron out the man for the convenience of the Machine." (p. 138) Krishnan rebels for the time being, as do Laila in *Sunlight on a Broken Column* and Mira in *Some Inner Fury*. The joint family may be a static force to rebel against but at the same time the joint family also stands for security, relaxed comfort and a kind of sharing of joys and sorrows, qualities which Hasanpur and Jalnabad embody. Finally at times it acts as a chorus—commenting on the actions of the individual, e.g., in the remarks of uncle Kruger in *The Dark Dancer* or of Aunt Abida in *Sunlight on a Broken Column*. Thus the institution of the joint family is very conveniently used by the Indo-Anglian writer, in order to get a close view of the struggle between self and society. Society which is vague and amorphous becomes a concrete experience in the joint family.

The conflict between the two cultures of East and West is nowhere so obviously spelled out as in Nayantara Sahgal's first novel *A Time to be Happy* and nowhere is the resolution so unambiguous and simple. Here the protagonist Sanad Shivpal is the son of a rich man, a product of a public school, an executive in a mercantile firm, a good tennis player : in short, the stereotype of a particular social class. His problem is that of regaining his roots, of belonging : "it occurred to him that his parents had gone to a great deal of trouble and expense moulding him to be a figure that would never have any reality" (p. 113) and the dilemma is restated for further emphasis when Sanad mourns his fate : "I don't belong entirely to India. I can't. My education, my upbringing, and my sense of values have all combined to make me un-Indian. What do I have in common with most of my countrymen ?" (p. 147) His self-pity arising out of a sense of alienation and rootlessness is a very common theme in Indo-Anglian literature, even though it is not always so explicitly stated. We remember Laila in *Sunlight on a Broken Column* breaking out into a burst of self-pity at the sight of an ugly shape in *burqua* heaving into a curtained car : "She is closer to the people than us, sitting, standing, eating, thinking and speaking like them, while we with our Bach and Beethoven, our Shakespeare and Eliot, put 'people' into inverted commas" (p. 258); and Krishnan in *The Dark Dancer* trying to unite himself to things "that are real and rooted, that belong to India," even if he does not.

Alienation in all these cases necessitates sentimentalisation of the objects one has been alienated from. In the case of Sanad Shivpal in *A Time to be Happy* it becomes an obsession to know the 'people' and the way he does it is the most unconvincing element in this novel of naive conflicts. In each of the three novels (*Remember the House, Sunlight on a Broken Column* and *A Time to be Happy*) the resolution comes through marriage. In *Remember the House* after some blundering misadventures Baba marries the right person and settles down to a life that adheres to the traditional code. In *Sunlight on a Broken Column* Laila achieves selfhood by marrying the man of her own choice even if it means defying convention and loyalty to family, though the resolution is later weakened by the fact that after Ameer's death Laila rediscovers a cousin of hers, and probably marries him. This in effect means a return to the family she had forsaken. In *A Time to be Happy* Sanad attains his goal of coming close to the 'people' by marrying the unsophisticated, non-westernised daughter of a college lecturer and by (incredible as it might seem) learning Hindi and spinning.

Kusum, Sanad's wife, conforms to that type of idealised Indian womanhood to which Premala of *Some Inner Fury* and Kamala of *The Dark Dancer* also belong. All of them derive their strength from service and sacrifice and they believe in non-violence as a creed and in right action rather than happiness. In *Some Inner Fury* although the central figures are an Indian girl and a young Englishman, they are merely themselves, and not intended to be representatives of two cultures. If anyone is representative of Indian culture it is not the heroine, but Premala with her Eastern calm and acceptance. The impact of the West is also seen more clearly on the minor characters than on the protagonist himself, in Kit, for example, Mira's westernised brother in the civil service whose "feeling for the West was no cheap flirtation... it was understanding and love" (p. 142), or at the other extreme, Govind, to whom the western way of life "was the product of a culture which was not his own—the culture of an aloof and alien race, twisted in the process of transplantation from its homeland and so divorced from the people of the country as to be no longer real." (p. 142) Between the two extremes of love and hatred for the West stands Roshan who, the author tells us, understands the West "but she belonged to the East also." This to the author seems to be the golden mean. Roshan's case is offered as the solution of a dilemma that is essentially complex.

To talk of West and East with capital W and E, as Kamala Markandaya does is, always a dangerous abstraction, especially in fiction where abstract notions must never obscure the particular and concrete realisation of individual human experience. Kit, because he is entirely a product of the West becomes more of a stereotyped *burra sahib* than a living character, and his actions and responses are predictable. Premala, Kit's wife, who feels ill at ease in westernised environments is idealised to the extent of being unreal. West, here as in Nayantara Sahgal's novel has a very limited connotation. In each case it means the external forms and empty rituals of westernised living in India—a variation of Forster's Chandrapore Club—more trivial, because it is an ineffectual imitation. This, of course, is the most superficial definition of West possible, and if nothing else, this limited definition seriously hampers the quality of these novels.

Some Inner Fury also attempts to work out another familiar dilemma, familiar at least in fiction, thanks to E. M. Forster, between personal relationship and racial prejudice. In the other three novels discussed above, the resolution came through marriage and there was an element of choice for each protagonist. But in this novel the climax is brought about by riot and violence in which Mira is separated from Richard. Because Mira is not a free agent, and has no power of self-determination, this novel cannot be regarded as the quest for self-discovery as the other three can. Mira is merely the victim of forces beyond her control, the forces of history as it were. As she leaves Richard in the midst of the angry mob, she thinks :

Go : leave the man I loved, to go with these people. What did they mean to me, what could they mean, more than the man

I loved ? They were my people those others were his. Did
it mean something then—all this 'your people' and 'my people' ?
...I know I would go, even as I know Richard might stay. For
us there was no other way, the forces that pulled us apart were
too strong. (p. 285)

Though rather melodramatic, these lines carry a faint echo of the
famous last line of *A Passage to India* : "The earth did not want
it... the temples, the tank, the jail, the palace... they didn't
want it, they said in their hundred voices, 'no, not yet,' and the
sky said, 'no, not there,' "—reminding us that *Some Inner Fury*
also ends on the note that East and West cannot meet because the
forces that pull them apart are too strong.

The name of Forster tends to stray into any discussion of East-
West relationship in fiction, but comparison or contrast with him
is not very relevant in the present context because what he attempted
in his masterpiece was something very different from what most
Indo-Anglian writers are trying to do. Personal relationship—
communication between, and understanding of, men who happen
to belong to two races—is part of Forster's theme in *A Passage to
India* while the Indo-Anglian novelist more often than not is trying
to reconcile within himself two conflicting systems of value. In
this tension between two views of life any easy solution is bound
to be an inadequate one as the four novels discussed above
demonstrate.

B. Rajan's *The Dark Dancer* comes closer to the crux of the
problem than any of the novels analysed so far. But even here
one feels dissatisfied with the treatment of the theme and the denouement. Krishnan's alienation is apparent from the very
beginning. After two years in Cambridge "he was coming back to
an indifferent sky, an anonymous teeming of houses." His indifferent attitude towards his family which was ready to arrange
his life for him, his cynical view of the society around him, and his
lack of involvement in his surroundings, all these mark him as an
outsider right away. The outsider as protagonist is a recurrent
figure in much of twentieth century fiction in Europe and in
America. We have celebrated examples of the artist as an alien
(*Portrait of the Artist as a Young Man*), the Negro or the Jew as an

outsider (as in Ralph Ellison's *Invisible Man* or Saul Bellow's *Herzog*), or the sensitive adolescent as an outsider (as in J.D. Salinger's *Catcher in the Rye*). In a similar way, the Indian who has spent a considerable time abroad may become an alien in Indian society.[16] One advantage of this device is that if the protagonist does not belong to the society he writes about, he can be more objective in his evaluation of it. But Krishnan is not an outsider in this sense, because his non-conformity does not influence his actions. In spite of his constant hair-splitting and analysis of the unreasonable demands of society, he submits to every family decision. Secondly, he wants very much to belong, which is indicated by at least two deliberate actions : his taking part in the non-violent demonstration by the seaside and his agreeing to an arranged marriage. His failure in both merely shows that estrangement cannot be overcome merely by accepting the symbols of belonging. The civil disobedience march is ruined by Krishnan's active show of violence, and his marriage by his wavering of will between Cynthia, and Kamala. Cynthia, who urged him to 'be and not belong' (pp. 98-99) for him represented individuality and self-hood, write his wife Kamala' represented the strength of acceptance and belonging. About his wife Krishnan thinks : "Kamala's Indian, intensely so, not simply in what she knows and does but deep down, in ways that I can only sense, and don't even want to understand." (p. 82) Krishnan is temporarily attracted towards Cynthia because her insistence on the importance of the self counter-balanced Krishnan's own streak of resignation. Like Baba's infatuation with the Nicolls, in Santha Rama Rau's novel Krishnan's infatuation with Cynthia is based on the fact that she has qualities that are lacking in Krishnan's own personality. Krishnan himself analyses the differences between them thus : "She [Cynthia] came from a tradition which included non-conformity and dissent among its attributes... His on the contrary was a background completely conformist, where the map of one's life was drawn even before one's first cry." (p. 165) From accepting the family's decisions he passes on to accepting Cynthia's decisions, which is easy, because she has a stronger will, until Krishnan suddenly realises the mistake of his choice. The reason they finally break their relationship is trivial and unconvincing. During his visit to a temple Krishnan suddenly discovers that while the priest would bless him, he would not bless Cynthia. This leads to a sudden realisation of the basic difference between him and Cynthia. Cynthia fails in the tug-of-war between loyalties and Krishnan goes back to his wife, who to drown her own unhappiness is serving the people of the riot-ravaged area of Shantipur. He thus finds the right path, learns abandonment of the self from Kamala, and even when she dies trying to save a Muslim woman Krishnan finds serenity and a meaning in life.

The resolution of Krishnan's East-West dilemma ultimately hinges on his choice between Cynthia and Kamala, and the two women are more representatives than convincing individuals. Cynthia with her strubborn individualism, her sense of fairness, her non-conformity, is an embodiment of British liberal humanism while Kamala, like the earth, with her source of mysterious strength, her belief in non-violence and right action rather than happiness, her patience and self-sacrifice is an idealised portrait of Indian woman-hood. But even more than the static nature of the characters, the real weakness of the novel lies in the fact that Krishnan's final resolution does not arise out of the conflicts and tensions that he goes through. Rather, it comes as a preconceived solution that has nothing to do with the series of crises described in the book. One knows from the way Kamala is presented that she is India, and she is bound to win ultimately and she does, even though she has to die for it.

The Dark Dancer brings to mind a novel by the Nigerian author Chinua Achebe,[17] also about a man returning home from England to a coveted government position (in Nigeria) and his adjustment thereafter. In spite of the initial similarity of their themes, the two novels are studies in contrast as far as treatment of the theme goes. For one thing Achebe's book *No Longer at Ease* is less ambitious than Rajan's, it does not have symbols (like Rajan's *nataraja* or *gopuram*) or myths (in *The Dark Dancer* the story of Karna, the son of Kunti who could not belong is a central myth) woven into its structure, nor does it aspire to a tragic depth, and yet it succeeds. Unlike *The Dark Dancer*, *No Longer at Ease* ends with the failure of its protagonist. If the novel is something less than a tragedy it is because Achebe does not see Obi Okonkwo

as a tragic hero. The pressures that pull and mould him are all
pressures making for compromise and accommodation; these are
not the stuff of tragedy, but of failure and decline. *The Dark Dancer*
on the other hand attempts to be profound from the very beginning.
Krishnan's dilemma is not seen for what it is, through events and
actions, but is invested with a philosophical aura even before any
action has taken place. Take this passage for example, which
occurs fairly early in the novel, about Krishnan's reaction to his
family's interference in his private life :

> It should have shocked him, and to some extent it did, but
> was the shock anything more than superficial, a tingle on the
> skin of his upbringing ? And under the skin did his muscles not
> move to surrender, did his blood not sing in that deep fascinated
> curiosity of acceptance which his reason resisted while his
> emotions curved to the pull ? He had the strange sense of
> detachment once again, of being both the dancer and the dance,
> of being the ritual and the ritual's object. (p. 14)

This passage demonstrates at once several reasons why Rajan's
novel falls short of its overambitious goal. Firstly, the exalted
style and the self-conscious rhetoric hardly suit the occasion.
Secondly, Rajan is so busy making generalisations from such an
early stage in the novel—generalisations about the polarities
between Krishnan's upbringing and education, between reason and
emotion, between the East where he was born and the West where
he was educated, that his later conflicts lose much of their con-
vincingness. This contrasts somewhat unfavourably with Achebe's
brief, almost laconic style. The predicament of Obi Okonkwo
is more convincing than the predicament of Krishnan because
Achebe is taking a hard look ot Nigerian society as it is, without
indulging in any comforting generalisations about the African
psyche and the western impact. It is possible for Rajan to write a
sentence like the following to explain the incompatibility between
Cynthia and Krishnan : "It was impossible to share the sense of
community with her (Cynthia) when the sense of being Indian
mounted in one's blood." (p. 158)

The phrase "the sense of being Indian" betrays the falsity of

Rajans' attitude, especially his admission that this sense is something that can mount in one's blood occasionally and lie dormant at other times.

Like Cynthia and Kamala, Krishnan, the hero of *The Dark Dancer*, is also a type rather than an individual. He is the representative of inter-cultural tension, a common enough character in Indo-Anglian fiction. Since the novel deals with types rather than individuals, it is not surprising that it should contain stock situations. The "England-returned" young man who deserts his patient suffering wife for a glamorous English woman, the brilliant scholar who is forced by his family to take up a government job that does not give him intellectual satisfaction, the advocate of individual freedom who willy-nilly submits to an arranged marriage, all these are stereotyped situations in Indian fiction today.

Rajan's novel merely underlines what was already evident in the discussion of the four novels earlier : that the direct opposition between two sets of values sometimes tends to oversimplify action and conflicts; that this oversimplification affects the characters also, making them static abstractions rather than dynamic, changing individuals. These static characters fall mainly into two groups : the representatives of the West (Alix Nicoll in *Remember the House*, Kitsmay in *Some Inner Fury*, Girish Shivpal in *A Time to be Happy* and Cynthia in *The Dark Dancer*) and those who embody the virtues of the East (Baba's mother in *Remember the House,* Premala in *Some Inner Fury*, Kusum in *A Time to be Happy*, and Kamala in *The Dark Dancer*). And lastly, we find that the resolution in most cases does not arise out of the conflict but follows a set pattern along preconceived lines. Except in *Some Inner Fury*, where the protagonist has no power to affect the denouement, in every one of these novels the East finally wins. This triumph of the Indian values does not emerge naturally out of the situations depicted, but is often arbitrary. One strongly suspects that this is so because the novelists themselves, like their portagonists, feel alienated from these values and they therefore tend to sentimentalise and idealise them. The denouements seem unsatisfactory not only because such facile solutions are patently false in real life where neither East nor West ever really wins, but also because it does violence to the integral logic of the novels.

IV

In Raja Rao's *The Serpent and the Rope* (1960), the East-West theme assumes a depth and validity not achieved before in Indo-Anglian fiction. Here East however, is no general term : it is India, Brahminical India, which represents the quintessence of advaita philosophy. India at all other levels is excluded. The moral puritanism of India is rejected as something essentially weak :

> I hated this moral India... Lakshmi was not India. Lakshmi was the India that accepted invaders, come Muslim, come British with sighs and salutations. Lakshmi would not read the Maha-bharata the whole night, cut her finger, and anointing her Lord with her young blood burn herself alive. (p. 354)

Industrial, metropolitan India is equally rejected as irrelevant : "Bombay... simply had no meaning to a Brahmin like me... Bombay had no right to exist." (p. 46) The modern, cosmopolitan India of the northern cities is rejected as alien to the traditional pattern of Indian life :

> I could not understand the northerners going from strict purdah to this extreme modernism with unholy haste. We in the south were more sober, and very distant. We lived by tradition... (p. 34)

But the West is considered in more general terms. The Provencal taxi-driver, the Parisian notary, the Russian scholar, the Spanish refugee, the British students, Ramaswamy's French wife, however different from each other as characters, all partake of a single value system which may be regarded as "western" in its insistence on the particular and the concrete, on the personal and the immediate— in other words, in its recognition of the object as something outside oneself.

The complex and amorphous theme of the novel has been summed up in one concise sentence by a reviewer : "In the marriage of Rama and Madeleine, two contrary world-views, two contrary epistemologies, come together, and the novel is a study of that

encounter."[19] In spite of their sharply differentiated attitude
towards life, Ramaswamy and Madeleine have one striking similarity
as characters : they are both intensely self-conscious about the
epistemologies they represent. Hardly ever do they regard themselves or each other simply as individual human beings. Instead,
they are constantly interpreting their own and each other's actions
in terms of their national and cultural differences, invariably ending
up with generalisations about "Indian" and "western" traits of
character. Thus when Madeleine is indignant about some social or
political injustice and Ramaswamy fails to be aroused, he attributes
it not to their differences in temperament, but to his "thin Brahmin
blood" and her "warm southern blood." (p. 20) When Ramaswamy
feels an affection for Catherine and talks to her like an elder brother,
he hastens to explain, "I acted no doubt from my Indian instinct...
Left to himself the Indian would go on tying *Rakhi* to every
woman he met, feel her elder brother, protect her love..." (p. 137)
Even minor events and small actions like buying a pepper-grinder
or carrying a suitcase are invested with Madeleine's "Frenchness"
("I must use it some day—you know, I am French and nothing
should be useless") or Ramaswamy's Indianness ("How incompetent
we two Indians felt before things") Ramaswamy's inability to deal
with the practical side of life, his haphazardness "like the towels
in the bathroom that lay everywhere"), is attributed not to any
personal shortcoming but to his Indianness. This representative
burden falls most heavily upon their personal relationship. When
Madeleine is impatient with Ramaswamy's heavy seriousness
and his refusal to grapple with tangible reality, she does not regard
these as characteristics of an individual human being ; these are
related immediately to the larger cultural, philosophic and religious
background of the country of his origin. Madeleine writes to him
"I wondered whether I could really love you—whether anyone
could love a thing so abstract as you... I wonder if Indians
can love." (p. 42) And when Madeleine feels no warmth for
Ramaswamy's family in Hyderabad, a group of people whom she
has never met, she thinks it is because of her reading of Gide and
Sartre that she cannot conceive of a large and loose unit as a family.
(p. 262)

But in spite of their representative function, both Ramaswamy and Madeleine are completely convincing and recognisable as individuals. Their self-consciousness about culture and history and heritage is the way they have been conceived of as characters and it sets them apart from other characters in the novel. Little Mother is in every way the exact opposite of Madeleine. It has been observed that Madeleine lacks that "mother principle" and "feminine principle" so richly and abundantly present in Little Mother.[19] But a far more fundamental difference between them is that Madeleine is actually aware of the values she stands for, while Little Mother's whole strength lies in her unconscious and unquestioning identification with a set of ancient values. If it is argued that Little Mother in any case lacks the intellectual training to recognise comparative culture patterns and thereby realise her own special role, this cannot be said of Savithri and Saroja. Yet both of them are unself-conscious characters and neither is striving deliberately to live up to the ideals of a culture. Savithri may be the ideal of Indian womanhood for Ramaswamy, but as a character she comes alive most vividly when she is her own self—the argumentative, rebellious, cigarette-smoking under-graduate fascinated by the wisdom and philosophy of a South Indian Brahmin who for her has the additional glamour of possess-ing a French education and a French wife—rather than when she is enacting the representative and symbolic role of Radha. The fact that both Savithri and Saroja finally submit to a marriage arranged by custom has sometimes been wrongly eulogised : "The sacrifices of Saroja and Savithri to the impersonal principle of marriage, and through it to the upholding and sustaining of the world... should therefore be seen in the context of the metaphysical emphasis of the book."[20] If Saroja and Savithri really did accept their marriages for metaphysical reasons, the book would have been a mere tract upholding the traditional values of Indian society, and lost much of its artistic authenticity. As it happens there is enough evidence in the novel to suggest that both these girls fought bitterly against their marriages, but they lost because they were not strong enough by themselves. While in London Savithri had once exasperated Ramaswamy with her fatalistic resignation to marriage (p. 199), but when she was actually faced with marriage she lost courage and sent a desperate appeal to Ramaswamy :

> No Hindu woman would wed a Turk. I feel besieged. The Turk
> is at the door. Help me to jump into the pyre... (p. 295)

The total world-view which sustains the novel may regard marriage
as an 'impersonal' principle, where the element of personal
fulfilment is irrelevant, but the characters involved suffer acutely
nevertheless. Saroja cannot get reconciled to her cruel fate even
on the day of her marriage :

> She (Saroja) wished she had been a European woman ; it
> would have given her so much freedom, so much brightness.

> "What freedom !" I exclaimed. "The freedom of foolishness.
> In what way, Saroja, do you think Catherine or Madeleine
> is better off than you."

> "They know how to love."

> "And you ?"

> "And we know how to bear children. We are just like a motor
> car or a bank account." (p. 259)

These individuals who refuse to conform to the cultural pattern
keep the book from becoming too abstract, too symbolic to
have any connection with reality, or too general to be a novel,
because a novel must be concerned with the fabric of actual life.
Ramaswamy is moved to declare at one place "... but I am
not telling a story here, I am writing the sad and uneven
chronicle of a life, my life..." (p. 233), and critics have also
wondered whether a story so digressive and amorphous can really
be called a novel. But if *The Serpent and the Rope* is an autobiography, it is the autobiography of Ramaswamy and not of Raja
Rao. Ramaswamy is a clearly conceived fictional character, and
though he often represents Raja Rao's point of view, he cannot
be identified with his creator. He is artistically realised and
recognisable as a character who is nostalgic for the past, who
lapses easily into sentimentality, who dramatises himself as Krishna
and who fulfils to the best of his ability the role of an Indian as
he conceives it. He finds strength in the conviction that he fits
into a familiar and permanent pattern. To him the value of the
individual is subordinate to the role allotted to him (as husband

or as brother or as the head of the family), and he admits :

My own countrymen, outside my country, terrify me. They seem to come from nowhere—from no particular province, caste, or profession. (p. 193)

Ramaswamy is disturbed by such people because he can function only when he can place a man in his social pigeon-hole. (This attitude may be regarded as an answer to Question No. 3 on page 73, namely, "What is man's relation to man ?") And part of the reason of his unsatisfactory relationship with Madeleine lies in the lack of his recognised role there. Ramaswamy's entire life is based on a role-expectation that operates on the impersonal principle.

While most critics have regarded Ramaswamy as a representative Indian, David McCutchion argues that his "type is not confined to India at all. *The Serpent and the Rope* has all the heavy-lidded pathos, the weary sadness of Pater's haunting book (*Marius the Epicurean*). It is the mood of disenchantment and gentle tolerance disguising indifference, that comes at the end of an age—the *mal du siecle*, the fatigue of ancient families and races..."[21] This critic's observation can be substantiated by Ramaswamy's own words :

I am a tired man. I am of a tired race which for three (four or five) thousand years has led such a studious thin-fed sadentary existence, that our nose and throat, our ears and eyes, have lost somewhat in native agility. (pp. 146-47)

Whether Ramaswamy represents India or he symbolises decadence may lead us to fruitless discussion. Those who share Ramaswamy's Brahminical background, his traditional childhood of hymns and rituals, and his advaitic grounding, will easily identify him with India. Those who do not have this background will inevitably feel uncomfortable at his excessive emotionalism with regard to certain objects and gestures (for example : the cows of Benares, the touching of the feet with kumkum). This diametric opposition in reactions has been present in all evaluations of *The*

Serpent and the Rope.

But if Ramaswamy is regarded as a fictional character and not the embodiment of Raja Rao's philosophy of life, then in his predicament we see just another variation of the familiar East-West motif—only, this variation touches many depths and spreads out to cover many aspects. As the title suggests, the novel involves two ways of apprehending reality : the recognition of the object as object, and the recognition that the object exists because the perceiver perceives it. The novel merely presents the confrontation of these two modes, but does not come to a definite preference of one over the other. Madeleine slowly excludes Ramaswamy from her life, and Ramaswamy brings his burden of infinite pathos back to India. And there is just a hint towards the end that in Travancore he might find a new mode of apprehending reality and a new meaning in life. With admirable restraint, Raja Rao has steered clear of the facile solution of concocting an easy assimilation of the two cultures. If there is an enduring solution, it is a private solution, and may not yield its secret to any public discussion.

NOTES

1. In this connection, an interesting issue raised by Khwaja Ahmad Abbas, an Indo-Anglian novelist as well as a film-maker, may be noted. During a talk on "Indian Films in the 'thirties" (given to the members of the Film Cultural Centre of Poona on 14th November, 1967), he made the point that since it would have been sedition in pre-independence days to portray an Englishman as the villain, the Indian film-makers often used a westernised mill-owner as the target of their attack; it was understood by the audience of the time that the Indian capitalist was a product of western values. This pattern, which operated in pre-independence indian films, was equally valid for the novels.

2. *Contemporary Indian Literature* (New Delhi, 1959), p. 93.

3. Perhaps 'choice' is not the right word here. Ideally, a writer has no choice about the language he writes in; it should be a matter of inevitability. In the last ten years there has been a great deal of controversy about the desirability of an Indian writer's writing in English, about the reasons that motivate him, and about the chances of his success—all based on the assumption that his writing in English is a deliberate and conscious choice.

4. "Identity and Nationality" *Commonwealth Literature*, ed. John Press (London, 1965), p. 109.

5. According to B. Rajan, it may be an advantage : "... the presence of two cultures in one's mind forms a wider and therefore saner basis on which to originate the quest for identity, and... the discordance between these two cultures can be creative as well as merely confusing. Perhaps one can go further and suggest that the man with mixed allegiances is contemporary *Everyman...*" *Commonwealth Literature. op. cit.*, p. 108.

6. *The Diary of a Writer*, trans. Boris Brasol (New York, 1954), p. 342.

7. *The Letters of Henry James*, ed. P. Lubbock (New York, 1920), Vol. I, p. 13.

8. Quoted, George Steiner, *Tolstoy or Dostoevsky* (London, 1959), p. 32.

9. Steiner, pp. 32-33.

10. "Values and Value-Orientation in the Theory of Action," *Towards a General Theory of Action*, ed. L. Parsons and E. Shils, (Cambridge, Mass., 1951), p. 410.

11. "The Cultural Interplay Between East and West," *The East and West Must Meet : A Symposium* (East Lansing, Michigan, 1959), p. 7.

12. In her summary used above, Cora Du Bois admits to have taken into consideration the formulations of Charles Morris, Ethel Albert, Clyde and Florence Kluckhohn.

13. When we speak of 'western' values we however refer only to the modern, post-Renaissance values of the West, because only in the last few centuries has the West shown a remarkable change in its attitude to nature, time and man. Today modern western man, generally speaking, seeks to conquer nature through technology, believes in the possibility of progress and gives more emphasis on the secular worth of the individual rather than on his place in a hierarchy.

14. See his paper in the section, "East-West Dialogue," in *Indian Writers in Conference*, ed. N. Ezekiel (Bombay, 1964), p. 108.

15. In an article, "English in India," *The Times of India*, December 2, 1964. See also his paper with the same title in *Commonwealth Literature*, p. 123.

16. Another alien in the Indian context is the Eurasian, whose predicament has not yet been seriously tackled in Indo-Anglian fiction. Malgonkar makes a passing reference to the Anglo-Indian's "awareness of root-lessness, of not belonging, not being wanted in the teeming brown world of India." (*Combat of Shadows*, p. 99)

17. Chinua Achebe (born 1930), author of *Things Fall Apart, No Longer at Ease*.

18. S. Nagarajan, *Sewanee Review*, LXXII (1964), 513.

19. See S.P. Ranchan and B.M. Razdan, *The Illustrated Weekly of India*, April 6, 1966.

20. *Ibid.*

21. *Writers Workshop Miscellany*, No. 8, p. 96.

5

Renunciation as an Ideal

THE CONCLUSIONS of *The Serpent and the Rope* and *The Dark Dancers* (discussed in the previous chapter), in spite of the differences in their themes, techniques and levels of meaning, have one basic similarity. Krishnan, the protagonist of Rajan's novel finds ultimate peace through suffering. When after the death of his wife, his desire, passion, quest for happiness and concern for belonging all are left behind, he emerges a freer and more detached man. This newly acquired non-attachment adds a dimension to his realization of self which is beyond the limited concept of happiness. He no longer worries about his identity or his goal in life. A new equanimity replaces the previous tension and pangs of adjustment. The quotation from the *Bhagavad Gita* that appears on the last page of the novel is not without some significance when we notice the recurrence of the same ideal in so many other Indo-Anglian novels :

> He who seeks freedom
> Thrusts fear aside
> Thrusts aside anger
> and puts off desire;
> Truly that man
> Is made free forever.

In *The Serpent and the Rope* the conflicts and tensions are of a different nature, but the final solution comes again through renunciation. After the estrangement between Madeleine and Ramaswamy is complete, Ramaswamy broods in Paris, the purpose of life obliterated before him :

> Yes, I say to myself: "I must leave this world, I must leave, leave this world." But Lord, where shall I go, where ? How can one go anywhere ? How can one go from oneself ? I walk up and down this mansard, and say : "There must be something that exalts and explains why we are here, what is it we seek."
> (p. 404)

And the explanation, there is more than a hint at the end of the novel, comes from his Guru in Travancore. "No, not a God, but a Guru is what I need," Ramaswamy exclaims (p. 408), because only a Guru can show the path that leads away from one's self.[1] Ramaswamy's thesis, and his love—the two reasons that kept him in France—both being over he turns eastward, back to the origin of his being, to find a deeper meaning of life, an explanation of "why we are here, what is it we seek."

Renunciation has always been an Indian ideal of life, be it renunciation of worldly goods and possessions, or the renunciation of selfish motives, passion and emotional bondage. Like all ideals it is a distinctly difficult condition, attainable only by a very few. In real life one hardly ever sees an ideal realised. But in literature, it is not impossible to create a credible individual by the complete realisation of all the fragmentary attributes one sees in different human beings. Such a character will adhere to the ideals of non-attachment, conquest of the senses, and selfless love towards all humanity. In Raja Rao's novels one nearly always finds one such saint figure. In his earliest novel, *Kanthapura*, Moorthy obviously corresponds to this ideal. A young boy, he rises above the desires of the flesh and the fear of suffering, of excommunication or censures of his fellow beings. Govindan Nair in *The Cat and Shakespeare* is a further development of the same kind of character. Moorthy being young still has to fight with himself to achieve equanimity, but Govindan Nair is past the phase of struggle. Even in Raja Rao's short stories one occasionally comes across

45-94/71 (7)

this ideal figure under the name of 'Master.'

Moorthy's struggles with himself are often referred to in *Kanthapura*, though they are mentioned only incidentally and never become an important issue. For example, his attraction towards Ratna, a young widowed girl, is hinted at. But he overcomes his desire and is able to work together with her in the Satyagraha movement in a detached way. His momentary anguish at being excluded from the social functions of the village (p. 111) and his instinctive revulsion on entering an untouchable's house (p. 99) indicate, however briefly, the struggle that went on within him constantly. When he first went to the house of an untouchable and drank milk there, it was in order to test his own capacity to rise above narrow prejudices. But breaking an age-old belief was a difficult ordeal :

> But Rachanna's wife quickly sweeps a corner, and spreads for him a wattle mat, but Moorthy, confused, blurts out. "No, no, no," and he looks this side and that. Surely there is a carcass in the back yard and it's surely being skinned, and he smells the stench of hide and the stench of pickled pigs and the roof seems to shake and all the gods and all the manes of heaven seem to cry out against him, and his hands steel mechanically to the holy thread, and holding it, he feels he would like to say 'Hari Om ! Hari Om !' (p. 99)

At such moments Moorthy is swayed by his emotions and prejudices, and occasionally loses his equanimity. He still needs the external aids of Ganga water and sacred thread to make him feel clean again. After a visit to an untouchable home, "taking the Ganges water he feels a fresher breath flowing through him." (p. 101)

Moorthy is young and is still in the process of conquering his senses. His vow of fasting in order to purify himself as well as the society of Kanthapura, indicates the tasks he sets upon himself. But Govinda Nair in *The Cat and Shakespeare* has already attained the ideal. He has realised the state of a *jivan-mukta*, which has been defined thus in *Yoga Vasistha* :

The *jivan-mukta* state is that in which the saint has ceased to have any desires... He may be doing all kinds of actions externally, though he remains altogether unaffected by them internally... He is full of bliss and happiness, and therefore appears to ordinary eyes to be an ordinary happy man... He is wise and pleasant and loving to all with whom he comes in contact... though unaffected within himself, he can take part in the enjoyment of others, he can play like a child and can sympathise with the sorrows of sufferers.[2]

Although this definition appears in *Yoga Vasistha*, the concept of a man enjoying a superior bliss through detachment and inner calm appears in many other Sanskrit philosophic texts (*Advaita Vedanta* or the *Bhagavad Gita*, for example). The traditional symbols of this blissful state of being, when a man is totally undisturbed by outside forces, are the tortoise within its shell, the lotus leaf on the pond, or a flame that is still and unmoving. In the *Bhagavad Gita* the description of the *sthita-prajna* comes very close to the definition of the *jivan-mukta*.

It must be remembered however, that the *jivan-mukta* or the *sthita-prajna* is not necessarily a man who has renounced the world. He could very well be a man living among the temptations of life, and doing many things that ordinary men do, and still be different internally. This is a fundamental and all-pervasive ideal of Indian life, an ideal that cuts across the boundaries of language and regional culture, and as such it becomes a motif that can be traced in Indo-Anglian novels profitably. This Indian ideal is derived evidently from Sanskrit sources, but it has permeated all levels of society and even people who may not be able to formulate the ideal in words have an instinctive respect for the qualities that comprise it. The traditional veneration for the ascetic arises mainly out of the popular faith that the ascetic has attained the state of being that others can only aspire for.

I

In a number of Indo-Anglian novels we come across characters who embody some or most of these ideal qualities, although they are seldom the central characters. In Santha Rama Rau's *Remember the House*, the mother is a character who has renounced

the possessions of this world, a rich household, an eminent husband
and a full life, and lives like a recluse far away in a town in Kerala
where her Guru lives. It is an unusual situation for a married
Hindu woman, but the blissful calm that she radiates, we are made
to feel, makes the propriety or the rightness and wrongness of her
mode of life quite irrelevant. The author, however, has employed
her not as a living character but as a symbol to counteract the effects
of the exuberance and quest of worldly happiness as represented
by an American woman. The heroine stands between these two
opposite systems of value and makes her own decision.

A different kind of contrast is developed in Anita Desai's first
novel, *Cry, the Peacock*. Maya, the central figure is alive through
all her senses and lives intensely for each moment. Her husband,
Gautama, is remote, detached, intellectual and somewhat
bewildered by his wife's hypersensitiveness. There are moments
when one feels that Gautama comes very close to our traditional
ideal of life, and achieves an inner calm. In one of his attempts to
explain to his highstrung wife the ideals of existence, he says :

> You should be capable of far greater detachment than I, hence
> of greater peace of mind and stability. That is the end of our
> philosophical aspirations—to exist like a lily upon water, rooted
> in water, yet with its petals dry, untouched by it, the lamp placed
> in a windless corner unflickering, the tortoise with its limbs with-
> drawn from the external world, the entire cult of symbols that
> we have for this ideal existence. But who is capable of it ? I
> with my books, my work, or you with your sensual pleasure of
> living ? Christ, who went out in the world to mingle with people,
> acquainted himself with their suffering, and involved himself
> in a series of miracles whereby to bring about physical well-
> being and salvation, or Buddha who meditated beneath the bo
> tree, his eyes closed to death, misery, pleasure, the temptations
> of helping, the temptation of saving, the temptation of attaining
> success? (p. 102)

This elaboration on the theme of ideal existence brings out the
essential ambiguity in the author's approach to it. There is not
one path that leads to equanimity, Gautama believes, and he has
nothing against his wife's intensely sensuous approach to life, be-

cause this could very well be another way towards the same ideal condition. But since the novel is narrated from the point of view of Maya, the ideal itself seems to be challenged. Gautama's aspiration to stability and calm appears to her to be a negation of life in all its vivid aspects. The fact that ultimately Maya turns insane and kills her husband may contain an indirect comment on their different values of life.

In Nayantara Sahgal's *A Time to be Happy* the central theme is stated thus : "At heart the sensualist is as Indian as the ascetic. The difference between the two is usually a matter of time." (p. 160) Therefore the narrator, who is an elderly man, comes close to the ideal of detachment described earlier, while the young hero Sanad Shivpal is shown to be very much involved with emotions and worldly ties. The narrator is tranquil, undisturbed by, though not indifferent to, what is happening around him, and he can take a sympathetic interest in the career of young Sanad Shivpal. His detachment never becomes the central focus of the novel, but the author tends to regard the narrator's attitude to life as harmonious, because he has achieved what should be the ideal at his time of life. The emphasis on time should be noted throughout the novel. Non-attachment cannot be the aim of every man at every phase of life—it is only the final stage in the development of an individual.

In R.K. Narayan's novels it is possible to trace this ideal unobtrusively operating behind certain situations and characterizations. As early as in *The Bachelor of Arts* we find the hero wanting to give up "a life full of distracting illusions and hysterics," which is an adolescent's groping effort to describe the state of the unflickering lamp. But only in *Waiting for the Mahatma* do we come across someone who has actually succeeded in achieving this. The Mahatma himself emerges here as a saint who can sympathise and remonstrate with ordinary men (true to the definition of *jivan-mukta*) and at the same time retain an internal calm. In some translations of Indian philosophical texts, the *jivan-mukta* has been called a 'saint' in English, but one must use the word 'saint' in the Indian context with tucaion because of its existing Christian associations. In Narayan's novel, however, Gandhi corresponds also to the idea of a Christian saint in becoming a martyr : he accepts a cruel death like Christ's to redeem the suffering of others. Later, in *The Guide*, the martyr motif is reiterated with a different emphasis in the character of Raju, who was very far from being a *jivan-mukta purush* in his life.

The fictional characters referred to so far are men who live in this world and yet strive for detachment from it. But a large number of spiritual aspirants in Indo-Anglian fiction seem to be actual ascetics who have renounced this world and have donned the saffron robe. In a recent survey of Indian fiction, K.R. Srinivasa Iyengar remarks on the important part *sannyasis* have always played in Indian fiction. Talking of Bankim Chandra Chatterjee's early novel *Anandamath* (1882), Professor Iyengar writes : "In this and other novels, Bankim introduced *sannyasis* (wandering ascetics) into the story—and, like the widow, the *sannyasi* too, often figures in Indian fiction, sometimes as a beneficent, and sometimes as a malevolent, influence."[3] Professor Iyengar places emphasis on the *influence* these ascetics have on other people's lives, and not on the ascetics themselves as central fictional characters.

In Indo-Anglian fiction the ascetic appears frequently, but hardly ever as an individual character, except in the two well-known examples of Raju in *The Guide* and Kalo in Bhattacharya's *He Who Rides a Tiger*. As a rule he exists as an agent influencing other lives. Iyengar's incidental distinction between sadhus who exert a beneficial influence and sadhus who exercise a malevolent influence should not distract our attention from the further shades of difference among ascetics in literature. One has to take into account the author's attitude to the sadhu as well as the attitudes of the other characters of the novel to him. These distinctions are not purposeless, because the ascetic in the saffron robe is a readymade symbol at the disposal of the Indian novelist, and much depends on how he uses this symbol for the purposes of his novel. Because the saffron robe automatically generates respect and adoration, a sadhu's role is a complex public one. Whether people derive beneficial influence from him or not often depends on the attitudes and expectations of the people themselves. The sadhu can very easily be turned into a symbol of evil, too, because he can play upon the faith of man by exerting an insidious influence.

But there are some novels, e.g., Kamala Markandaya's *A Silence of Desire*, where the sadhu has a more complex and ambiguous function.

The ascetics who influence the other characters in a benign way are a common feature of Indo-Anglian novels. They often solve problems raised by worldly men or bring peace to a troubled situation. This is the simplest pattern, seen in novels as different as Bhabani Bhattacharya's *A Goddess Named Gold*, Sudhindranath Ghose's *The Flame of the Forest* and Kamala Markandaya's *Possession*. In *A Goddess Named Gold* 'the wandering minstrel' ultimately resolves the crisis brought about by a vicious cycle of avarice and misunderstanding. The crisis however is partly of the ascetic's own making, because during one of his infrequent visits to the village he had given an amulet to Meera which, he said, would turn copper into gold the day she performed a real act of kindness. One of her friends exchanges her gold ring with Meera's copper ring when Meera is asleep. This is no miracle or magic, but merely a joke; yet out of this small practical joke grows an enormous misconception. This girl is then believed to have the power of turning baser metals into gold, and the rich industrialist of the locality takes her into partnership. The miracle is not repeated. The rich man believes that it might happen again if she is made to perform more acts of kindness. People are made homeless, children are dropped into wells so that she might have a chance of helping them out and displaying her kindness. Her friends are alienated from her— in short, the poison of gold works into each heart until the people become suspicious of each other. When the situation gets beyond human solution the 'wandering minstrel' appears again and resolves the crisis, not by revealing the trick to her, but by throwing away the amulet into the river. Bhattacharya turns this act into a significant gesture, and by making the day coincide with 15th August, 1947 he adds a further suggestion of a new future. The wandering minstrel here is the ascetic and a builder of modern India rolled into one; the latter part of his function is merely stated, but not presented before the reader. The wandering minstrel, who even in his absence is supposed to wield so much influence, in fact never quite fills the role cast for him. He is supposed to be a large-

hearted man, a sage with great powers of good, but the reputation
built up for him remains unsubstantiated in the actual characterization of the man.

In the last novel of Sudhin Ghose's tetralogy, *The Flame of the
Forest*, the wandering ascetic is a young woman, an unusual figure
like most characters in Ghose. Mynah the *kirtani* (or singer of
devotional songs), is not merely a person who sings of God and
roams from place to place; nor is she only an aspirant for the ideal
of non-attachment. But she has had a mystic experience, a revela-
tion in the Himalayas that has changed her life. This experience
(on one level it is nothing but a narrow escape from a tiger; on
another level, it is an inexplicable miracle) is described in frightening and yet poetic terms by Ghose in a memorable chapter.
(pp. 222-230) After this experience Mynah became a visionary.
The mountains, hills, crags, trees all communicated with her.

> The bridegroom was looking for the bride, and the bride Radha
> was playing at hide-and-seek with the divine spouse Krishna;
> Purush was rejoicing with Prakriti, and she Mynah, was Radha's
> hand-maiden. (p. 237)

Out of the five paths that her people regarded as means of serving
Krishna and Radha, Mynah chooses the most difficult. The five
paths, we are told, are *Santi* (calm contemplation of the deity),
Dasya (willing servitude), *Sakhya* (friendliness), *Vatsalya* (filial
attachment like that of a child for its parent) and *Madhurya* (the
tender affection of a girl for her lover). Mynah chooses
Madhurya, and in her devotion all the Vaishnavic lore of rural
Bengal becomes alive.

In *The Flame of the Forest* this Kirtani comes in contact with the
hero of the novel. It is the same hero whom we find growing up
from childhood to adolescence and then to manhood in the three
earlier novels of Ghose. The young man whose name is never
mentioned but whom Mynah calls Balaram, has a tendency to get
into all kinds of scrapes because of his interfering nature. He is
a rationalist and an intellectual with no spiritual inclination, and
Mynah's mystic moods frighten him. He fights his fascination

for her because in his practical rational mind he does not understand Mynah. Mynah constantly remonstrates with him for the
amount of useless knowledge he is collecting around him. Her
voice is the traditional voice of Indian faith, which holds that
the knowledge that cannot help a man towards self-realisation is
not knowledge but learned ignorance. She asks him to join her in
her ceaseless wanderings. From Calcutta she leaves suddenly
for the Himalayas, and from each stage of her journey she
sends for Balaram. Balaram resists the temptation to join her.

> What would happen, I asked myself, if at the end of a Kirtan
> singing on a moonlight night Mynah said "come with me."
> What would I do if she proposed "you will play on the flute and
> I shall sing and we shall move on and on till we reach the throne
> of the 'Bestower of Bliss'. What could prevent me from
> accepting her invitation ?
> Self-preservation, I repeated to myself, is a man's first duty.
> Ulysses tied himself to the mast of his ship lest the siren songs
> should tempt him to plunge into the sea. But where was my
> mast ? What was there to hold me back ? Nothing.
>
> It was this fear that prevented me from revisiting Gilani when
> Mynah was there. (p. 221)

Later on he gets into a number of political complications. He is
forced to leave Calcutta for some time. At the first stop in his
journey he meets Mynah and becomes a flute accompanist to her
songs. He becomes a pilgrim along with her and together they
wander from place to place singing the praise of Krishna, and
learning 'other forms of wisdom' that reveal one's affinity with
the universe.

This is the conclusion of the tetralogy. It is significant that a
sustained work of nearly a decade, four novels of considerable charm
and technical skill, should build up to this conclusion. The hero
leaves his worldly concerns behind and sets out to find "affinity
with the universe." Sudhin Ghose had lived abroad for a long time,
and he was in England at the time of the writing of these novels.
Therefore it is specially interesting to note that, like Rajan and
Raja Rao, Ghose also makes his hero turn back to the strength of

his own beginning. And Mynah the Kirtani is the most important factor in showing him the way.

Mynah is a vivid and unique creation—a girl with a swing in her hips and a magic in her voice, who calls herself "less than the red dust of Braja that Radha trod." Beside her the Swami of Kamala Markandaya's *Possession* appears vague and shadowy. He is hardly a living character, but he represents the other side in the tug-of-war for the possession of Valmiki. Lady Caroline Bell stands on one side. She claims to have discovered the artistic talents of the young goat-herd Valmiki, and therefore she has a right over him. The Swami was Valmiki's guide and mentor before the Englishwoman found him, but he makes no claim to him. Eventually however he wins in the tug-of-war because Valmiki after his global tour, fame and publicity, chooses to come back to his obscure South Indian village to the cave where the Swami lives. The conflict here is simple, almost predictable; between possession and renunciation, between wealth and fame on the one hand and freedom and obscurity on the other. The author weakens the impact of the novel by making the contrasts too clear cut, a solid black and white, cast in the now thread-bare pattern of the spiritual East encountering materialistic West. The oversimplification is rather surprising because in a previous novel, *Silence of Desire*, Kamala Markandaya had very sensitively depicted the nuances of relationship between the spiritual and non-spiritual spheres of life. In *Possession*, the Swami wins the battle because he does not try, because he has reached that state where pleasure or pain, victory or defeat makes no difference. That, the novelist suggests, is his real strength.

While in most of these novels the ascetic embodies the ideal of renunciation inherent in the culture of the sub-continent, it is also a well-known fact that not all sadhus are really ascetics. The saffron robe is a very convenient disguise for tramps, destitute people, and petty thieves because it assures some anonymity and privilege. Frauds and charlatans frequently try to pass for sadhus, and since this is a common experience in India its presentation in fiction is also inevitable. G.V. Desani's highly individual *All About H. Hatterr* deals with a man's encounters with a series of such fake sadhus. In K. Nagarajan's *Athawar House* several chapters are devoted to the description of how a man on the only occasion he came out of the protective orbit of the joint family was duped by an ascetic in Benares. The ascetic systematically went about his job by getting certain photographs of the man taken in a compromising situation and chased him across the country with the intention of blackmailing him. Mulk Raj Anand's novels also abound in hypocrites who pass for priests or holy men.

These counterfeit holy men are often treated on the comic level. G.V. Desani's book[4] consists of seven episodes in which seven sets of imposters manage to make a fool of Mr. Hatterr. Six of them are holy men. Written in a mock-serious style *All About H. Hatterr* is the supposed autobiography of an Anglo-Malayan orphan who grew up in India. In the introduction he tells the reader that he has been the disciple of the "Sages of Calcutta, Rangoon, Madras, Bombay, and the Right Honourable the Sage of Delhi, the wholly worshipful of Mogalserai and his naked majesty number one, the sage of all India himself !" (p. 19)

The subsequent chapters deal with the various steps of his education at the hands of these sages. After the third chapter the situations begin to repeat themselves. The first sadhu of Chapter 1 becomes the prototype of the rest of the sadhus in the book. Hatterr goes to interview the holy man as a reporter of a newspaper, but he has to come back without his clothes because the sage and his brother deal in second-hand garments. Hereafter this becomes the recurrent pattern. The sage called All-Happy (Sadanand), the one called Hira Manek Mukti (Cardinal Diamonds and Rubies), Master Ananda Giri-Giri, the sadhu of Ajmere Marwara, and the fellows of Sat-Sang, all seem to be members of a disreputable gang of swindlers. Nudity, or being cheated out of one's clothes, is a common occurrence. Admirers of *All About H. Hatterr* may find a symbolic significance here, but it is possible to regard the novel merely as a study of different varieties of human deception. Characters in ochre robes have a special advantage in deceiving men because they can exploit the simple faith of a credulous people. Hatterr stands for the eternal dupe who is an easy prey to all kinds of swindlers; to use Hatterr's own terminology, he is the "ruddy crab who takes the hitting" while the imposters belong to the class of 'hitters.' The theme of the book could have

been 'the education of H. Hatterr,' if one could see some development or progress in his character. But as it is the book is
an admirable tour de force with interesting linguistic and technical
experiments.

Mulk Raj Anand's holy men are also obviously fake. His
attitude towards them is not one of comic acceptance, but of
righteous indignation. The priests and Mahants who frequently
appear in his novels are censured by the author not for their lack
of spiritual authenticity, but for the tyranny and hyprocrisy they
practise. In almost every Anand novel one comes across the three
inevitable figures of evil : the landlord, the money-lender and the
priest. Mohant Nandgir of his trilogy is a characteristic example
of an Anand priest; he smokes hemp, drinks *bhang*; he punishes the
village people for supposed wrongs, but he himself indulges in
fornication. It is in his interest to keep the village people unenligh-
tened so that they may never question his authority. Like the
landlord and the money-lender he is against progress, and therefore
an evil force in society. The priest in *Untouchable*, who complains
of pollution when his advances towards Bakha's sister are frustrated, is another typical character. In *Coolie* an ascetic seeks physical gratification under the pretence of performing religious rituals
to bring fertility to a childless woman. Pandit Suraj Mani,
the lascivious priest in *The Road*, is the same character appearing under a different name. The devout Brahmin, self-righteous
religious leader of society who is at heart merely an old lecher, is
a recurrent character in Anand's novels. This is in keeping with
his ideals of progress and enlightenment, because religion often
becomes a reactionary force, an instrument of oppression and an
obstacle to the development of independent thought.

II

There is no ambiguity in Anand's attitude to the holy men he
creates. But in Kamala Markandaya's *A Silence of Desire* the
author's stand towards the spiritual powers of the Swami remains
complex and elusive to the end. At first the Swami's influence
appears to be malevolent, because it breaks up a normal
comfortable domestic life. Sarojini, a traditional Hindu-
woman, a good mother and a submissive wife, suddenly becomes

distant and incomprehensible. Dandekar the husband, who is a clerk in a Government office, feels that his stable universe is shaken because his wife has withdrawn herself from the family. At first it is sexual jealousy that drives him mad, but later his wife confesses that she goes to a Swami in order to be cured of a growth in her womb. When Dandekar asks her why she kept this a secret Sarojini answers :

> Because you would have stopped me going to be healed... Yes you. You would have sent me to a hospital instead. Called me superstitious, a fool, because I have beliefs that you cannot share. You wouldn't let me be—No ! You would have reasoned with me until I lost my faith because faith and reason don't go together, and without faith I shall not be healed. (p. 87)

This becomes the crux of the conflict between faith and rationalism, a very significant issue in the context of Indian society today. The gulf between the husband and wife widens. The wife completely ignores her household duties; the hungry children come back to an empty house, and the tightly balanced economy of the family is disturbed because Sarojini begins to give away to the sadhu whatever money or jewellery she can lay her hands on.

Dandekar wants to confront the enemy who is destroying his peace and his happiness. He walks long miles, crosses a river and arrives in the village to see this Swami whose baleful influence has blighted his life. When he actually meets the man he finds that he can hold nothing against him. Dandekar feels a calm, a peculiar detachment from the everyday affairs of life in the presence of the Swami but he knows this to be only temporary. Dandekar has the same feeling of rising above the body and the worries of the world when he meets the Swami for the second time. But once he comes away from him he feels "the pains crept back, the worry, the misery, the lust for gold chains and silver cups." (p. 159) He tries desperately to get Sarojini away from the Swami because he realises "our worlds do not mix. It is disastrous to try make them."

The author scrupulously avoids taking sides in the conflict. Just as one can sympathise with poor Dandekar whose orderly life is threatened with ruin from a power that he cannot fight, so one

can admire Sarojini's strength in standing alone in her faith. From
an ordinary passive wife she becomes a woman with a will
of her own, a will that happens to be different from her husband's. In this struggle the Swami has only a vague distant part.
He is brought before the reader only on two or three occasions,
and on none of these occasions what he has to say is of much
significance.

One thing however is clear. The Swami has some solace to offer
to individuals who are torn by worries. Even a sceptic like
Dandekar does not question the Swami's power to bring tranquillity as long as one is in his presence. But Dandekar reasons that
"his reality is not ours." (p. 199) Since one cannot remain with
him for ever, and since the worries and frustrations return as soon
as one comes away from him, it is practical wisdom to stay away
from a man who disrupts the even tenor of one's daily life. To
Sarojini however, the tenor of daily life has ceased to matter. She
does not mind the children going hungry or dust gathering on the
floor because these are insignificant matters compared with the
deeper wisdom and peace she has received from the Swami.

The situation reaches an impasse. In order to bring about a
solution, the interference of an outside agent becomes necessary,
and this outside agent comes in the shape of Dandekar's superior
officer Chari. To him Dandekar pours out his woes. When
Dandekar wails "I want my wife back," Chari wants to know if
his wife has really left him.

"She is still with me," said Dandekar, "but it's only the shell.
All that's real is left with the Swami. Sometimes when I look
at her I know she has even forgotten that I exist. I know in the
Swami's world it is not easy to remember—I've been in it. I
know the forgetfulness it brings—but I want to exist, to exist for
her, I want my world back, my children happy, my floor swept."

"Is that important too ?"

"Yes, yes, yes," he cried. "In the world I'm in, it's most
important, all the small things are important, and I know it's
small and petty, but I'm a small and petty man." (p. 197)

The tension now takes on a different hue. It is no longer the
conflict between reason and faith as it was in the beginning of the

novel. Dandekar is not so emphatic about the inefficacy of the faith cure. He merely asserts the difference between the two levels of existence. An ordinary man cannot afford to live on the higher level on which the Swami lives. And it is uncomfortable for him to know that his wife can tread a path that is beyond him.

Thereafter the private problem of Dandekar becomes a public issue. Government officials start an inquiry to determine whether the Swami is a charlatan or a saint. The people of the town divide themselves into two sides. Some complain that the Swami has enticed away their wives and daughters, taking advantage of their ailments to establish a dominion over them for his material ends. Others want him to stay because they have faith in him. On the official level, Chari and his subordinate Ghosh represent the two points of view. Chari, a local man with an instinctive understanding of the people wants to let the Swami alone ("It doesn't really matter what I think. Or what you think. It's the people that count"), while Ghosh, in his enthusiasm for rationality and abolition of superstition, zealously wants to prove that the Swami is a fraud. Ultimately the Swami himself solves the problem by leaving the town of his own accord. Sarojini is restored to Dandekar, but her calm acceptance of the Swami's departure itself is something that she has learnt from the Swami and for a few stray moments Dandekar is possessed with jealousy at the thought that he is indebted to this man for the return of his wife. But he has her back and that is all that matters. And she even agrees to undergo surgical treatment for the growth in her womb, because the Swami has told her to do so. At the end of the novel we find her recovering from the operation.

But that is not all. It is not enough that the Swami, even when he voluntarily leaves the field, remains the more powerful adversary, because his influence is abiding. There is also a public side to this issue. The Swami supported a hundred destitute and ailing people from what he received as gifts from his devotees. When the Swami leaves, these men remain behind and as the resources slowly dwindle, they reach the point of starvation. Dandekar, to assuage his sense of guilt at the departure of the Swami (he believes to the end that he himself was responsible for the removal of the Swami) makes one more visit to the Swami's deserted residence, only to come face to face with these starving people herded together in despair.

The question whether the Swami is a saint or a charlatan remains unanswered, or perhaps at this point the answer is not relevant any more. The Swami functions not as an individual who lives his own life, but as a public figure—a fulfilment of certain needs of society. He satisfies the needs of the people who want an object of faith. And the insistence finally appears to be not on the spiritual but on the social function of the Swami.

The figure of the *sannyasi* in Indo-Anglian fiction thus appears sometimes on the comic level, sometimes on the serious level, sometimes as a source of benevolent influence, occasionally as an evil power that blights other people's lives, or (as in the novel just discussed), as an ambivalent and complex character who fulfils certain needs of society. In none of the novels discussed above, however, does the ascetic appear as the central figure. Normally he appears either as an abstraction or a vague power in the background influencing the action and behaviour of other characters.

III

Only in three Indo-Anglian novels—widely different from each other—do we find an attempt to put the holy man in the centre of focus. Anand Lal in *Seasons of Jupiter* makes his hero pass through seven years of hard yogic discipline away from human habitation, while Bhabani Bhattacharya and R.K. Narayan in their novels *He Who Rides a Tiger* and *The Guide* attempt to probe into the issues of reality and pretence behind the saffron robe.

Seasons of Jupiter is an ambitious philosophical novel where the hero is on a life-long quest towards a completeness of being, where spiritual elements will become fused with sensual elements. If the novel fails to achieve the purpose of the author, it is because the tensions and conflicts are not sufficiently objectified, and the novel remains the brooding monologue of an introverted man.

Gyan Chand, the heir of a rich land-owner, after several fruitless attempts to establish a satisfying relation with other persons, leaves his house and property and becomes the disciple of an ascetic. For the first few months he learns nothing beyond a certain self-discipline through voluntary physical hardship. Only after watching him carefully for some time does his Guru agree to 'instruct' him, and part of the instruction consists in repeating the different verses of the *Upanishad* until his ears are filled with the rhythmic pattern of sound. The next lesson is meditation; this is difficult because Gyan Chand is a man of intense sensitiveness to the world around him, and his own five senses are acute. There are days when he is so alert to the smell of the mango blossoms or sight of the yellow mustard fields that he forgets to meditate. But slowly, imperceptibly, he learns the secret of the inner stillness that transcends the experience of the senses. The steps in Gyan Chand's development in the mystic path are minutely described and the author attempts the difficult task of conveying through words a feel of the startling experiences Gyan Chand has during his meditations. At the end of the third year he begins to understand the bliss of existence : "the free awesome contemplation of, and pleasure in, the creation." At this point the sadhu, his mentor, takes leave of him because Gyan has no further need for him.

Gyan Chand himself moves forward after a while because an ascetic must not stay in one place too long lest he grow attached to it. At the first step of his journey an incident takes place that is curiously reminiscent of the central situation of *The Guide*. When Gyan stops at the village Paramanand, the people of the village urge him to stay on because they need his help in combating an epidemic that is raging there. Gyan Chand protests, telling them he does not possess any supernatural power. But by some miracle or accident he stops the epidemic by taking the disease upon himself.

Considerably weakened by the sickness, he moves on in his travels along the Beas until he reaches the Kulu Valley, where two consecutive emotional experiences shake him and make him realise that the path of detachment and renunciation is really not for him. First it is a little hill boy to whom he becomes deeply attached, and second, a bird of which he becomes inordinately fond. When the boy leaves, and the bird dies, his sorrow belies all pretensions of non-attachment. In his outbursts of grief he realises his failure to attain the unruffled calm expected of an ascetic. After this incident he comes back to his land and property in Amritsar.

The period of renunciation for Gyan Chand is only an interlude,

45-94/71 (8)

but it leaves a deep impress on his life afterwards. The essential
need for simplicity remains with him, and he learns to look at the
trivial things of life with the right kind of detachment. In many
ways his personality blossoms forth, and when he marries again
at a late age it is a completely satisfying experience because he has
learnt to "love without burdening the beloved with the false attempt
to focus my whole life on her." Anand Lall has attempted to
relate the sexual experience of a man with a total realisation of
life. This is in close connection with the view of life that gave rise
to the temple sculptures of Khajuraho and Konarak, when the
physical and the spiritual aspects of life are seen as parts of a whole.
In *Seasons of Jupiter* the secret room in Gyan Chand's ancestral
home, the central symbol of the novel, assumes a special significance
after Gyan Chand's solitary retreat in the hills and valleys. The
room is hung with rust and gold sensuous draperies and a series of
Rajput paintings depicting love. It has a heavy erotic atmosphere,
but it assumes an unexpected dimension when Gyan Chand comes
back after seven years of ascetic life: "I turned to the room again
and went up to the pictures... I gasped in surprise : in miniature
they were reminiscent of the greatest of my own flights into space
in my periods of meditation." (p. 232)

Anand Lall attempts the difficult task of recreating through words
the mystic experiences which are generally regarded as something
that can only be lived through, not described. This problem is
bypassed by most novelists dealing with *sannyasis* by not probing
too deep into the experiences that make them what they are. Lall,
in spite of his knowledge of philosophy, and of human nature,
lacks the skill of externalisation that turns a discourse into a novel.
Too much is stated in the novel, too little presented through action
or behaviour. The other characters remain shadowy, and although
Gyan Chand spends his life in trying to establish a continuous
harmonious relationship with other people, these other people
seem to lack any existence beyond their relationship to him. *Seasons of Jupiter* contains excellent ideas for a novel that could
have been written.

He Who Rides a Tiger is a totally different kind of work where
Bhabani Bhattacharya is concerned not with the mystic experiences
of a yogi, but with the deception of an imposter. The spiritual

element is treated on the social level where the ochre robe of an ascetic becomes the symbol of power. It is the story of Kalo, a village blacksmith, and his revenge on society. Hunger and famine drive Kalo from his village to Calcutta, where a petty theft of food sends him to jail. Once out of jail, his hunger compels him to accept the job of a procurer for a brothel where one day he happens to find his own daughter. Totally embittered with the society that turns innocent girls into prostitutes and honest men into thieves, he prepares for revenge.

His success exceeds his expectation. By a clever trick he makes an image of Shiva rise out of the soil before hundreds of eyes. A great temple grows up in the place, and Kalo, disguised as a Brahmin, becomes the prosperous master of the temple.

So far it is an easy success. But to continue the fraud becomes increasingly difficult. Kalo could pretend to defy the limits of caste in one rebellious moment, but to accept the role of a Brahmin for a sustained period is no easy task for a man rooted in the tradition of rural India. Putting on the sacred thread, which only the higher castes are qualified to wear, itself involves a moral struggle. When the crowd gathers round him on the first day with reverence and holy fear it is a crucial moment for him.

> He had closed his eyes. He had held his breath. Clutching the sacred thread in his hands he had passed it lightly over his shoulder and across his bare chest. The daring of that gesture made him tremble. With that gesture he had thrown off the heavy yoke of his past and flouted the three thousand years of his yesteryears. Putting on the sacred thread he had made himself rootless. (p. 82)

But did Kalo have the intellectual strength to accept the rootlessness? The novel raises this question very unobtrusively. Kalo's jail-mate and friend, 'B-10', had the strength to renounce his caste. In fact he gave up his given name because that betrayed his Brahminic origin, and preferred to be known by the number he was given in the jail, so that he could be equated with all other human beings. But B-10 is an educated man brought up in an industrial city where caste divisions are not so deeply ingrained. And he has his intellectual conviction to support his castelessness. Kalo, an uneducated blacksmith from a remote village, cannot have the same background and the same mental preparedness. And therefore he feels the need to belong much more than 'B-10.' Since now he cannot belong to the blacksmith caste in which he is most at home, his next attempt is to identify himself with the Brahmins. He tries to rationalise this attempt in his own mind. He argues with himself :

> Is not your purpose already served ? Have you not had enough? It is better that you rinse the bitterness out of your mouth, purge it from your blood, so that you, a self-created Brahmin, may take your place in the new order of living, the place that they are offering you.

The initial inspiration of his deception had come out of his anger against society. This was his revenge : he had wanted the people in power to bow to him. But he is now dazzled by his own success and when the elite of the city shower him with honour and respect, Kalo's weapons lose their edge, the revenge loses its sweetness. Instead, out of an instinctive need to belong to a caste, he almost begins to believe that he has achieved genuine Brahminic powers. At a certain point Kalo even becomes concerned about pollution from non-Brahmin touch, and becomes as rigid as the hired priest of the temple about the customs and rituals of worship. Kalo would have entirely identified himself with his new Brahmin role, but for occasional reminders from his daughter Lekha.

Lekha is her father's associate in the temple, but she never shares her father's exultation at the success of the scheme. She too has enough reasons to rebel against society. She has been through the same hell of starvation and suffering. In a way she has suffered more than her father at the hands of society, because she was forced into a brothel. But her listlessness over the whole project of her father raises another complicated moral issue : how far is deception justifiable even if it means paying back to a cruel society what it has given to its defenceless poor ? Does Lekha worry about the moral aspect of the venture, or is it only the fear of being found out ? Or is her indifference the result of the nervous shock that she receives in the brothel ? Whatever the reason, the contrast between the attitudes of she father and daughter is obvious. When her father gloats over the deference he receives from the eminent men of Calcutta, Lekha merely moves about mechanically doing her work, completely detached from the whole show.

Kalo becomes so sure of his Brahmin identity that he plans to arrange his daughter's marriage into some Brahmin family. What began as a fraud is passing into reality. The metaphor of the title becomes relevant at this point because neither Kalo nor his daughter has the courage to go back. Their deception is the tiger they are riding—and to dismount would be to court death.

Kalo's ambition slowly transcends the revenge motive, and without admitting it to himself he becomes greedy for more power. Most of the time he identifies himself with his new role, but occasionally there are moments of truth, when he realises with anguish that his deception not only affects the rich, the exploiters whom he hates, but also the poor, who are spending their hard-earned money on a fake god created by a trick. But his final moment of illumination comes when he discovers with horror that his own daughter is going to be sacrificed at the altar of his ambition. The temple authorities are going to transform Lekha into "The mother of Sevenfold Bliss," a living goddess, and Lekha submits to this deception because she has no will left to protest.[6] The tragedy of the situation can be viewed from two angles. First : a human being is made into a tool in the hands of powerful men; the victim is denied all the natural pleasures of youth and the fulfilment of the normal instincts of life. But the second tragedy lies in the fact that she herself, however hesitantly, comes to believe in her sacred powers. Lekha, who to begin with wanted no part of her father's huge game of deception, later reaches a stage when she agrees to touch with her toe the forehead of a sick child in the hope that this would cure him. The child dies and the violent curses of the mother bring Lekha back to her senses. But even then she does not rebel against the role that has been imposed upon her.

The final outburst that frees Lekha from her bondage comes not from herself but, quite unexpectedly, from her father, who makes a clean breast of his deception to a large crowd that has gathered to see the anointing of "The mother of Sevenfold Bliss." The tensions and complications that have slowly been mounting in the novel are all resolved, though a little too easily, at the end. The issues involved in the novel have been difficult issues, fraught with dangerous implications, and the facile solution at the end robs the novel of some of its seriousness.

When Kalo confesses his fraud, and tells the people that the Shiva they have worshipped so devoutly is a fake stone, installed through the trick of a blacksmith, the people rise against him in anger. Kalo has no means of saving himself from the consolidated attack of the insulted Brahmins, but at this point providential help comes to him from the outer fringe of the crowd, in the shape of the poor, the low caste and the destitute men. They come forward to fight Kalo's battle because they feel that Kalo has avenged the wrongs done to them, by duping the proud Brahmins. Hereafter the conflict becomes simply the conflict between the exploiters and the exploited, the haves and the have-nots, the proletariat and the bourgeois, the Brahmins and the non-Brahmins. While this Marxist class war goes on, Kalo and his daughter leave the temple built on a lie and take the dusty road together.

To stick to the metaphor of the title, one may say that the man who rode the tiger ultimately did have the courage to kill it in order to dismount. But the killing of the tiger is made to appear too easy a job. The end simplifies the complex issues involved in the novel. Kalo is made to escape the consequences of his confession and the doubts raised earlier about Kalo's capacity to go back and be satisfied in his original station in life, remain. Kalo had always wanted to rise above his caste as the naming episode in the earlier part of the novel indicates. When his daughter was born he had called her Chandralekha, as suggested by a Brahmin customer. He had been fascinated by the beauty of a name uncommon in his caste. Only Brahmins and educated people gave such names to their children, and Kalo not only had named his daughter differently but had educated her in a way unknown in his caste. He had expressed his regret more than once that the beauty and brains of his daughter were not properly appreciated by the people of his backward community. Therefore when circumstances raise him to the status of a Brahmin it is the fulfilment of his own submerged wishes.   How is one to reconcile Kalo's sudden renunciation of his power, his money and his status with this background ?

R.K. Narayan's *The Guide* invites obvious comparisons with Bhabani Bhattacharya's *He Who Rides a Tiger*.   Both are stories of a man who deceives society by passing for a spiritual man, in both the man is carried away by his deception until a point comes when it is difficult to undo the enormous lie. But the superficial similarity hides a very fundamental difference. If both these novels deal with the theme of a man wearing a mask, in one the man at the end throws away the mask and goes back where he began.   In the other the man finds it more and more difficult to tear off the mask until he finds that the mask has become his face.   In Bhattacharya's book Kalo's deception is a deliberate act of revenge against society.   Raju in *The Guide*, on the other hand, drifts into the role of a sadhu willy-nilly, and once he finds himself cast in the role of an ascetic he attempts to perform the act with gusto, partly for the sake of self-preservation, partly because it suits his personality wonderfully.

This drifting into the role of a sadhu fits in with the general pattern of Raju's life.   The account of his past as narrated to one of his disciples makes it sufficiently clear that Raju never *did* anything; things always *happened* to him. His illustrious career as a tourist guide also began very casually, almost as an accident. When tourists happened to ask him about the spots worth visiting around Malgudi, Raju who was then only the owner of the sweetmeat-stall on the railway platform exaggerated the beauty and importance of these spots, even when he knew nothing about them.

> I never said 'I don't know! Not in my nature, I suppose... I am sorry I said it, an utter piece of falsehood.   It was not because I wanted to utter a falsehood, but only because I wanted to be pleasant. (p. 49)

Soon he found himself escorting the tourists to these beauty spots, giving them historical and geographic information, and before he knew it he had become a full-fledged guide, and the stall in the railway station had become merely a part-time business.

Raju's second role as an entrepreneur also came upon him quite by accident. Once he had tried to win Rosie away from her husband, but failed in his attempt, and had settled down again to his old way of life. He would have got over his disappointment if Rosie herself had not reappeared in his life. He found himself acting as Rosie's business manager and publicity agent without making any conscious plans about it. Rosie more or less willed him into accepting this role. Once cast in a particular part, it was Raju's nature to perform it with relish and perfection, and he excelled as an impresario and manager.

In the third stage of his career he happened to become a convict, and even this role he performed with enthusiasm, becoming an ideal prisoner. Raju did not drift into jail of course; he was taken there for a deliberate act of forgery. This was the one act that Raju did voluntarily and deliberately, it did not happen to him. But Raju was bewildered that such a trivial action should bring down such frightful consequences on his head.

Once out of jail Raju finds himself drifting into the role of a sadhu. Not once does he deliberately try to pass himself off for a holy man, but when he finds that people want to believe in his spiritual power, he cannot disappoint them. He wants to tell the villagers of his shady past of his stay in the jail, but he cannot : "It looked as though he would be hurting the other's deepest sentiment if he so much as whispered the word." (p. 8) Once he is accepted as a sadhu, Raju, with the characteristic thoroughness, pays attention to details like his appearance, his beard, his fluency in uttering mystifying statements. As in his earlier roles, he learns his trade while practising it. As a guide Raju had learnt through some empiric lessons in popular psychology what kind of sentiment went down well with the tourists :

I found that everyone who saw an interesting spot always regretted that he hadn't come with his wife or daughter, and spoke as if he had cheated someone out of a nice thing in life. Later, when I had become a full-blown tourist guide, I often succeeded in inducing a sort of melancholia in my customer by remarking, 'This is something that should be enjoyed by the whole family' and the man would swear that he would be back with his entire brood in the coming season. (p. 51)

Raju while performing the role of a guide also learns to modify the historical statistics of a place according to the quality and temperament of the tourists he is accompanying.

In the second phase of his life Raju picks up enough jargon about dancing to pass for connoisseur of Bharat Natyam when actually his knowledge of this art goes no deeper than his historical knowledge of the relics around Malgudi. The same ready wit helps him in the final role of his life as an ascetic. He soon learns that the essence of sainthood seems to lie in one's ability to utter mystifying statements. When the villagers talk about the crocodile in the river, Raju says

"What can a crocodile do if your mind is clear and your conscience is untroubled..." It was a wonderful sentiment to express. He was surprised at the amount of wisdom welling from the depths of his being. (p. 41)

Raju's entire life is a series of improvisations. His quick adjustment to the part of a sadhu falls in line with similar improvisations done throughout his life. Living for the moment, and postponing the crisis indefinitely, these seem to be the principles that guide his action. and the five-rupee adjournment lawyer merely projects an aspect of Raju's own personality. During the court case between Raju and the Sait, the businessman whom Raju has not paid for months, there are moments when Raju finds the whole business very tiresome, and refuses to think about it. "By not talking about money, I felt I had dismissed the subject." (p. 147) This hints at his habitual refusal to look beyond the present moment.

The act that confirms Raju's career as a sadhu is his establishment of a night school in the temple. This school becomes the nucleus around which the village people gather every evening to listen to Raju's discourses and story-tellings. These evening sessions grow in popularity until Raju becomes a public figure. But the idea of the school originates quite by accident. During his early days as a sadhu when Raju is not very sure of the manner he should adopt, he tries to make conversation with the children in "the manner of big people he had seen in cities." He asks them about their schools.   When he realises that these children do not go to school, he is taken aback a little, and to cover his embarrassment he utters some pompous exhortations on the need for education. And out of that casually uttered idea develop the evening classes that bring him prestige and popularity.

Even the final episode of fasting originates in a similarly insignificant and casual manner. During the prolonged drought the nerves of the village people are tense, and some minor quarrel flares up into a riot.   This news upsets Raju, not because he is genuinely concerned about the welfare of the village people, but because he is afraid that a disturbance might attract public notice to the village, and if the newspaper reporters and policemen arrive there, Raju's identity might be disclosed. It a is purely selfish reason that makes him announce that if people go on doing such foolish acts, he would not eat. The young man to whom this message is given is not very bright, and when he goes back to the village, he gives a completely different version of the message.   "The Swami will not eat until it rains."   The others believe him because only a few days ago Raju has told them of a saint who brought the rains down by his fast.

Hereafter begins a series of misunderstandings that gradually narrows down his path of escape.   In an excess of zeal his disciples stop bringing him all food.   This has an ironic side to it, because food had been the first link that had connected Raju with the inhabitants of the Mangala village.   He had accepted the role of a saint because it gave him unconditional and free supply of food. Fresh out of a jail, Raju had appreciated the value of this and at first when they used to leave food for him Raju used to be "filled with gratitude and prayed that Velan might never come to the stage of thinking that he was too good for food and that he subsisted on atoms from the air." (p. 30)

But the very stage that he was afraid of was duly reached. People gathered round Raju for *darshan*, and brought him their reverence but no food.   Raju had no alternative to fasting now.   And in their zeal, the disciples kept a twenty-four hour vigil with their famished Guru.

Before this stage is reached, being the sadhu has merely been a bit of play-acting for Raju, and by his excellent histrionic talent he had even persuaded himself of his authenticity :

...he began to feel that it was but right they should touch his feet; as a matter of fact it seemed possible that he himself might bow low, take the dust of his own feet and press it to his eyes. He began to think that his personality radiated a glory. (p. 96)

Like Kalo the blacksmith who came to believe that he had acquired genuine Brahminic powers, Raju had nearly convinced himself of his own exalted status. But this was a familiar feeling for Raju. He had always been in the habit of surprising himself with his own excellent performance. Years ago when he was launching Rosie on her career as a dancer he was impressed by his own oratory :

Heaven knows where I had found all this eloquence. I delivered such a lecture on the importance of our culture and the place of the dance in it that they very simply had to accept what I said. (p. 161)

Even as a guide he had achieved such an eloquence that he more or less came to believe, even if momentarily, all the historical data he had cooked up for his clients. Part of Raju's success is his ability to identify himself completely with whatever role he is playing.

But in his part of a saint he has at last reaches a stage when the situation is no longer familiar. When the shadow of famine stalks the countryside, and cattle begin to die, Raju for the first time confronts a situation in which he does not know how to act :

Something was happening on a different level over which he had no control or choice and where a philosophical attitude made no difference. (pp. 83-84)

And it is at this point that the penance of purification through fasting was thrust upon him. Raju now realises that he has worked himself into a position from which he cannot get out.[7] "He now saw the enormity of his own creation. He had created a giant with his puny self." (p. 99)

Raju is called upon by the community to undergo an act of vicarious suffering to purify the sins of others.   It is dangerous task and even Raju, who has so far always lived for the moment, improvising and acting the part that is convenient, senses the destructive risk of the situation.   During the early days of the fast, in desperate attempts to escape, Raju contemplates running away from the whole show.   What keeps him back is not practical considerations or fear of being caught; but very surprisingly, the faith of the people : "He was moved by the recollection of the big crowd of women and children touching his feet." (p. 100) At last the collective faith of the people transforms Raju from what he really is into a worthy object of its devotion.   Towards the end Raju loses the feeling of an actor performing an act; the act becomes the reality, the mask becomes the man, and Raju the guide turns into a Guru.

Whether his fasting really brought the rains down or not is an irrelevant question.   The superb ambiguity at the end serves its purpose.   More important is Raju's moment of transcending his limited self. The unquestioning faith of the people around him drives him on until he identifies himself as an instrument of their will :

If by avoiding food I should help the trees bloom and the grass grow, why not do it thoroughly ?   For the first time in his life he was making an earnest effort; for the first time he was learning the thrill of full application, outside the money and love; for the first time he was doing something in which he was not personally interested. (p. 218)

This is a moment of illumination, a moment in which an individual acquires the power to go beyond his self. We can see the measure of his growth when we compare these lines with Raju's earlier statement before the fast began :

I am prepared to fast for the sake of your people and do any-

thing if I can help this country, but it is to be done only by a
saint.   I am no saint. (p. 101)

When he said this he had broken down all barriers of pretension
and duplicity and this was the beginning of his change.   At this
point he began relating his life story to Velan, his chief disciple.
Going through the event of his life chronologically obviously
helps him to understand himself better.   And when he has unfolded the whole shabby story before Velan, he has no doubt the
feeling of removing one by one all the layers of disguise from his
true self.   Telling his autobiography to Velan is Raju's last attempt
to escape from the trap of fasting, but by the time he has finished
telling the story he is a changed man.   Velan's respect for him
does not diminish after hearing about Raju's past, and one wonders
if this should be attributed to the blind faith of the foolish peasant
or to the instinctive wisdom of a man who feels that it is the quality of his own faith that matters, not the quality of the object of
that faith.

In the story of Raju, we see the created object transcending
its creator.   The sainthood that Raju has created out of
his deception ultimately transcends his control and obliterates
his former self.   The theme gains its strength through repetition,
because earlier, in the Rosie episode, the same pattern had been
established.   Raju had more or less created Nalini the dancer, and
his motivation was not exactly an artistic passion for Bharat
Natyam.   But Nalini does not remain a doll in Raju's hands.
For her dance is not a profession, a means of making money,
but a cause, a devotion, and as Raju gets more deeply involved
in the forgery case, Nalini begins to lead an independent life of
her own.   Finally she goes out of Raju's influence altogether to
become an illustrious artist on her own strength and lead a fuller
life devoted to her art.

The parallelism between the Rosie episode and the final episode
of Raju the holy man is too pronounced to be accidental.   In both
cases the first phase involves a little struggle, but in both, once
launched in the field Raju never has to look back.   Both as a
business manager and as a sage Raju's success exceeds all his
expectations. The episodes begin very casually, almost by accident,

and in both cases Raju makes every effort later on to fill in the
details of his part. In both cases he becomes a public man eventually. In one he makes a slip and lands in jail. In the other,
owing to a misunderstanding, he is pushed into fasting, which at
first appears as disastrous an experience as a prison sentence.
At the end in both cases Raju's creations transcend him. Nalini
soars high above him, leaving him below behind the bars, and
the saint that Raju unwillingly creates passes into a different
level of reality leaving the imposter behind.

The ideal of asceticism runs through Indo-Anglian fiction as a
recurrent and compulsive motif. Even writers who are seemingly
indifferent to the spiritual aspects of life have not been able to
ignore it altogether because this is a pervasive cultural ideal in
India. We have seen how sometimes a saint figure in the novel is
made to embody this difficult ideal. This ascetic however rarely
becomes the central character of a narrative. Usually he remains
in the background, influencing the other characters and shaping
the events. This influence can be either positive as in *The
Cat and Shakespeare* or *Possession* or *The Flames of the Forest,*
or destructive and negative as in the novels of Mulk Raj Anand
where the hypocrisy of pseudo-spiritual men is presented in a spirit
of righteous indignation. In some other novels the man in the
saffron robe in seen obviously as a charlatan in disguise, and writers
like Desani and Nagarajan have in their different ways exploited
the comic possibilities of the situation. Occasionally the role of
the holy man appears complex and ambiguous as in *A Silence of
Desire* where a Guru is seen not only as a spiritual force, but also as
a person who satisfies certain social needs. There are at least
two novels in which the study of the significance of the saffron robe
is extended even further to include the psychological changes it
brings about in the wearer. *The Guide* and *He Who Rides a Tiger*
both deal with men whose holiness is only a convenient disguise,
but in both these novels the men undergo such transformation that
the fraud ceases to be a fraud. Narayan and Bhattacharya deal
with this apparently similar theme in totally different ways. The
ascetic in a saffron robe is a readymade symbol in Indian literature,
and in their several uses of this symbol the novelists reveal a great
deal of themselves and of their art.

NOTES

1. "The path that leads away from one's self," one can see, had been part of Ramaswamy's preoccupations even earlier in the novel. His dissertation was on the Albigenses, who constituted a branch of the Catharist and among whom the *perfecti* or the selected ones practised a rigid asceticism. Their one sacrament was the *consolamentum* and their act of final perfection was the *endura* or suicide. Ramaswamy's professional interests also thus centred on a group of people who sought a path that led away from the 'self'.

2. V. 77. Trans. Surendranath Das Gupta, in his *A History of Indian Philosophy*, (London, 1961), Vol. II, 246.

3. *The Novel in Modern India*, ed. Iqbal Bakhtiyar, (Bombay, 1964), p. 3. This volume contains papers read at the symposium on the subject at the fifth P.E.N. All-India Writers' Conference at Bhubaneshwar held in 1959.

4. One wonders if it should be called a novel; the author himself calls it "a gesture."

5. P. Lal, in an assessment of Indo-Anglian literary traditions, mentions G.V. Desani's name along with Sri Aurobindo, Raja Rao and Bharati Sarabhai at the "parent figures of the new trend." He refers also to T. S. Eliot's comment that *Hatterr* was the first major step in stylistic development in Indian writing in English. He also mentions Shaun Mandy's appreciation of the novel. Lal's own comment is that "Hatterr is that rare thing : a 'total' novel," *The Illustrated Weekly of India*, September 25, 1964, p. 35.

6. This forced transformation of a living being into an embodiment of divine power is a theme that has been treated very well In a Bengali short story by Prabhat Mukhopadhyay on which Satyajit Ray based his film called *Debi*.

7. In a Bengali novel, *Putul Nacher Itikatha* by Manik Bandopadhyaya, a similar theme is treated with considerable skill.

6

Myth as Technique

THE WORD 'myth,' owing to constant use over the last few decades, has now become something of a cliche of literary criticism.
Moreover, since the concept of myth interests not only the literary
critic but also the anthropologist, the sociologist, the psychologist,
the philosopher and the student of comparative religion, the term
is used in a variety of meanings, each field of study investing it
with different connotations. A term which is used to cover a
multitude of meanings soon becomes one of Ruskin's chameleon
words. Therefore, before we can discuss the ways in which myths
operate in Indo-Anglian fiction, we must define the specific context in which the word 'myth' is used in this chapter.

The important distinction between the conscious and unconscious use of myth must be made at the very outset. The conscious
use of myth is an easily recongnised literary device and part of a
modern trend—the method of Eliot in *The Waste Land*, of Joyce
in *Ulysses*, of O'Neill in *Mourning Becomes Electra*. Eliot, Joyce
and O'Neill differ widely in their techniques and intentions, but
there is one element common in their diverse methods : each of them
uses mythical (or classical) situations or characters in a modern
context, thereby seeking to illuminate the predicament of contemporary man, viewing him in a larger perspective of time. The
uninitiated reader reads the narrative for its own sake, but when
the mythical (or classical) parallel is recognised, his response
(assuming of course that he knows the myth) to the work is

enriched by an element of recognition. To clarify the matter one could borrow Wilhelm Wundt's analogy of a picture-puzzle drawn in the shape of a tree :

> In the picture of the foliage of the tree there are sketched the outlines of a human face or the head of a cat. An uninitiated observer sees at first only the foliage. Not until his attention has been directed to it does he discover the head. Once however he has seen the latter, he cannot suppress it, try as he may...[1]

Thus, the awareness of the concealed design makes the experience of the picture more complete. This conscious use of myth is now a familiar technical device used by many contemporary writers.[2]

Secondly there are literary works where the writer may not have been aware of using a mythical situation, but critics have discovered the unconscious way in which myths have operated in them. There is the example of *Hamlet* which Gilbert Murray traced to a primitive myth connected with the ritual battle of Summer and Winter, of Life and Death. This kind of archetypal criticism, claiming descent from Jung's theory that modern man preserves, though unconsciously, those prehistoric areas of experience which he interpreted in myth, is undoubtedly a fruitful and fascinating approach to literature, but is not the one we shall follow here. We shall rather limit ourselves to the study of the conscious use of myth by Indo-Anglian writers, mostly as part of their technique. For this purpose we shall consider not only the literary myths used by them, e.g., stories from the *Ramayana*, the *Mahabharata* and the *Puranas*—but also local legends, folk-lore as well as primitive rituals like the ritual for rain, for harvest or the fertility ritual for land or for a woman. Our discussion will include the novels that are constructed on a single sustained myth as well as those works where myths, rituals and folk tales are used as digressions, embellishments or illustrations.

One basic question arises here. Why are myths important in the study of literature? It is interesting to speculate why poets and writers have always been drawn towards myths and legends. One reason may be their quality of timelessness. Myths, in spite of their distance from contemporary reality, do have, for that particular group of men to whom they are culturally relevant, a kind of fundamental significance. Another reason is pointed out by Northrop Frye. Myths, along with folk tales and legends, he says, provide abstract story patterns : "Writers are interested in (them) for the same reason that painters are interested in still-life arrangements, because they illustrate essential principles of story-telling."[3] Moreover, Richard Chase has emphasised the literary nature of all myths; according to him, writers are attracted to myths mainly because myth *is* literature.[4]

Christian, pagan and classical myths have always provided a rich area of reference to English poets and writers. Achilles and Hector, Diana and Apollo, Job and Judas, have frequently appeared in the literature of the eighteenth and nineteenth centuries as allusions and decorations. But the structural use of myth is clearly a twentieth century literary phenomenon. In English literature, the revival of interest in myth derives largely from the works of W.B. Yeats, T.S. Eliot and James Joyce, each of whom in a different way made myth meaningful in the modern world. It can be shown that the literary artists' concern with myth is part of a broader twentieth century tendency, shared by anthropologists and scholars in other allieds fields of learning. The importance of the discoveries of Jung and Frazer in this revival is also well known. It is not necessary to go into the origin of the movement, partly intellectual and partly emotional, that rediscovered myth, because, for the Indo-Anglian writer it was an existing trend, already manifest in English (as well as other European) literature of the 'twenties and the 'thirties.

It will not be unfair to point out that many of the 'trends' or 'movements' in Indian literatures have been derivative in nature, though not always consciously imitative. In Hindi literature the *Pragativada* movement of the 'thirties was clearly a counter-part of the Leftist writings in Europe at the same time. In Bengali literature of the 'thirties the post-war European disillusionment was reflected, especially in the work of the young writers of the *kallol* group, although the situations that gave rise to that dis-illusion and despair were not present in exactly the same form in India at that time. In the 'sixties one notices a predominantly existentialist movement in Bengali fiction, which one strongly suspects, is not a natural growth, but primarily inspired by the contemporary existentialist writers in Europe. It is true that conditions in India are also those leading to despair and futility, but one must remember that the despair in western literature is of an intellectual and spiritual origin, while the despair that an Indian experiences is born of the inability of getting his minimum needs satisfied—the needs of food and shelter and clothing. The two are totally different experiences and cannot naturally produce the same kind of literature. Just as most European trends have found their echoes in India (sometimes immediate, often belated), the western writer's concern with myth was bound to be reflected in Indian literature.

But here was an area in which direct derivation was not possible. The Indo-Anglian writer, like the Bengali or Hindi or Marathi writer, could benefit from the technical experiments of their European models, emulate their stream-of-consciousness method, or share their existentialist philosophy. But when it came to the use of myth in literature, he found that he could not draw his material from the Graeco-Roman or Judaeo-Christian mythical framework. This was a more creative challenge because he had to turn to the mythology of his own culture to create significant patterns of fiction.

In one sense it should not have been difficult at all, because the Indian people are still closer to their mythology than the modern Irish or British people are to Celtic folk-lore or Greek legends. Children in India still grow up absorbing the legends of the land. The public recitation of tales from the *Ramayana* pointing out its contemporary relevance is even now a living tradition. If a world-view is required to make literature meaningful in terms of shared human experience, then the Indian epics offer a widely accepted basis of such a common background which permeates the collective unconscious of the whole nation. Besides, the epics and the *Puranas* are among the few common links that constitute an all-India frame of reference, equally valid to the Tamilian and the Punjabi. In this case the Indo-Anglian writer should have been easily attracted towards this rich material.

But in actual fact, the consciousness of myth was very slow to

evolve in Indo-Anglian fiction. It could be held that too close a
proximity of the writer to these myths was itself perhaps a hindrance
to their objective realisation. But it may be nearer the truth to
admit that most Indo-Anglian writers happened to be men or
women who were more exposed to western culture than to Indian, if
not in actual life at least in literary training.[5] They were, therefore,
unused to finding meaningful patterns in Indian myths for possible
use in literature. It is not until the 'fifties that we find any significant use of myth in the Indo-Anglian novel, and even then it is
only in writers as exceptional as Sudhin Ghose or Raja Rao whose
encyclopaedic knowledge and eclectic interests traverse with equal
ease Indian folk-lore and Sanskrit classics as well as the history and
culture of Europe.

There seem to be two distinct ways in which myths have been
used in Indo-Anglian novels : as part of a digressional technique,
of which Raja Rao is the most outstanding exponent, and as structural parallels, where a mythical situation underlies the whole or
part of a novel. There are writers who have tried their hands at
both the methods. Sudhin Ghose's writing, for example, is normally
digressional. Usually he weaves various legends and folk tales
and myths into the fabric of his novel to attain some desired effect.
But at least in one novel, *The Cradle of the Clouds*, we find him
using one particular ritual as the central design. This second
method of using myth as a structural parallel is sometimes used
consistently throughout a novel (as in Narayan's *The Maneater
of Malgudi* or Anand's *The Old Woman and the Cow*) but more often
it is done in a fragmentary way, illuminating a character here or
enriching a situation there. For example, B. Rajan in his novel
The Dark Dancer identifies his hero with the *Mahabharata* character
Karna, because Karna could not belong anywhere. But the
analogy is not extended far enough to become significant. In the
same novel the post-partition Hindu-Muslim riots are seen as a
re-enactment of the fratricidal battle of Kurukshetra.

Whatever the method employed, each Indo-Anglian writer has
his own unique vision that colours his attitude towards myths.
For Sudhin Ghose, the myths are so real that sometimes the line
that divides mythical time from historical time is quite blurred.
Raja Rao uses the mythical parallel to extend our understanding of

a present situation, but Anand does the exact opposite. Anand
follows the mythical design to a certain point and then changes
it totally, intending perhaps to indicate that the same ending is no
longer possible (or desirable) in our time. This difference in
method is quite revealing because it suggests a basic difference of
attitude (between say, Raja Rao and Anand) towards the past.
However, before we proceed to a detailed discussion of these and
other aspects of the conscious use of myth by Indo-Anglian novelists,
one incidental observation may be made about the way in which
myths sometimes unconsciously operate in these novels. This is
seen in certain archetypal figures, situations and relationships
that recur in novel after novel. Sita as the archetype of Indian
womanhood in all her suffering and sacrifice appears in *Some Inner
Fury*, *The Dark Dancer*, *A Time to be Happy* and *The Dark Room*,
where suffering almost becomes a virtue. Another figure is the
elemental earth-mother (Little Mother in *The Serpent and the Rope*,
Akkaya and Lakshamma in Raja Rao's short stories) for ever giving
abundantly without expectation of return. An archetypal situation
encountered in many novels is a sacrifice done in order to gain
divine favour, for example fasting unto death to end a drought as in
The Guide, or the fasting of Moorthy in *Kanthapura* for the purification of self, or the sacrifice of the village women to bring about rain
in *The Cradle of the Clouds*. In the relationship between man and
woman, two chief archetypes are seen : the Radha-Krishna motif
where the woman is the playmate as well as the beloved (sometimes
Radha is Meera, the devotee) and the Rama-Sita relationship where
the woman is the submissive sufferer, who through her suffering
enhances the nobility of her husband. These archetypes appear
time and again, not necessarily because the authors are trying to
give a mythical colouring to their work, but because these are part
of our cultural pattern, our ideals of aspiration, that may or may
not have any basis in the actual conduct of real human beings.

The digressional method of story-telling is perhaps the oldest
device in narrative literature. Weaving in stories within a story,
or pausing to narrate a parable to drive home a point, these are
characteristic devices of the *Panchatantra,* the *Vishnu Purana* and
other Sanskrit narrative treatises, and of the *Mahabharata* and the
Ramayana as well. In the now famous foreword to *Kanthapura*

Raja Rao claimed that this was a characteristically Indian technique
of narration. "Episode follows episode, and when our thoughts
stop our breath stops, and we move on to another thought. This
was, and still is, the ordinary style of our story-telling. I have tried
to follow it myself in this story." Since one finds the same style
of narration in the Bible as well as in the Greek epics where episode
follows episode in a meandering fashion, it would perhaps be better
to call it the oral tradition of story-telling. The earliest narrative
works of any literature—religious or secular—are closer to the oral
tradition and therefore they have this leisurely digressional manner
of unfolding. Sometimes numerous interpolations are added to
the original work through the centuries, and even if it was not an
oral composition in the beginning, it soon acquires the distinctive
marks of an oral tradition in the process of being spoken aloud or
recited by succeeding generations.

The sharing of a common mythology between the narrator and
the audience is a general condition of the oral tradition of story-
telling. The two important Indo-Anglian writers who have deliberately adopted this method—Raja Rao and Sudhin Ghose—have
both drawn very largely from mythological sources. The myths
they use in their work are mainly of three kinds. Firstly, the well-
known epic or *puranic* myths which are easily communicable to all
Indian readers; for example, the polarities between good and evil
as exemplified in Rama and Ravana, which Raja Rao uses as the
basis to describe the Gandhian struggle against the brute force of
the red demon in *Kanthapura*; or Sudhin Ghose's repeated rendering of the idyllic yearning of Radha for Krishna to represent,
on one level, human love—"Every woman in love," he says, "is
Radha, and her lover is Krishna" (*The Flame of the Forest*, p. 99)
—on the other, "the human soul's longing for reunion with the
Divine as symbolised by Krishna." (*ibid.*, p. 99) Secondly, there
are localised myths that do not have a pan-Indian appeal. This is
what Raja Rao has called 'sthala-purana'—the legendary history of
a place or village. If the novel *Kanthapura* itself is a complete
rendering of one such *sthala-purana*, connected with a village in
the western coast of India, each novel of Sudhin Ghose's fascinating tetralogy contains many scattered examples taken from North-
Eastern India; for instance, the history of the Penhari Parganas,

where the people were ruined five hundred years ago through their exessive love of wrestling, related in *The Cradle of the Clouds*. In the same novel we are told the history of the Gola, a Penhari landmark which goes back to the time of the Maratha marauders called the Vargis. In *The Flame of the Forest*, the legend of Ati, the Nemesis, and its connection with the Calcutta landmark, Omichund's Tower, is given in some detail. The difference between a well-known pan-Indian myth and a *sthala-purana* is that the reader's acquaintance with the former can be taken for granted, and therefore variations and nuances are possible, while the latter has to be told in some detail before references can be made to it. But as soon as the local legend has been narrated and established, its function becomes the same as that of a more well-known myth.

Thirdly, there are the rites and rituals which strictly speaking do not form part of myth but provide a frame of reference; for example, the ritual for rain which forms the main motif of *The Cradle of the Clouds*, the esoteric *tantric* rite of reviving a dying man by exchanging his soul with another (*The Flame of the Forest*), or the ritual of *arathi* with *kumkum* and camphor censer or the offering of coconut and betel nut that one frequently finds in Raja Rao's work.

But weaving in of myths, legends and rituals will not by itself give a novel a special stature unless there is an underlying design holding together all the digressions, all these tales within tales, and mere description of the rituals will weaken rather than enrich the structure of a modern novel. One of the most articulate critics of *The Serpent and the Rope* has said that "the major fault of the book is its philosophical garrulousness. Raja Rao cannot (does not wish to ?) control his material,"[6] and it would appear at first that the same criticism is applicable to Ghose's work also. Sudhin Ghose's four novels all are richly laden with myths, legends and rituals. I shall attempt to examine in some detail his last, *The Flame of the Forest* to determine whether the profusion of parables and legends serves any useful structural purpose.

I

The four novels of Ghose deal with the childhood, adolescence

and youth of his central character, who is the first person narrator
of this tetralogy.   The first two volumes were set in the Penhari
Parganas (another name for the Santal Parganas situated along the
border between Bihar and West Bengal), but the background of
the last volume is Calcutta, where the hero is looking for a job
after completing his university education.   There is a curious
blend of reality and fantasy, and of the comic and the serious,
in all of Ghose's work.   The earlier volumes were replete with
local legends, myths of the tribal people and rituals of the village
folk, and he carries the same technique to the impersonal locale of
a big city.   For him the roads and landmarks even in Calcutta are
rich with *sthala-purana*.   Fairly early in the novel we are told the
story of the origin of Calcutta's Chowranghee. And it is here while
narrating the story of Jungal Giri Chowringhee that Ghose introduces another recurring concept of this novel : the concept of
matra or the sense of measure. (pp. 80-81) According to Indian
tradition, men who transgress their *matra* (i.e., natural limits) are
punished for it,[7] as in this novel, by the visitation of *Ati*, a kind of
Nemesis.   All the legends and fables related in the novel appear to
have this common underlying pattern—how men who overstep
their *matra* are finally punished.   Take for example the story
describing the origin of Omichund's Tower.   This may be quoted
in full because this is the shortest anecdote in the novel :

'Eight-cornered columns are loved by the God Vishnu,' Omichund was told by the soothsayers.   He sought their advice as
to the best means of appeasing the dread deity *Ati*—Nemesis.
'A worshipper of Vishnu has nothing to fear from Ati.   Vishnu
protects his adorers and repentant sinners.'   Omichund was at
that time—the middle of the eighteenth century—concerned
about a dirty deal.   He had in the preceding year succeeded in
cornering the grain market and in ousting his former employers,
Boistab Sett and Manik Sett; this success was followed by still
greater successes with forged documents : he was now the richest
merchant in Hindustan, the biggest property owner in Calcutta,
and the principal black-marketeer in Chandernagore.   'An easy
success,' the soothsayers warned him, leads to an easy fall.
The goddess Ati is a jealous goddess.   She should be appeased.'

(*The Flame of the Forest*, pp. 68-69)

The means of appeasement, the story goes on, could be to erect an eight-cornered tower and to practise "the three R's : Restraint, Rectitude and Righteouness." Omichund laughs at their suggestion, but decides to build the tower all the same, for its publicity value. The tower which he wants to be higher than any other tower in the land is a measure of his egotism. He does the right thing for the wrong reason, and, therefore, the erection of an eight-cornered tower does not save him from disaster.

Although the moral of the story is clear enough, at this point of the novel its relevance to the total structure is not apparent. Omichund is destroyed obviously because in his vanity he oversteps his *matra* and refuses to humble himself before Vishnu. Not until the pattern has been subtly repeated a few more times (with enough variation so that it does not obtrude) do we discover that it is the central metaphor of the plot. A little later comes another story of a basketmaker's widow and a rich Diwan's wife, both of whom sought God's blessing. The poor widow knew her *matra* and therefore received a blessing in exchange for a basket made by her, while the Diwan's wife received a curse because in her eagerness she overstepped her *matra*. She attempted to revive her dying son with the help of a *tantrik*. The *tantrik* took the life of a lower caste boy and put it into the body of the Diwan's son which made the son live, but he became a source of untold misery to his parents. This life-long punishment was a reminder that it is a transgression to resurrect the dead with magic rites.

There are numerous minor anecdotes and legends to reiterate the pattern, but only two more will be briefly mentioned to illustrate how all the legends point in one direction, and the general drift of the plot itself runs parallel to it.

Towards the end of the novel, a casual reference is made to the main street of Gilani (a village at the foot-hills of the Himalayas) which is paved with huge flag-stones covered with Devnagari inscriptions, faded beyond recognition. The local tradition maintains that these stones cover the tombs of a number of Brahmins who once came to the village to bless a wedding that never took place. Then the story is unfolded of the proud king of Kanauj who wanted for his harem the handmaidens of Nanda Devi, the presiding deity of the mountain, and came to Gilani with a powerful army to fight the goddess. The Brahmins accompanied him to give their benediction at the time of the wedding. The villagers were shocked at their presumption and pleaded with the Brahmins to have a sense of *matra*. The Brahmins refused to dissuade the king. But the wrath of the goddess destroyed the king and his followers. The Brahmins were then buried in the streets of Gilani, and inscriptions were written on the stones to remind the villagers of *matra*.

The last story is the well-known one of Nahush, the unscrupulous villain who secured a kingdom by enchanting the people with honeyed words and putting them in a trance with his unblinking gaze. He insulted and humiliated the wise men of the land and became invincible until one day the sage Agastya broke the spell that Nahush had cast on the people. Nahush was transformed into a reptile because he had forgotten his *matra*.

These are but four tales taken from the dozen or more that are scattered all over the novel. These stories are neither digressions nor decorations strictly irrelevant to the story. Diverse as they are (local legends, national myths, individual history) they all have a basic underlying pattern which is repeated in the total design of the plot.

Among the various shuttlings back and forth in time, and among the numerous episodes that at first seem unconnected, the story that emerges in the novel is that of a youth from the Penhari Parganas trying to make a living in the impersonal city of Calcutta. He is too confident of himself, too sure of his superiority over others and too quick to challenge the knowledge of other people. He meets the Kirtani (singer of devotional songs) Mynah from his home district, who gently tries to bring him back to his senses, but he, a rational modern man, is afraid of Mynah's mystic moods, and fights the temptation to join her. Finally this youth, whom Mynah calls Balaram,[8] gets into trouble by trying to do things beyond his power and is forced to run away from Calcutta. When Myna meets him again, she chides him : "Have you forgotten Balaram went on ploughing his field even when a great battle was raging in his neighbourhood ? The main thing is to cultivate your own field—instead of meddling with many things—like improving the universe !" (p. 286) Unlike the mythical Balaram, Krishna's brother, who refused to have anything to do with the battle of Kurukshetra, the Balaram of this novel, gets involved in a political feud far beyond his concern and oversteps the line of chalk,[9] the limiting boundary. The central theme is thus concerned with the sense of *matra* and man's transgression of it. The use of myth in Sudhin Ghose, therefore, is not arbitrary, but done with the definite purpose of delimiting his total scope and imposing deeper pattern on the literal level of his narration. Nor is the parallel design as obvious as this paraphrase might suggest, but is complicated enough to make a sudden recognition of the total design at the end a gratifying experience. Northrop Frye speaks of two kinds of recognition in fiction : "One is the continuous recognition of credibility, fidelity to experience. The other is the recognition of the identity of the total design, into which we are initiated by the technical recognition of the plot."[10] Sudhin Ghose's delightful rambling novels suddenly assume a new meaning as soon as the second recognition has been experienced.

II

The material Raja Rao works with is also rich in myths and legends, but his technique is quite different from Sudhin Ghose's. His method is that of mythologising contemporary reality. His gifts as a myth-maker can be seen even in his early short stories, later collected in the volume *The Cow of the Barricades* (1945). These tales do not have the cohesion of structure one expects from modern short stories, but are more in the oral tradition of story-telling where the narrator meanders at will and no focal point is necessary to hold the story together. The two serpent stories in it, 'Companions' and 'Kanakapala,' are most certainly made up of the elements of a folk legend or myth : a dream vision, a curse, a quest, fulfilment and finally something tangible (a tomb, or a temple) as testimony to the truth of the legend.

Kanthapura is again another and a larger attempt at creating a *sthala-purana*, i.e., a legendary tale of a specific locality. Just as in a myth "some of the chief characters are gods and other beings larger in power than humanity,"[11] in this tale Moorthy is

presented as a figure much above the common run of men. A
dedicated selfless soul, he is idealised to the extent of being
regarded as a local Mahatma. And of course, there is the real
Mahatma also, always in the background though nowhere physically present. The village women think of him as the Sahyadri
mountain, big and blue, and Moorthy as the small mountain.
Range Gowda, the village headman, thus describes Moorthy :

> He is our Gandhi. The state of Mysore has a Maharaja but that
> Maharaja has another Maharaja who is in London, and that one
> has another one in heaven, and so everybody has his own
> Mahatma, and this Moorthy who has been caught in our knees
> playing as a child is now grown up and great, and he has wisdom
> in him and he will be our Mahatma. (p. 103)

Just as there is the local goddess Kenchamma who protects the
village Kanthapura and a greater god who protects all, Moorthy is
the local *avatar* while Gandhi is the greater deity. This pattern
of having two figures larger than life, one beyond the other, can
be seen in two of Raja Rao's earlier short stories ('Narsiga' and 'The
Cow of the Barricades') also. In both these stories an idealised
local character referred to as 'Master' appears, and in both the
Mahatma occupies an all-pervasive God-like position. Just as in
'Narsiga', the little pariah boy equates the release of the Mahatma
from the jail with Sita's release from Lanka—"He is going to fly
in the air in a chariot of flowers drawn by four horses, four white
horses" (p. 116)—in *Kanthapura* the Harikatha-dasa raises Gandhi
to the level of a god by identifying his activities with one particular
feat of Krishna, though it does not always mean fidelity to facts :

> You remember how Krishna when he was but a babe of four had
> begun to fight against demons and had killed the Serpent Kali.
> So too our Mohandas began to fight against the enemies of the
> country... Men followed him, as they did Krishna, the flute-
> player; and so he goes from village to village, to slay the serpent
> of the foreign rule. (p. 16)

If here the 'Kaliya-daman' offers a parallel to the destruction of the foreign rule, later on the battle between Rama and Ravana offers a similar mythical analogy. None of these analogies can be systematically followed through to find exact points of correspondence, but they do temporarily illuminate the historical situation of the 'thirties, and give an insight in the unlettered mind of the village people that Raja Rao has attempted to present in *Kanthapura*, the kind of mind in which myth and fact are not clearly distinguishable. Moreover, for such a mind a fact does not become significant until it can be related to a myth. Narsiga rejoiced at Mahatma's release from the jail, equating it with Sita's release from Lanka. For the grandmother in Kanthapura, Swaraj is Sita, Mahatma is Rama, and Jawaharlal is brother Bharata :

> He will bring us Swaraj, the Mahatma. And we shall be all happy. And Rama will come back from exile and Sita will be with him, for Ravana will be slain and Sita freed, and he will come back with Sita on his right in a chariot of the air and brother Bharata will go to meet them with the worshipped sandal of the master on his head. And as they enter Ayodhya, there will be a rain of flowers. (p. 251)

This mythicising of facts serves a two-fold purpose in *Kanthapura*. Its narrator is an old illiterate woman, and mingling of myth and fact would be her natural manner of observation and reflection. Thus, it is a device of characterization. Secondly, Raja Rao adheres to the Indian classical tradition by idealising or mythicising the central character. Valmiki held that the dominant accent in art should be on the dignity man gains when he accepts obligations implied in an ideal character. "The serious...(work)...which seeks enduring human significance should, thus, deal with the idealised man, because it seeks to make man move nearer to the ideal."[12] Moorthy is an idealized character, who like Christ takes all the sins of the people upon himself and undergoes a penance for purification, a young man who conquers physical desire and self-interest. Indeed, in the context of modern European realistic tradition, he will appear unreal as a character. But this is not meant to be fiction in the realistic tradition; it is a local legend, and therefore the presence of a god-like hero is more appropriate here. A myth necessarily deals with an idealised man or a man larger than life and Raja Rao uses the device of mythicising facts in order to give his hero that exalted status.

Apart from the literary myth of Krishna and Rama, *Kanthapura* is full of references to local rituals, e.g., the ritual of yoking the bulls to the plough under the Rohini Star (pp. 151-155), or to the traditional belief that at the beginning of Kartik, gods can be seen passing by, "blue gods and quiet gods and bright-eyed gods" (p. 113), or to the different modes of appeasing the goddess Kenchamma. All these make up the fabric of living of which the narrator is a part. Thus the reference to the rituals of ploughing, of worship and sacrifice, becomes a means of establishing the atmosphere in which the villagers live, as well as a device for concretising the 'point of view', i.e. delineation of the character of the unsophisticated narrator who can assimilate all facts into a mythical structure, for whom no fact becomes really significant unless it can be identified as part of a myth.

The 'point of view' in *The Serpent and the Rope* is that of Ramaswamy, a character much more sophisticated and widely travelled than the grandmother of *Kanthapura*, and the mythology here is consequently far more eclectic. While on the one hand it contains the legends of Satyakama and the *budumekaye* (pp. 121-123) or the retelling of Rama's story every Saturday and the blessing it brings, on the other hand it also contains the Chinese fable of Wang-chu and Chang-yi (pp. 127-128) and the tale of Tristan and Iseult. Besides, the telling of the legends is much less concrete now, and far more elusive, one legend often blending into another from a different civilisation. This is appropriate, and perhaps consciously done, because the protagonist of *The Serpent and the Rope* is, like Raja Rao himself, a product of many cultures—"born in South India and into the Sanskrit tradition, having a French intellectual discipline, and writing in the English language."[13]

Moreover, Ramaswamy's research project in the university is an attempt to connect the Albigensian heresy with Brahminical influences. His friend Georges is studying the relationship of the lotus and the cross, the Holy Grail and the begging bowl. Such is the cross-cultural, assimilating atmosphere of the novel. It is, therefore, hardly suprising that the narrator will not only be familiar with the myths of different civilizations, but will be agile in perceiving parallels between legends and forging a link between the past and the present by comprehending the essential oneness of history. Take, for example, the passage where he speaks of the impersonal principle of kingship. He equates the ailing king (George VI in the year 1951), who had succeeded to the throne only after his brother Edward had abdicated his claims, with Bharata, King of Ayodhya, who merely substituted for a brother far nobler than himself and

> apologized every time he spoke saying 'you think I am your King, but I am only brother to the King; I tremble, I hesitate, I wish my brother were here !'... Kingship is an impersonal principle, it is like life and death, it knows no limitation... and when a king apologizes for being a king, he is no king; he establishes a duality in himself, so he can have no authority. (p. 206)

Here two isolated incidents, the exile of Rama and the exile of Edward VIII, one belonging to myth, the other to history, one to India the other to England, one taking place in a world above or prior to ordinary time, *in illo tempore* in Mircea Eliade's phrase, and the other in very recent past, suddenly become fused into an identical predicament.

This is not an isolated example of perceiving links in a vast area of time and space—the novel abounds in such recognitions. There is, for example, a long description of, and reflection on, the coronation of the queen towards the end of the novel (pp. 357-370) where the Queen of England is seen as the feminine principle that makes the universe move. "To Mitra she is Varuna, to Indra she is Agni, to Rama she is Sita, to Krishna she is Radha." She is Iseult for Tristan, and Savitri for Satyavan, for Ananda (the reader is reminded of the opera Wagner wanted to write called *Savitri and Ananda*) as well for Ramaswamy. She is the *Prakriti* that makes *Purush* manifest. The *matrishakti* of Hindu mythology thus gains a universal significance through Raja Rao's panoramic application of it.

These are, however, incidental reflections, not integral parts of the structure of the novel. The only recurrent mythical allusion is the Radha-Krishna legend which forms the dominant motif in the relationship between Ramaswamy and Savithri. This is an archetypal relation between the seeker and the sought, the woman and her beloved, that has been used in India thousands of times in devotional songs, in Vaishnava love-lyrics, in novels of sentimental love, and more recently in popular films. Sudhin Ghose succeeded in handling this theme without creating an aura of vague emotionalism, partly because in the case of his Kirtani Mynah in *The Flame of the Forest* for the Communist worker Ramoni in *The Cradle of the Clouds* (both identify themselves with Radha), Krishna is never personified. Union with Krishna remains an unrealised symbolic longing for the Absolute. But in the episode between Ramaswamy and Savithri in *The Serpent and the Rope*, two corporeal beings are represented as Krishna and Radha, and their relationship—as illustrated in her washing his feet with *kumkum* water and offering him *arathi* with camphor censer— appears ritualistic without being sufficiently human, A mythic parallel becomes significant only when a situation is primarily and recognisably human and real. A concrete and particular situation gains an extension into infinity by being absorbed into a corresponding situation in mythology. But substitution of a contemporary situation by a mythical one may not always gain the same extension. Such substitution demands of the reader a transition from one level of fictional reality to another which he may not be able to make—at least that is what Raja Rao seems to demand in his depiction of the relationship between Ramaswamy and Savithri in the scene referred to above.[14] Their identities as flesh-and-blood human beings are allowed to lapse as Savithri, the sophisticated Cambridge University undergraduate, says to Ramaswamy, the learned research scholar of world history :

> I wish you could sing me a song, and I would lie on your lap, far away where there is no land or road, no river or people, no father, fiance, filigree, palace or elephants—perhaps just a mother —and on some mountain... (p. 210)

One could accept this emotional outburst as idle talk between young lovers, if Raja Rao did not strive to invest their relationship with an aura of sublimity. Savithri performs certain rites in Rama-swamy's hotel room in London. She washes his feet and anoints them, performs *arathi* three times, places her head on his feet, and sobs. He, in return, touches her head with *kumkum* and gives her coconut and betelnuts. Whereupon she says, "I have known my Lord for a thousand lives, from *Janam* to *Janam* have I known my Krishna ..." (p. 214) All these details are supposed to be an actual enactment of Radha's adoration of Krishna, and thereby meant to elevate a merely human relationship into a symbolic one.[15] This act of worship, however, does not seem quite natural to the character of Savithri, who has been depicted as a non-conformist, somewhat rebellious girl. Unlike the traditionally brought up Indian woman, she is fond of asserting her own will, and has, earlier in the novel resisted an arranged marriage. It is arguable, therefore, that the fond description of these rituals has its birth in the sentimental longing of the writer himself, an expatriate Indian, who sees all traditionally Indian actions enveloped in a mist of nostalgia.

The structural unity of *The Serpent and the Rope* is based more on a philosophical concept than on a mythical parallel, and this raises certain controversial issues. The novel in the sense we understand it today is concerned with circumstantial reality, with the concrete and the particular that are influenced very largely by time and place. In this sense *Kanthapura* is a modern novel, and its oral tradition of mythicising facts is a well-chosen technical device. In *The Serpent and the Rope*, on the other hand Raja Rao unearths metaphysical propositions everywhere, personal relations do not always count unless they correspond to some archetypal pattern, abstract truth is read into the smallest action; hence the inter-weaving of myths, instead of steadily illuminating a particular situation, merely adds to the flux of general observa-tions about cosmic truth. The myths and legends are part of the characterization of Ramaswamy, but not integral to the progress of events.

III

It has already been pointed out by critics that R.K. Narayan's
The Maneater of Malgudi has a definite sustained mythical structure.   The *New York Times* reviewer read this as an allegory, and
Edwin Gerow, in a perceptive analysis of the novel, has pointed
out how closely the novel follows the classical pattern of Sanskrit
literature.[16] Any casual reader will notice the allegorical nature of
the novel. The polarity between Nataraj, the meek and tolerant
printer, and Vasu, the dynamic man of action, is too clear to be
overlooked. Nataraj is mainly passive, things happen to him and he
has very little power to influence events; while Vasu is the great
advocate of individual achievement. Vasu is alone, he comes from
outside, and sets up his business of taxidermy unaided by anyone,
fighting with the Forest Department on one hand and the Malgudi
people on the other. He secures a room, a jeep and a game licence
on his own initiative, and kills, processes, stuffs animals, packs
them in boxes and sends them out to different places singlehanded,
while "I (Nataraj) noted it all from my seat in the press and said
to myself 'from this humble town of Malgudi stuffed carcasses ra-
diate to the four corners of the earth'." (p. 52)

If action and inaction are the two attributes of Vasu and Nataraj,
associated with them are also the qualities of tolerance and
intolerance :

"Look here Vasu," I said, with a sudden access of foolhardiness,
"You should leave others alone; it will make for happiness all
around."
"I can't agree with you," he said, "We are not lone dwellers
in the Sahara to live self-centred lives, and, there is no point in
living like a recluse..." (p. 104)

It should be noted, however, that in spite of his insistence on man
being a social animal, it is Vasu himself who is anti-social in his
isolation and egoism. He frightens children, kills dogs, repels
neighbourhood people with the stench of his workshop and defies
social conventions by bringing prostitutes home. All these negative
acts set him apart from common human beings. Fairly early in

the novel, Sastri of the printshop identifies him with the *rakshasa*, embodying the forces of destruction. Vasu corresponds to the letter with Sastri's definition of a *rakshasa* as a demoniac creature, possessing enormous strength, strange powers and genius, but recognising no sort of restraint of man or god. (p. 75) The definition reminds one of the 'sense of *matra*' which was discussed earlier as the dominant concept of one of Sudhin Ghose's novels. In *The Maneater of Malgudi* also, the demon gets swollen with his ego. He thinks he is invincible, beyond every law, but finally he oversteps his limitations, and is destroyed.

The opposition between Nataraj and Vasu is so clearly marked, that one is tempted to read in the story of their conflict an allegorical or mythical implication. Theirs is the opposition between *Satva* and *Rajas*. The battle between the gods and demons, the *sura* and the *asura* is a recurrent motif in Hindu mythology. The *asura* were powerful, sometimes even more than the gods, and many times they triumphed, threatening Indra in heaven with chaos and confusion. But every time Indra's throne was saved by some miracle or divine strategy whereby the demons caused their own destruction and order was restored in the cosmos again.

The structure of the *Maneater of Malgudi* more or less follows the same *puranic* pattern. The drawn blue curtain of the printer's room stands for order and normalcy, as it were, and from the day the six-foot tall, broad-shouldered giant called Vasu crosses the threshold intruding into the privacy beyond the curtain, confusion begins. Vasu's very philosophy of life is in opposition to the peaceful ordered universe of Malgudi. He announces himself a sa rival to nature soon after his arrival :

...after all we are civilized human beings, educated and cultured, and it is upto us to prove our superiority to nature. Science conquers nature in a new way each day : why not in creation also ? That's my philosophy. Sir, I challenge any man to contradict me. (pp. 15-16)

He goes on relentlessly in his fight against nature by stuffing dead animals to make them look real. The conflict is not between Vasu

and Nataraj alone, but between Vasu and society in general, and
Vasu's seeming superiority over so vast a force merely underlines
the fact that evil is often far more dynamic than forces of goodness. Nataraj's fascination for Vasu and his attempts to re-estab-
lish friendly relations with the taxidermist indicates that evil is not
merely stronger but also more attractive than goodness. Edwin
Gerow in his extended study of the novel says that Vasu does
not really represent evil. "In a sense the *rakshasa* represents
evil, but this puts too moral a cast on it; he is rather an aspect of
creation—the chaotic, the disruptive; his weakness is not that he
is bad, but that he is ultimately not real."[17] Gerow goes on to
state that the settled order of the cosmos is in the Indian view
the fundamental ontological fact. This settled order was threatened
with dislocation by Vasu. But the threat is finally dissipated and
the novel ends where it began—with the enduring cosmos.

There can be no disagreeing with Gerow's general line of argument, though his interpretation in details, that even the names
'Vasu' and 'Nataraj' are symbolic may not find equal acceptance.
It is evident, however, that the story of *The Maneater of Malgudi*
follows the familiar pattern of a tale from the *Puranas* where a
demon gets too powerful, threatens the heavens with his elemental
forces of disorder, but finally goes up in the air like a bubble,
leaving the universe as calm as before. At the end of the novel,
the blue curtain of the printer's room is peacefully drawn again,
and Sastri disappears behind it to print the labels for K.J.'s Soft
Drinks.

Undoubtedly, the novel has a mythical structure. But doubt
arises when we try to judge whether Narayan was consciously
using myth as technique, or was it an unconscious manifestation of
his basic outlook which sees in the existing order of things a
desired stability that should be permanent, and any external element threatening to change this order as something illusory. At
the beginning of this chapter a distinction was made between the
conscious use of myth and the archetypal pattern which sometimes
unconsciously operates in a work of art. In which category should
The Maneater of Malgudi be placed ? Like everything else in
Narayan, this at first seems to be an elusive issue. Narayan was
not totally unaware that he was creating an *asura* in the person of

Vasu, because in a radio interview he said :

> The man-eater is a man, not a tiger, an ego-centred man for
> whom the objective world is non-existent—a modern *rakshasa*
> who wants to kill the elephant that belongs to the local temple.[18]

Granted that Vasu was conceived as the *rakshasa* who is opposed
to the benign aspects of life (represented by the temple festival,
where thousands of men, women and children reaffirm the positive
values of life through their celebration) it is still debatable how
much of the total pattern of Order—Disorder—Order was consciously conceived, because surprisingly enough, each of Narayan's
novels when closely analysed, reveals the same basic pattern. The
only exception seems to be *The Guide* and *The Guide* is different
from the other novels of Narayan in many other ways also. His
first novel *The Bachelor of Arts* begins with a picture of normal
ordered existence. A young man, the son of a retired District
Magistrate goes to college, takes some interest in debating and
in the other usual group activities of a college. Complication is
created through an illusory love affair which makes the young
hero run away and even become a *sannyasi* for a few days. But
ultimately normalcy returns when he comes back, takes a respect-
able job, marries according to his father's choice, and begins to live
happily ever after. *The Financial Expert* begins with Margayya
sitting under a banyan tree in front of the Co-operative Bank
with his tin box. This is the settled norm—the stable background
of the novel. After various ambitious ventures and turns of fortune's
wheel, when the novel ends we find Margayya on the point of
returning to the banyan tree. In between he had become
immensely rich, but his riches, like all sudden changes in
Narayan's world, were illusory; stability returns only when
Margayya loses his wealth. In *Mr. Sampath*, Srinivas, a
typical Narayan hero, son of a lawyer, graduate of the Albert
Mission College, Malgudi, edits a weekly paper called *The
Banner*. That is the norm—his not too prosperous life as an
editor and a householder. Suddenly the arrival of Mr. Sampath
changes the tenor of his life; he gets involved in the film industry
with its lure of big money. The usual complications arise. At

the end, the central character simply walks away from his vanishing creation, back to the dingy office of his weekly rag. Even in *The Dark Room*, where the pattern has an unhappy colouring, the norm is set at the beginning : the lopsided family life of Ramani, where there is little understanding between husband and wife but life goes on. The wife makes an unsuccessful attempt to run away and live a life of her own, but ultimately she comes back to the life she had left behind—and we come back full circle to where the novel had begun.

In a way which is perhaps traditionally Indian, Narayan sees any sudden change not for what is produces, for what new possibilities it brings into existence, in other words, not as a positive factor of being, but much more negatively as a play of shadows, an illusion, an unreality like a bubble, which will burst sooner or later, and the normal order of the cosmos will prevail again. In this sense very few of Narayan's novels (*The Guide* is again an exception) have a plot which shows a development of the story to a conclusion through interaction of different forces. Usually there is no conclusion as such, but reintegration of an original state of stability and normalcy. The return to this state of repose does not come logically out of the complications of the plot, but the complications are seen as an error which is protracted until such time as the individuals rediscover themselves in their true and original light. Thus action is often seen as a mistake or an unreality. In *The Maneater of Malgudi*, the stability of the printshop, the sanctity of the blue curtain, is re-established at the end not through the inept efforts of Nataraj, but because Vasu carried the seed of his own destruction. The repetition of the pattern is so regular in Narayan, that we may surmise that it operates unconsciously because it is part of his world-view. In this sense the mythical structure of *The Maneater of Malgudi* is only partly a self-conscious device, it is largely the same archetypal pattern that is to be found in all his novels.

IV

The Maneater of Malgudi thus has a clear mythical design (order—dislocation of order—restoration of order), reiterated by references to the *Puranic* conflict between *sura* and *asura*. Here the use of the myth is structural, i.e., relevant to the total concept of the plot, and not incidental, as in the novels discussed earlier. Another novel to use a central mythical structure consistently (though in a different way) is *The Cradle of the Clouds*, the second novel of Sudhin Ghose's tetralogy, where the ploughing ceremony, a magic ritual for bringing the rains, is the focal point towards which all incidents and episodes move. The myth behind the ploughing ceremony or *halakarshan* is explained in some detail. Kansa, the tyrant king wanted to burn down Brindaban and subdue its inhabitants. It was a summer of extreme drought. The men of Brindaban had to take their cattle to distant pastures. While the men were away Kansa set fire to Brindaban, taking the undefended women and children by surprise. They fled from their homes and in the darkness sought shelter in the mango-grove, thinking of the means of their survival.

> "Will you help me to pull my plough?" asked a little boy. "I want to plough the fields round about here. In the morning when Kansa sees the furrows he will think that our men have not only been back, but have already been at work and getting ready to wreak vengeance on him..." (p. 89)

This boy was Balaram, the brother of Krishna, and the pulling of his toy plough with the help of the women not only deceived Kansa, but also pleased the rain god Indra, so that he poured down rain on them.

The actual enactment of the myth comes towards the end of the novel, but throughout the novel the myth is shown to touch contemporary reality at various points. Firstly, the drought of one particular year in the Penhari Parganas and the distress that accompanies it forms the basic situation of the novel, corresponding to the dry season of Brindaban before Kansa set fire to the town. The cattle are taken away to distant pastures, and the sky is tinged with a strange glow. Secondly, it is made known from the beginning that the first-person narrator of the novel is commonly referred to as Balaram, because he has the same birthday as the mythical Balaram, Krishna's brother. The villagers believe that Krishna

himself is personified in the Second Master of the village school,
Hem Chandra Nahar, who like Krishna, is eighth child of his
parents and is born on *Janmastami* day.   Just as Kansa set fire to
Brindaban, the villagers set fire to the neighbouring village, hoping
that the holocaust will make the enactment of the ritual complete.

The impending *halakarshan* ritual towards which all actions and
movements proceed in the novel is seen at various levels of meaning.
The village people have a firm belief in the efficacy of the ritual to
bring rains, but the Second Master, who is to enact Krishna,
mocks at their irrational superstition. Balaram, the narrator, does
not mock, and yet he cannot share the enthusiasm of the villagers
for this sympathetic ritual.   Balaram takes his doubts to Panditji,
the wise man of the village, and asks :

> "But will they get any (rain) by simply repeating a ceremony
> performed aeons ago ?"   "Of course they will."   He (Panditji)
> spoke as though he was making a matter-of-fact statement...
> "Whatever you ask," he affirmed "you will get.   Provided you
> know how to ask for a blessing.   That's why it is important
> to master the art of thinking correctly." (p. 90)

Thus there is on the one hand the blind faith of the village people
who believe in the literal truth of the ritual, and on the other hand
the impatient irreverence of the Second Master.   In between there
is the attitude of the Panditji, whose belief is not in the ritual itself,
but in the faith of the people performing it. Balaram wavers among
these views, but finally at the moment of crisis the collective faith
of the people pulls him through, and without knowing how, he
brings about the miracle.

The question of faith, miracle and superstition here is a
variation of the question raised in R.K. Narayan's *The Guide*
where also the climax hinges on a ritual for bringing down the rain
(fasting, in this case).   While in Sudhin Ghose's novels there is a
considerable intermixture of fantasy and reality which makes
miracles probable, it is far more difficult in Narayan's world with its
realistic tone and ironic understatements.   But even in *The Guide*
there is a faint suggestion, though a very ambiguous one, that
the rains do come, that is, the miracle does happen at the end.

The faith of hundreds of people has a certain strength in itself, that can transform even a shady character like Raju into an agent of divine grace. Perhaps this interpretation oversimplifies the elusive quality of Narayan's novel, but it should be noted that both Raju and Balaram are at first reluctant instruments, who are later changed through the power of the collective conviction of the people in general.

To come back to the question of the central myth in *The Cradle of the Clouds*, the *halakarshan* ceremony which is a tribal ritual, embodies a literary and a religious myth. Balaram, the brother of Krishna appears in the folk legends concerning the idyllic exploits of Krishna in Brindaban, and also in the *Mahabharata*, where he plays a neutral role. Balaram refused to take sides in the great battle of Kurukshetra, and remained home to plough his patch of land. Balaram in the novel also does not take sides in the battle between the rationalists and traditionalists. He remains an observer who acts without much involvement.

The *halakarshan* is one of the many rituals for rain found among village people. In *The Golden Bough* Frazer has described several such rituals for rain in different parts of the world.[19] Frazer does not refer to the legendary background of the Indian ritual, but there can be little doubt that among others he has mentioned the one which Sudhin Ghose describes. Even the details like the naked women pulling the plough on all fours, tally. The only point of divergence is that while Frazer refers to a total absence of men, the ceremony Ghose describes allows two male participants —one, the naked boy Balaram who will hold the plough; the other Krishna, the only fully clothed person present, who will play on the flute "to beguile the hours of trial and travail." (p. 90) No other men are permitted to stir out of their houses that night. "If any other man comes across us tonight, he will be struck with blindness," we are told by Balaram's aunt. (p. 255)

The legendary ceremony is enacted in the novel in exact details. The nakedness of the women is made less shocking by the introduction of a subsidiary myth. Mashima, Balaram's aunt, relates the story of a woman who appeared before Chitra Gupta (the recorder of Man's sins and virtues) stark naked :

'She is guilty,' everyone whispered. Why does she not
extinguish her lamp, and make herself less conspicuous ? The
cloak of a woman is her virtue... Shamelessness is the vilest
of all sins for a woman... Chitra Gupta asks her, 'Were you not
aware that other sins might be expiated more readily than im-
modesty ?'   (p. 245)

But finally the woman is redeemed when it is proved that her love
was greater than her shame. Later this legend is linked up with
the shamelessness of the women who took part in the ploughing
ceremony.   Their love for the land was greater than their modesty :

They were convinced that the ploughing ceremony would
procure them abundant showers, provided none of the participants doubted its efficacy.   And I wondered what entries were
made by Chitra Gupta, the Recorder of the Nether World in his
great Register against the mothers, wives and daughters of my
village... on that occasion when I acted the role of Balaram.
(p. 273)

Tension builds up, beceause the ritual has a frightening aspect.
If the rain charm were to fail none of the women would be allowed
to return home, and Balaram's house would be burned down.
But the Second Master, who was supposed to enact the role of
Krishna introduces an element of disbelief and mockery. His
crude remarks on the naked women suddenly enrage Balaram who
has so far been merely passive, and with the aid of the miracle-wand
'Mahendra Chandal', he not only vanquishes the Second Master,
but also brings down rains. Thus Kansa, who comes disguised
as Krishna, is defeated and Brindaban saved.

All the different strands in the novel which seem separate at first
—the story of Panditji's magic wand called 'Mahendra Chandal',
the feud between the traditionalists and the modernists, the con-
spiracy to blow up the *Golah*, the prophetic statue made by Kumar
the village potter—all come together on the night of the *halakarshan*
ceremony. The 'Mahendra Chandal' frightens the disbeliever
and becomes an instrument to bring down the rains. In the feud
between faith and rationalism, faith is more powerful, and the blow-

ing up of the underground passage near the *Golah* coincides with the electric storm that brings rain to the Penhari Parganas. The piece of sculpture made by Kumar suddenly acquires a new meaning in view of the drunken behaviour of the Second Master at the *halakarshan* ceremony.

Sudhin Ghose builds his novel around a village ritual that has its basis in folk-lore. But in doing so he probably attempts also to give a mythical colouring to his own tale. It should be noted that the action takes place in a kind of unspecified time (*in illo tempore*). The time can be recognised as the twentieth century, but the novel does not give any more definite clue. The characters are not restricted by demands of verisimilitude to life. *Dakinis* and *Yoginis* (witches and wise women of supernatural power) are allowed to appear at will ; fantasy and reality mingle in an elusive manner. The magic wand is a kind of emblematic object (like a ring or an amulet) that one often finds in a myth. Its supernatural power works a miracle at a moment of crisis. Panditji tells Balaram : "A myth impels a man to action regardless of the limits of apparent truth." (p. 77) The novel thus builds up deliberately a myth-like atmosphere, inducing a willing suspension of disbelief. In the feud between the champions of faith and the champions of science, the narrator is made to appear neutral at first, but the author's sympathy does not remain hidden. Among the two advocates of science, the Second Master (who is an admirer or Cromwell) is almost diabolic. The evil in him comes to surface during the ploughing ceremony. The other advocate of rationalism, Kolej Huzoor, has a mine of information, a great deal of theoretical knowledge, but no essential wisdom, and he lacks the sense of *matra*. In one sense both Kolej Huzoor and the Second Master are like Lezo in *The Serpent and the Rope*, whose learning has not penetrated his being.[20]

But the three traditionalist characters in *The Cradle of the Clouds*, Panditji, Padre Johan and Kumar, are portrayed with sympathy and respect. One of them is a Brahmin, the other a Christian, and the third a low-caste Hindu, but they are similar in their belief in the faith of the people. All three of them are very much against the building of a dam in the area and the prosperity and material progress that such a construction will bring. The reader may not

share their point of view, but there is no denying that these beliefs
set the mood of the novel. The area of the Penhari Parganas
presented in the novel has of course a historical and geographical
reality, but in another sense it exists outside time and outside the
realistic framework of most contemporary novels. Hence the ritual
enactment of the ploughing ceremony becomes more than a mere
technical device to hold the plot together—it becomes a symbolic
test of the power of faith over the impersonal power of science.

V

Finally we have the example of authors who use myth not as
part of a digressional technique (as in *Kanthapura*), nor as a central
structural device (as in *The Maneater of Malgudi*), but employ
mythical parallels only incidentally to illuminate certain situations
or characters. B. Rajan's *The Dark Dancer* whose central theme,
the problem of identity, has been discussed in an earlier chapter
at some length, uses the Mahabharata character Karna as a symbol
of not belonging :

> "Which son of Kunti do you suppose I am ?" he asked her.
> "You're Karna," she replied without hesitation. "The man
> who could not belong." (p. 133)

Karna at first seems to be a convenient figure to represent the predicament of the modern man who is uncertain of his identity;
but looking closer we find that Krishnan's situation in *The Dark
Dancer* is by no means parallel with that of Karna. In the Mahabharata the question 'what is my place?' is crucial because it was
a strictly hierarchical society where every man had his prescribed
dharma, a given role to perform. If there is any 'lost' character in
the Mahabharata, any man who is caught between two worlds, it
is not Karna, but Ashwathama. Ashwathama was born a Brahmin,
and he had the training of a Kshatriya. Yet he could never properly understand the *dharma* of a Kshatriya. He had learned the
use of terrible weapons, but he did not use them to bring victory
to Duryodhana; after everything had been lost, he used them only
for his own revenge and safety.

   Karna's case was different. He was born a Kshatriya and grew up a warrior. He had his definite *dharma* to follow. There is no doubt that Karna always knew his Kshatriya origin. In the Udyogparva, Book V, he tells Krishna : "Before her wedding with Pandu, Kunti conceived me by the Sun God and at his command she abandoned me as soon as I was born. I know I was born this way."[21] What Karna lacked was not a sense of belonging, but social recognition, until it was given to him by Duryodhan. Krishnan, the hero of *The Dark Dancer*, whose main preoccupation in life is self-analysis, and worrying about his identity, offers no real point of comparison with Karna the man of action, even though such mythical parallelism may look attractive by investing a modern novel with a certain sophistication.

Rajan's hero seems to share a common romantic misconception about Karna's motivation; he believes (along with many other people whose reading of the *Mahabharata* is casual) that Karna had wanted Draupadi, and failed to win her because of his inferior social status. Krishnan says : "What was the use of bending the great bow and all that if Draupadi would not give him the go-ahead signal? His father was a charioteer, that's the trouble." There is nothing in the *Mahabharata* to indicate that Karna wanted to win Draupadi by trying to bend the great bow. He was present at the *swayamvara*, but not as a suitor. As for Karna's desire for Draupadi, the *Mahabharata* never gives any clue, and it can only be a modern romantic fancy that attributes this motivation to Karna's action and behaviour. In the Udyogparva Karna was given a chance to change sides, when first Krishna, and then later Kunti implored him, appealing to his sentiment, tempting him with equal status with the Pandava brothers which included a share in Draupadi. But Karna was not tempted. He knew his *dharma*, and never wavered from it.

Karna is thus very different from the Hamlet-like hero of Rajan. References to Karna or to the sons of Kunti (it should be noted, that the last chapter of the novel is entitled 'Son of Kunti', making the reader feel that the mythical undertone is significant at the end) thus serve no real purpose in the novel apart from giving it a pseudo-mythic appearance. Similarly, in Rajan's second novel, *Too Long in the West*, the device of the *swayamvara* with five suitors rouses in the reader the expectation of a mythic parallel. But the reader is disappointed, as he is in *The Dark Dancer*, because the references are merely arbitrary; they do not cohere into a pattern.

In a chapter dealing with the use of myth in Indo-Anglian fiction, Mulk Raj Anand's name seems out of place because his work is generally characterised by a forward-looking vision, while myths and legends, along with village superstitions and rituals, form part of the old world that he as well as his young heroes reject. But in one of his more recent works, *The Old Woman and the Cow*, for the first time Anand uses myth as part of his technique. Gauri, the meek heroine of the novel, offers a parallel to Sita in her suffering. Like Sita she has to leave her home, and Sita's stay at Lanka can be said to present a parallel to Gauri's stay at Hoshiarpur, in the house of a lecherous Sahukar, to whom her uncle had sold her. Like Sita she refused to yield to the demon. But it is after her rescue and return to the village that Gauri's predicament comes closest to Sita's. Her chastity is doubted by society because she has been away at the city with unknown people. Gauri's husband refuses to accept her if she cannot somehow prove her purity. But unlike Sita who was swallowed up by Mother Earth to save her from humiliation, Gauri has no one to rescue her. Instead of meekly surrendering to further humiliation, as she had always done before, Gauri for once stands up against her oppressor. She leaves her husband and her village behind and walks to the city to find an independent existence. Gauri has earlier been a weak docile character, and before taking this final decision she wavers once :

> for a brief moment the thought that the earth must open up to rescue her as it had opened up to receive Sita, came as an echo from the memory of her race. But the ground was hard and solid under her feet, and showed no signs of opening up to prove her innocence. She waved her head to forget Sita, and thought of the road to the town. (p. 284)

Gauri at the end conquers her diffidence and acquires the courage of self-assertion. It is in this final development that the analogy to Sita breaks down. The novel is not a saga of suffering and patience but is intended to be the portrait of a woman who through suffering and misery finally discovers herself as an individual, not merely as a wife or daughter. Whatever may be our opinion of its execution there is no doubt that the central theme of the novel is Gauri's transformation from "the gentle cow's acquiescence" to an individual "with a will of her own". (p. 284) Thus, the Sita-myth is introduced only to be exploded at the climactic point.

It is part of Anand's technique that in his novel a myth should be pursued upto a certain point and then suddenly reversed. This contains an implicit comment on the values of the past, and reveals Anand's rejection of the ideal represented in the particular myth. *The Old Woman and the Cow* is not a particularly successful novel, but Anand's negative use of myth is worth special mention, because this novel is unique among Indian novels in rejecting rather than extolling the time-honoured womanly virtues of patience and submission.

In his *Studies in Classical American Literature* D. H. Lawrence had considered certain fictitious characters like Natty Bumppo or Hester Prynne and certain plots as fulfilling the archetypal patterns of the culture. Similarly in Indian literature one may notice characters who adhere to certain ideals. These ideals assume a mythic quality in their permanence within the cultural context of India. In connection with Anand's novel *The Old Woman and the Cow*, we have just noted one prominent archetype of the patient, submissive, ideal of womanhood as exemplified by Sita that has occurred many times not only in Indo-Anglian fiction, but in novels in every Indian language. The man-woman relationship in which the man's role is dynamic and the woman's passive is a pattern that goes very deep into the Indian ethos. This ideal is so much a part of the Indian mind, that an Indian reader never pauses to wonder whether the numerous novels that portray this relationship and present the woman as the symbol of purity and goodness draw their material from real life, or merely follow a literary convention. It takes an outsider like Dorothy Spencer to ask this pertinent question : "As we observe with the mind's eye this procession of devoted, submissive, faithful, loyal self-sacrificing woman, the question arises, are these characters intended as realistic portrayals?"[22] Miss Spencer goes on to prove, with various quotations from Prem Chand and Bankim Chandra Chatterjee, that the authors have intended these idealised creatures to be taken as real human beings. What is true of Bengali and Hindi literature is true of Indo-Anglian literature also. The distinction, especially in the case of women, between the real and the ideal is almost obliterated. Even in the limited range of Indo-Anglian novels over a period of thirty years we find not less than twenty novels where the women adhere to an archetypal pattern, where women are like Sita, Savitri or Shakuntala in their suffering and forbearance. These women exemplify the ideal, and thus express the society's values.

Not all mythical heroines however are so popular with fiction writers. Draupadi, for example, has never been a prototype of the characters of fiction. Nor have Gandhari or Kunti, two other characters of extraordinary power and complexity who appears in the *Mahabharata*. The reason for this is more sociological than literary; in fact none of the *Mahabharata* characters has ever become everyday models of reference in Indian life as the characters of the *Ramayana* have. Not only does the *Ramayana* provide us with the literary archetype of womanhood, but also of the ideal king, the ideal brother, the ideal subjects, and even an ideal villain. But the *Mahabharata* presents no ideals. It is a record of a human struggle where the participants are human in their weakness, deceit, and petty jealousies. No character in it is without a flaw, no character is totally villainous. It is more ruthlessly faithful to life than the *Ramayana*. Although in English both the *Ramayana* and the *Mahabharata* are called epics, Irawati Karve maintains that in Indian languages a distinction is made between *kavya* and *itihas*. She describes how the *Ramayana* corresponds to the literary conventions of a *kavya* :

> A courageous hero, a virtuous heroine—all the stuff of the Sanskrit *kavya* tradition, category for category; there is a description of each kind of love : first love, mature love, and separation. Even the war is but a literary device and is unreal......the flames of war did not touch Ayodhya, they remained in the realm of romance.[23]

The war in the *Mahabharata* on the other hand was a real war, bringing desolation to the victor and the vanquished alike, and its heroes and villains are more recognisably human.

The theme and motibs of the *Mahabharata* have a contemporary relevance to the twentieth century Indian, and in the last five or six years one notices a renewal of interest in this epic among younger winters in the regional languages who are using symbols from the *Mahabharata* in their work.[24]

The fact that most of the literary myth of the fiction we have analysed in this chapter is drawn from the *Ramayana* and the *Puranas*, and hardly any from the *Mahabharata*, may be a significant commentary on the idealistic nature of Indo-Anglian fiction.[25] Even Krishna, when he appears, is not the stern apostle of duty, the ruthless charioteer of *Mahabharata*, but the romantic young lover of folk-lore, who frolicked with the Gopinis on the banks of the Jamuna. This total neglect of the *Mahabharata* as a source material for myths reveals what is part of the characteristic inability of Indo-Anglian fiction to face life in the harsh and unflinching light of reality, without softening it with idealism and sentiment. Perhaps this is inevitable, because literature reflects the culture of the people and the aspirations people live by; idealism has until very recently been part of a literary tradition in India, whether the ideal is patriotism or sacrifice or Ram Rajya.

Another reason why the *Mahabharata* has never rivalled the *Ramayana* in providing literary inspiration is perhaps its treatment of evil. The *Mahabharata* deals with evil in its various forms—adultery, deception, rape, treachery, pride, lust; there is no form of human depravity that is not handled here in a matter of fact manner. Subsequent Indian literature has shown a marked refusal to go into the problem of evil. The *Ramayana* has its Ravana, but Ravana is more of a symbol than a concrete creature. I have already quoted Edwin Gerow's remarks that the *rakshasa* represents evil only to a certain limited extent.[26] That he is an aspect of creation which is unreal is more important This applies to Ravana as well. He is the villain of a *kavya*, therefore he satisfies the literary convention of a villain without being evil himself. Evil is a frightening quality only when it appears along with recognisably concrete human attributes. Indo-Anglian fiction has hardly any true figure of evil in the sense Henry James' Gilbert Osmond is evil or Dushasana in the *Mahabharata* is evil. Mulk Raj Anand's sahukars and landlords are villains without really being evil, because they are symbols rather than human beings. In a hierarchical society these men merely perform their roles, their function is representative rather than individual. One wonders why, after the *Mahabharata*, the Indian mind has shown itself unwilling to cope with the problem of evil unless it is made into a symbol. Is it an artistic inability or a metaphysical preconception that prevents the Indian writer from creating convincing figures of evil ?

At any rate, from our analysis of the use of myth in Indo-Anglian fiction it emerges that the use of myth so far has been more successful technically, than thematically; that the myths chosen are often part of an established literary convention and do not show any unusual insight on the part of the author in perceiving links between the present situation and its parallel situation; yet on the whole the experiments have been varied enough and the methods of execution diverse enough to make the study rewarding. Moreover the authors through their different techniques reveal a great deal about their attitudes to life and their aspirations in art.

NOTES

1. Quoted, Richard Chase, *Quest for Myth* (1949), p. 6.
2. Among recent instances are Archibald MacLeish's play, J.B. (1958) and John Updike's novel, *The Centaur* (1963).
3. *Fables of Identity : Studies in Poetic Mythology* (New York, 1963), p. 27.
4. *Quest for Myth, passim.* This view, however, is not widely accepted.
5. See Chapter 4 also in this connection.
6. David McCutchion, *Writers Workshop Miscellany*, No. 8, 95.
7. Nemesis, as a goddess of retribution, not only expressed the righteous indignation of the gods at human presumption, but also corrected the balance when fortune obviously favoured any mortal.
8. His real name is nowhere mentioned. He is sometimes called Balaram because he has the same birthday as Krishna's brother, and once in childhood he had played the part of Balaram in a ploughing ceremony in the *Cradle of the Clouds*.
9. The reference is perhaps to the line made around Sita before Rama went to bring the golden deer.
10 *Fables of Identity*, p. 29.
11. Frye, *ibid.*, p. 30.
12. Krishna Chaitanya, *Sanskrit Poetics* (Bombay, 1963), p. 169, where he interprets 'Bal Kanda', the first canto of the *Ramayana*.

13. Raja Rao described himself thus in *Tribute to E. M. Forster*, ed. Natwar Singh (New York, 1964), p. 27.

14. For a different reading, see S. Nagarajan's review of the novel in *The Sewanee Review*, LXXII : 3, 512-517.

15. There is, I understand a ritual observed in many parts of South India which exactly corresponds to what Raja Rao describes here. This ritual in which the wife worships her husband is known as *Dishagauri-vrata*, and its origin is said to be in *Mahabharata*.

16. See Edwin Gerow, *Literature East and West*, X (1966), where the *New York Times* review is also quoted.

17. *Ibid.*

18. AIR interview on September 8, 1961, published in *Writers Workshop Miscellany*, No. 8 (1961), 50.

19. For example, the Pshwas and the Chewsurs of the Caucasus, "have a ceremony called ploughing the rain which they observe in times of drought. Girls yoke themselves to a plough and drag it into a river, wading in the water up to their girdles." Frazer goes on to add that the Armenian and the Georgian women perform the same ceremony. "A similar rain charm is resorted to in some parts of India; naked women drag a plough across a field by night, while the men keep carefully out of the way, for their presence will break the spell."—*The Golden Bough*, abr. edn. (London, 1959), pp. 70-71.

20. This type of character (represented by Lezo, Kolej Huzoor and the Second Master) is not in tune with the traditional Indian goal of learning which has always regarded learning as a means to an end, the end being the understanding of the self. William Haas in *The Destiny of the Mind* (London, 1959) emphasizes this important distinction between eastern and western attitudes to learning by coining a new word *Philousia* (the desire for essence or Is-ness) and by opposing the western ideal *Philosophy* (the desire for knowledge) to it. Indian scriptures are full of parables showing the futility of knowledge that does not bring one close to the essence. One remembers the story of Yagnavalkya and Maitreyi. The sage had taught her all that he could teach, but at the end she asked "What shall I do with knowledge that will not lead to salvation ?" There is also the story in the *Chandogya Upanishad* of a young Brahmin very proud of his learning. Returning to his father after his period of instruction he enumerates his studies to his father, where-upon the father shows him that he has not been taught the one thing worth knowing.

21. *The Mahabharata* translated by Chakravarthi V. Narasimhan, Calcutta, 1965, p. 110.

22. *Indian Fiction in English* (Philadelphia, 1960), p. 16.

23.   Translated from her Marathi book, *Yuganta* (Poona, 1967).

24.   See the special issue of the journal *Vagartha* (no. 5, April 1974) on Mahabharata and Northern Indian Literature.

25.   Rajan's reference to Karna in *The Dark Dancer* as the symbol of a man who does not belong, or to the Kurukshetra fratricide as analogous to Hindu-Muslim riots, does not go far enough to be significant.

26.   Edwin Gerow, *op. cit.*

7

The Problem of Style

THE MOST significant challenge before the Indo-Anglian novelist is the task of using the English language in a way that will be distinctively Indian and still remain English. For a long time 'Indian English' used to be a term of disapprobation, implying an insecure grip on English idiom or an infelicitous use of English vocabulary.[1] That meaning still persists in many quarters, and a number of cultivated Indians even today refuse to be interested in the novels Indians write in English for fear that they may have to contend with specimens of 'Indian English'. But in other quarters, especially among the writers themselves, there seems to be an increasing awareness that English is a pliant language which each writer has to fashion anew to serve his particular purpose, that for an Indian writer this fashioning will have to be different from what a British or American writer does, and that the definition of good English varies not only from century to century but also from place to place.

In the last thirty years there has been a great deal of experimentation in the use of the English language in Indo-Anglian fiction. Not all these experiments have been successful, and some writers are perhaps not even aware that they are experimenting, yet the tendency itself deserves notice because it reflects an important change of attitude towards the English language. The few writers who wrote novels in English in the early part of this century used

the language carefully, with stiff correctness, always conscious
that it was a foreign tongue. Perhaps because of this consciousness,
some of the best creative talents kept away from it.   There may
even have been a kind of shame, a tag of servility, attached to the
writing of creative literature in English in the late nineteenth and
early twentieth centuries, in the era of newly awakened nationalism.
This, of course, applies to literary writing, because the case of
orators and writers of utilitarian prose was different. For Rammohun Roy and later for men like Tilak, Gokhale and Mahatma
Gandhi, English was a more useful medium than any Indian language because it ensured a wider audience. But for creative writers,
English, even if it came naturally, was to be avoided because it was
the language of the rulers. Bankim Chandra Chatterjee, before he
made his indelible mark as a Bengali novelist, wrote his first novel,
Raj Mohan's Wife (1864), in English; the reason for his switching
over to Bengali was partly a realisation of the inadequacy of
his medium of expression, and partly a growing nationalistic
awareness as illustrated in a novel like *Ananda Math*. Another
great Bengali writer, Michael Madhusudan Dutt, began his career
in English with *The Captive Ladie* (1849), but thereafter devoted
himself to Bengali; he later wrote a poem on the subject of his
return to his own language in which the goddess Saraswati admo-
nishes him for neglecting the treasure that lay at home and running
in vain after the wealth of others. A third example of an Indian
writer consciously making a choice between two languages was that
of Romesh Chunder Dutt who wrote his novels in Bengali but also
translated at least two of them into English—*The Lake of Palms*
(1902) and *The Slave-girl of Agra* (1909). But most of the major
writers do not seem to have felt the dilemma faced by Bankim and
Madhusudan and Romesh Chunder. More often it was a handful
of second-rate writers who chose to write literature in English,
and this may be the main reason why Indo-Anglian creative writing, in quantity as well as in quality, is very poor until the third
or fourth decade of this century.

In the 'thirties one notices a sudden development in Indo-Anglian fiction, in quantity as well as quality. This may be related to
a recognition on the part of the writers that English was no longer
a foreign language, but after a hundred years of domicile had be-

come just another of India's many languages. Out of this self-assurance came the confidence to bend the language to their will. The liberties one can take with one's own language—the language one has inherited by birth and by upbringing and been exposed to in daily life—cannot be taken as easily with an acquired language which has been learnt at school according to the rules of grammar. Hence the vigorous attempts to wield the English language in a different way must be construed as a sign that writers have ceased to regard it as an alien tongue. Mulk Raj Anand is the first conscious experimenter, followed closely by Raja Rao, and in the next decade by Bhabani Bhattacharya. Each in his own way took liberties with the accepted diction and syntax of the language which had been so carefully taught to them from childhood. Some of their attempts failed; others enriched their novels, giving a new range and potential to the familiar English language. It seems there will be a continuous experimenting in giving English a peculiarly Indian tone and colour by drawing on the resources of the Indian languages and infusing their essence into normal literary English. It is essentially a personal experiment where each writer has to forge the medium that will best answer his needs. It is an attempt to find an individual style, but, incidentally, a successful experimenter also finds a style that could be called Indian in that it is different from British or American English. It should be emphasised, however, that creating an 'Indian English' is by no means the primary duty of the Indo-Anglian writer. His success or failure will be judged not by the amount of Indian imagery he has used in his novels, nor by his capacity to capture the rhythm of the vernacular in English. These images and rhythms become important only if they serve some purpose in the context, become integral with the total pattern, and if they perceptibly enhance the scope of the language. A writer's first obligation is to himself, and in whatever language he writes, he has to remake it for his own particular purpose. In this sense the Indo-Anglian novelists' experiments are no different from the experiments of creative writers anywhere in the world.

But in certain other ways the problem of the Indo-Anglian writer is indeed unique. He is writing in English about people who do not normally speak or think in English. One could add as a second problem the fact that he himself is writing in a language that is not his own. Not too much importance need however be attached to this second problem. If a man is not perfectly at home in English, or if he is more at home in some language other than English, he should not be writing English at all. It is true that one could cite a number of minor Indo-Anglian writers whose mastery of the language is questionable, but their work is not significant enough to deserve detailed discussion or draw any important conclusions from. The writers who matter are not beset with these naive linguistic hurdles, but with more complex issues. Their problem is different from that of the American, Australian or West Indian novelist (with whom they are sometimes compared) who can make use of living speech, be it a dialect, or city slang, or the language of affluence and sophistication, to delineate character and to portray subtle nuances and distinctions of social level, and sometimes to create a new technique. In the West Indian novelist Vic Reid's novel *The New Day* a type of stylised Jamaican dialect is used to create a poetic effect. V. S. Naipaul in *A House for Mr. Biswas* handles the dialect of West Indies Indians with success. Another West Indian writer, Derek Walcott, has attempted to draw special effects from the Creole dialect of St. Lucia. Many American novels from *Huckleberry Finn* to *Catcher in the Rye* and *Herzog* depend for their effect largely upon dialect or slang or some specialities of spoken language. The Indo-Anglian novelist has no such device at his disposal because although Indians speaking in English do have certain characteristic modes of expression, he is not necessarily writing about that very small minority who speak English all the time, nor about those few situations in which many Indians are forced to speak some variety of English. He is generally dealing with non-English speaking people in non-English speaking situations. He has to overcome the difficulty of conveying through English the vast range of expressions and observations whose natural vehicle is an Indian language. And yet literal translation is not always the answer because he has to make sure that the translated idioms or images do not go against the grain of the English language.

Technically, the problem becomes most acute in the writing of dialogue and presenting conversation. This perhaps explains why drama has always been the poorest genre in Indo-Anglian literature. But apart from dialogue, even in description, narration and reflection, the Indo-Anglian novelist is dealing with modes of thinking, manners of observation, and instinctive responses of people whose awareness has been conditioned by a language other than English. A powerful writer does indicate through his use of the English language this basic difference in attitudes and responses. The sum of all these differences may be regarded as the 'Indian' quality of his novel.

But 'Indian' is a vague word, because even though the Indo-Anglian novelist is writing in English, which is a language prevalent all over India, generally speaking, his area of intimate experience is limited to a small geographical area. The quality that marks his writing is often the quality of that particular area, the characteristics of its speech, its typical responses and its distinctive spirit. For example, Mulk Raj Anand at his best manages to convey a Punjabi flavour through his English (how he does it, is a question that will be tackled later in the chapter), and when he attempts to write about life outside the Punjab, as in *Private Life of an Indian Prince*, he is not so successful. R. K. Narayan's novels are so satisfyingly Indian perhaps because they are so authentically South Indian. This means not only that he depicts the customs and manners of the Tamil people accurately, which he does, but what is more important, through skilful use of the English language he delineates people whose actions, behaviour and responses are shaped by a language different from English; not only different from English, but also markedly different from Punjabi which is the language of Anand's most successful fictitious characters, or Bengali, the normal mode of speech of the characters created by Bhabani Bhattacharya. What Narayan does very unobtrusively, Raja Rao does in a more conspicuous way in *Kanthapura* in dealing with Kannada-speaking characters. Particularising of characters is an indication of a novelist's skill and part of the means of doing it is through subtle nuances of language. Raja Rao does it so effectively in *Kanthapura* that even those who are not closely acquainted with the rigid social structure of a South Indian village will notice how a man's caste can be ascertained from his mode of speech. Bhabani Bhattacharya's English, where it does not jar, succeeds in recreating a Bengali rhythm, as does occasionally Sudhin

Ghose's, though Ghose's fictional world, being partly fantasy, is less rooted in regional reality.

As against these writers with a regional flavour, there are a few others with suave and competent styles whose English neither betrays their own origin nor gives any indication of the regional identity of characters they create. Santha Rama Rau, Kamala Markandaya and Manohar Malgonkar offer examples of this kind of writing. All of them are undoubtedly as much at home in the language they write in, as any educated, cultured native speaker, and their fictional characters could come from any part of India. When they attempt to present regional characters (e.g., the Malayalee headmaster in Santha Rama Rau's *Remember the House*, or the Bengali clerk in Malgonkar's *Combat of Shadows*) these are never central characters and often only caricatures. It may be a significant fact that in Kamala Markandaya's first three novels there is no mention of any specific locality. The style of all these writers has the smooth, uniform ease of public school English, which is highly readable, but it is doubtful whether it is the most desirable style in fiction where one has to deal with particular human beings rooted in their narrow regional identities.

These writers have generally by-passed the linguistic and stylistic problems inherent in the Indo-Anglian situation. But those who have confronted the complex problem, and have attempted to convey the particular and the specific reality through their novels, have done so through different experiments with language. These experiments can be broadly classified under three heads:

(1) Experiment in diction (literal translation of idioms).
(2) Experiment in syntax (changing the structure of sentences).
(3) Imagery.

While the first two are generally consciously and deliberately done, the third category includes a great deal that is spontaneous. Strictly speaking, imagery cannot be an experimental device, because it is part of a writer's mode of perception, but it is included here along with the other two for the sake of convenience because the term style here is taken to include idioms, tone and imagery.

I

The device of literal translation has been most consciously tried out by Mulk Raj Anand. He does it so profusely that it is impossible not to take notice of it, and many critics and reviewers have disapproved of the liberties he takes with English. "Is this any talk?" or "There is no talk, son," or "Are you talking true talk?" are literal translations of Hindi phrases, just as expressions like "may I be your sacrifice" or "to make one's sleep illegal" are transference of Hindi (perhaps Punjabi also) idioms to English. The pages of Anand's novels are crowded with such literal translations. They are too numerous to be listed here, but among the more prominent are phrases like 'eating the air' (to take a stroll), 'counterfeit luck' (rotten luck), 'breaking the vessel' (to expose a secret) or 'black in the pulse' (something wrong) which are very common in Hindi, but when rendered into English appear quaint and unusual. More interesting are instances where not merely single phrases or idioms but a number of sentences follow each other to resemble the sequence of vernacular conversation. Anyone at all familiar with the Punjabi (or even colloquial Hindi) way of speaking will immediately recognize the authenticity of the following exchange in *Across the Black Waters*. Sepoy Lal Singh asks the veteran soldier, Kirpu, whether at the end of the war the sepoys will be given land as reward :

"The son of land !" said Kirpu "Thank your luck that you are still alive... Land, he says, the brother-in-law !" (p. 188)

As a contrast to the racy vigour of Punjabi peasant speech, there is in Anand also the extravagant diction of a man from Avadh, whose speech is redolent of the flavour of Urdu. In *The Sword and the Sickle*, a killing is reported thus : "from the tail of Sheikh Hadayatullah's gun some pomegranate blossom made Nanda's head a sieve" (p. 199). The unusual image loses its strangeness once it is recognised as translation. Similarly "eating the dust of the roadway, drinking the blood of my liver," is immediately revealed to one who knows Hindustani as a stock phrase and not a startling metaphor. A welcome like "Come on our head, come on our fore-

head," or a polite inquiry like "How is your gentle temperament"
are merely translations of well-known formalities in North Indian
languages. Another Hindi colloquialism that sounds absurd in
English is 'potter of somewhere' which in Hindi is a sort of mild
abuse for a potter. Anand uses these literal translations deliberately
because this is how the common man of Uttar Pradesh or Punjab
would sound if his speech was rendered into English.

A common complaint against Anand's language is the excessive
use of swear-words and abuse. The only justification, however,
is that of realism : the Punjab peasantry with whom Anand's best
works deal does have a large repertoire of swear-words in its ordinary conversation. It would be hypocritical to bowdlerise their
speech merely because these might appear strange in the English
language. The same argument will explain the use of proverbs like
"your own calf's teeth seem golden" (*The Road*, p. 24), or "a goat
in hand is better than a buffalo in the distance" (*The Road*, p. 22),
or "the camels are being swept away, the ants say they float"
(*The Big Heart*, p. 206). Proverbs play an important part not only
in Punjabi speech, but in Indian speech in general, and the tendency to render Indian proverbs in English is a common trait of
most Indo-Anglian writers. Khushwant Singh is another Punjabi
writer who translates Punjabi sayings into English (e.g. "Sardar
Sahib, you are a big man and we are but small radishes from an
unknown garden," (*I Shall Not Hear the Nightingale*, p. 27) while
Bhabani Bhattacharya's novels are full of literal translations of
Bengali proverbs like "when an ant grows wings and starts flying
in the air, it is not far from its doom" (*A Goddess Named Gold*,
p. 118) or "you may be digging a canal from the river to the house
door and inviting the crocodile" (*Music for Mohini*, p. 53). Sometimes we get regional variations of the same proverb rendered
into English. "After eating seven mice the cat is going on a pilgrimage" is a saying that Anand's characters frequently repeat,
and Raja Rao's village women speak of the cat that has "taken to
asceticism only to commit more sins" (*Kanthapura*, p. 85).

When the proverbs are repeated indiscriminately one gets a
little tired of them, especially because this is not a common
characteristic of modern English. But if we compare this
tendency with that of some of the earlier Indo-Anglian writers, of

using original English text-book phrases, literal translation seems a more desirable device. Take for example Venkataramani who presents the following conversation between a master and a servant :

"Muruga, it is really *putting new wines into old bottles*, though you don't understand the metaphor. . ."*
"Swami, what is the use of *crying over spilled milk ?*" (*Murugan the Tiller*, p. 5)[2]

The fact that many Indians tend to overuse these cliches which the high school grammar books call 'idioms and phrases' is perhaps explained when one takes into consideration the system of teaching English in India.[3] But when a writer uses it consistently in a novel, it reveals his stylistic naivete, as in the case of Venkataramani, who seems to believe sincerely that use of these idioms helps him to write good English. K. Nagarajan's novel, *Chronicles of Kedaram*, is also full of similar expressions, though Nagarajan is perhaps less naive in the use of these hackneyed phrases than Venkataramani because he intentionally makes these part of a device of characterization of the pompous narrator. The narrator, Gokarna Sastri, has a commonplace mind and he speaks and thinks in terms of cliches; hence it is not inappropriate that his language of narration should be full of stock phrases like ". . .descended upon him with his entire household *lock, stock and barrel* as one might say. . ." (p. 245), or "he had shed *for the nonce* all his upto-datedness. . ." (p. 64). If idioms and phrases and proverbs must be used in Indo-Anglian writing, it seems more appropriate to use the genuine Indian ones, rather than ineffectively employ the out-of-date copy-book English phrases. The important consideration, however, is whether they are functional and relevant. When the old woman who is the narrator in *Kanthapura* and the grandmother in *Music for Mohini* punctuate their speech with numerous proverbs, it is appropriate to their character. Similarly the narrator of *Chronicles of Kedaram* can use stereotyped idioms and phrases learnt from English text-books because it fits in with his small-town personality and unoriginal manner of perception. But when young and old alike speak in proverbs as in Anand's *The Road*, or master and

---

*In this example and in others which follow, I have italicized words and phrases to draw attention to stylistic and linguistic devices.

servant converse in grammar-book phrases as in Venkataramani's novels, it strikes the reader as unnatural.

Apart from idioms, phrases and proverbs, another aspect of the device of literal translation is found in the coining of new compound words. Raja Rao writes of the 'that-house people' or 'next-house-women's kitchen' and Bhabani Bhattacharya writes of the milk-infant growing into a woman, or of a child ten-eleven years old. Occasionally such words illuminate a sentence with vividness, but used too frequently they can easily degenerate into a mannerism. Most of these words are translations of vernacular compound words, but Bhattacharya does something very strange and inexplicable. He uses expressions that are obviously not English, their deliberate quaintness being meant to suggest that they are translated from Bengali. In reality, however, they have no counterparts in Bengali either. For example, words like childling, wifeling, even starveling; terms like picture-play (for the cinema), sun-up (for sunrise), joy-moments (perhaps for moments of joy); sentences like "Villagefuls of folk were on the high road" (So Many Hungers, p. 111), "Two moons were gone since they were wed" (ibid., p. 125), "When over-much joy in his heart, he made a gift" (ibid., p. 77), "Keep well away from the vote-mote" (A Goddess Named Gold, p. 157). These are neither recognisably English, nor are they faithful renderings of any other living mode of speech. It is this falsification of language that is the most serious flaw of Bhattacharya's writing; only his best novel, He Who Rides a Tiger, is relatively free of this trick. When in his other novels Bhattacharya speaks of mockful arms, or of easeful bones, or of prideful village-folk, it is difficult to understand what is gained by coining these strange adjectives when legitimate English attributes would have served just as well.[4] Bhattacharya sometimes lapses into plain bad English in pursuit of strangeness and becomes capable of sentences like "She has such a white back, white as a lime plaster. Besides her I am a darkie" (So Many Hungers, p. 66), "Manju in a muse ate her fish" (ibid., p. 66), "Mohini was excited to have Harindra's full confidence as well as with his plans" (Music for Mohini, p. 208), "And they discharged you, the boss folk" (He Who Rides a Tiger, p. 151).

Allied to this device of literal translation, 'there are two other

stylistic devices used by these novelists, especially by Mulk Raj
Anand. The first is Anand's use of Hindi (or Punjabi) words
directly in English, usually as nouns (thus, *angrez-log*, *yar*, *khaichal*)
but sometimes more daringly as verbs—in '*sisking* with cold,'
'*burburred*' in his sleep, '*thak-thakking* at a cauldron.' The second
device is to change the spelling of English words to indicate the
illiteracy of the speaker—as in *yus* for yes, *notus* for notice, *Amrika*
for America, *Girmany* for Germany. This second device
is patently false because an Indian writer writing in English
prima facie accepts the unreality of the characters' speaking in
English since the characters would not do so in real life. Since it is
understood that their speech is being recreated in another language,
distorting the spelling of English words contributes nothing to the
effect of verisimilitude. The only possible reason for this mis-
spelling could be to indicate that these words have become part of
the Indian language spoken by his characters. The other device,
that of interpolating Hindi words in English, is something which
the English language can stand a very small dose of at a time. Too
many successive sentences of the following variety can distort
the character of the language altogether, besides becoming incomprehensible to a non-Hindi knowing reader :

"*Chup sale*," shouted Ram Din, striking Gupta a *thappar* on the
head" (*The Sword and the Sickle*, p. 256);
"Shut up, *sale*, stop your *tain tain*" (*The Sword and the Sickle*,
p. 284);
"Why don't you say it loudly ? Why this *phus phus* ?" (*The Old
Woman and the Cow*, p. 275).

Besides, this is an impatient evasion of a problem that cannot be
so dodged. It is a problem inherent in the Indo-Anglian situation :
how to convey through English, situations, moods and expressions
that are essentially Indian ?

Of Anand's three devices to achieve a solution of this task—
literal translation of idioms, direct use of Hindi words, and mis-
spelling of English words—the first two occasionally succeed,
especially in his earlier novels where there is a vigour in the experimentation and an eagerness to convey a certain mood at all costs.

He changes and modifies the diction of English and invents new words to get his desired effect. But in his later novels these experiments lose their force by getting congealed into mannerisms.

Using *han* for *yes*, *acha* for *very well* and *nahin* for *no* is a common feature in Anand, just as Bhabani Bhattacharya frequently uses *han* and *hoon* and *nah*. It is difficult to see what is gained by this simple substitution, except perhaps as a reminder that the characters are not speaking in English. Exclamations other than simple affirmatives and negatives are indeed difficult to translate, and one can understand why Anand sometimes bodily transfers them, transliterating them into English spelling. And Anand's 'Bale Bale' though obscure to a non-Punjabi reader is perhaps less jarring than Bhattacharya's 'Eat my head.' Raja Rao never uses Kannada words in English except for words like *kumkum* or *arathi* (which are really Sanskrit and therefore intelligible to most Indian readers) more for the sake of clarity than for any special effect. Nor does he use exclamations in Kannada. The flavour of Kannada, whatever there is in his English, comes out of the unobtrusive use of Kannada figures of speech and terms of reference. The following sentences taken at random from *Kanthapura* should illustrate this point :

(1) Postman Subbayya, who had no fire in his stomach, and was red with red and blue with blue... (p. 154);

(2) You are a Bhatta, and your voice is not a sparrow voice in your village and you should speak to your people and organize a Brahmin party. Otherwise Brahminism is as good as kitchen ashes... (p. 154);

(3) ...and mother and wife and widow godmother went upto their lighted lizard-clucking homes. (p. 185)

The important point in these three instances is not that the expressions used are literal translations, but that they serve their purpose in their context, and they are more vivid than any other accepted English expressions that might have been used in their place. In quotation no. 3, the words 'lighted lizard-clucking homes' for example, convey a completely satisfying sense of security associated with the interior of a house after lighting time which is essential to these women (mother and wife and widow godmother), who have spent a long and uncertain day of struggle, picketing toddy-booths. Moreover, these sentences contain nothing that would be unintelligible or jarring to the reader who does not know Kannada, and that is more than what can be said about the linguistic experiments of most other Indo-Anglian writers. Relevance and clarity are perhaps the two prime criteria in any experiment with diction, though no fixed rules can be formulated. Each writer has to experiment for himself and decide where a literal translation will do and where it will become an unnecessary impediment.

II

Among the Indo-Anglian writers who have attempted to alter significantly the normal structure and rhythm of English sentences, two stand out—Raja Rao and Bhabani Bhattacharya, writers who are otherwise vastly different from each other in theme as well as in technique. In spite of their differences, they share a common tendency : they tend to make their sentences sound archaic, even biblical. In Raja Rao this characteristic becomes very prominent in *The Serpent and the Rope*, but even earlier, in the stories of *The Cow of the Barricades* for example, we find sentences like "When they said 'Here's a coin' he said '*Nay*' and the snake was *right glad* of it" (p. 170), or "And people were *much affrighted*" (p. 177), or "His Sona, *he who is dead*, was once tied to a tree and beaten" (p. 149). In *The Serpent and the Rope*, where the tendency towards archaism becomes very marked, one notices two special stylistic devices aimed at creating the archaic note. The first is the use of 'be' instead of 'are'—for example, "what wonderful animals these be in our land" (p. 27), or "the sorrow of woman be indeed the barrenness of man" (p. 27). The second consists of attaching the name of the subject to the end of the sentence to explain the pronoun that has gone before. Thus : "He is so tender and fine-limbed, is my brother" (p. 12), or "He is the whole of himself, is Oncle Charles" (p. 87), or "She had become so beautiful, had Madeleine" (p. 88), or "Her hair was so long, she needed a comb wherever she went, did Madeleine" (p. 96), or

"They are so immoral, the English are" (p. 146). This is the most common feature of Raja Rao's style in *The Serpent and the Rope,* and it is possible to cite scores of instances.

It would be interesting to speculate what purpose these archaisms are meant to serve. David McCutchion dismisses all these devices as "dubious rhetoric" and "an irritating trick... presumably to strike a profound note,"[5] while S. Nagarajan has suggested a close relationship of Raja Rao's English prose with the rhythm of Sanskrit.[6] But there is also a possibility that these devices are intended to create a distance between the reader and the happenings of the novel and give the impression of timelessness. An archaic style ought to remove the events in the novel from contemporary reality and from normal expectations of logic and probability. In that case it is part of a larger technical device inherent in the novel, of creating a suspension of the ordinary demands of reality. These archaisms should then act as a reminder, in addition to the deliberately ambiguous rhetoric of his speculative sentences, that his work is not a novel in the accepted sense of the term, but rather a metaphysical treatise on non-dualism which just happens to deal with particular human beings. Take for example tortuous sentences like the following :

> But once having gone a hundred leagues I shall come back a thousand, for I do not really have the fear of fear. I only have fear. (*The Serpent and the Rope,* p. 9)

> It is a metaphysical comedy, and all I would want the reader to do is to weep at every page, not for what he sees, but for what he sees he sees. (on the dust jacket of *The Cat and Shakespeare*)

> So how shall I ever know if I love cats ? I must know cats and I know that I know that I love cats. When cats are there, where am I ? When I am there what becomes of the cats ? (*The Cat and Shakespeare,* p. 90)

For the reader only two reactions are possible to this kind of writing: either to throw the book away in exasperation, convinced that the author is exploiting the credulity of the reader with pseudo-profundity;[7] or to go along with the author believing that truth itself is complex, and what he wants to convey here could not have been conveyed in simpler language, in which case style becomes inseparable from the content.

Bhabani Bhattacharya's attempts at changing the structure of the English sentence are less complicated. When he uses archaisms like 'thine', 'goodly' or 'god forsooth', they serve no purpose other than adding quaintness. Sometimes they co-exist with modern colloquialisms, and the total effect is bizarre. One favourite device of Bhattacharya is putting a mark of interrogation at the end of a statement, thereby indicating that it is not a statement of fact but a question. For example, he writes "The new world order was an empty dream ?" (*So Many Hungers*, p. 25), instead of writing "Was the new world order an empty dream ?" This is not a very important deviation from the norm, and done once or twice it would not attract attention. But Bhattacharya repeats this pattern frequently to make it a very obvious element of his style. Thus : "What peril he muttered, worries plenty we have ?", or "Kanu— he was safe ?" (*So Many Hungers*, p. 204)

This peculiarity of style can be explained only in one way. In the Bengali language the form of a statement and of a question are sometimes identical, the difference being indicated in speech through tone, and through punctuation in writing. Perhaps Bhattacharya deliberately tries to recreate the Bengali rhythm in the English language by doing away with the syntactic distinction between a question and a statement. Also, Bengali sentences, unlike English or Hindi, often leave out the verb 'to be'. Bhattacharya seems to transfer this feature to his English occasionally, as in "Who more proud than I on this day. . ." (*Music for Mohini*, p. 88) instead of "Who *is* more proud etc." Again, such sentences are not unknown in English but the constant repetition of such construction makes it a feature of Bhattacharya's style.

A third device is to use short sentences, a number of them together, in a way that does not sound natural in English. For example :

"Why speak ? what use ! Trees and rocks have a heart. Not man. Why speak ?" (*So Many Hungers*, p. 76)

"Fear is left far back... A little more way to go, a bare hundred oar strokes. That thicket at the water's bend. Good spot.

The boat will have hiding safety. . ." (*ibid.*, p. 72)

The basic sentence patterns of English are altered so frequently that the language appears violated.

Whatever the degree of Bhattacharya's success, his intention is laudable. Like Raja Rao he also attempts, through experiment with sentence structure, to indicate a different ethos. Both have experimented with a number of devices to make it clear that these novels are different from contemporary English novels, that they deal with people who think and act and speak differently from English-speaking people. Moreover, Raja Rao also attempts to convey the philosophical nature of his novel through a special kind of rhetoric. Mulk Raj Anand, characteristically enough, uses neither archaism nor metaphysical riddles in his writing. He is a 'progressive' forward-looking writer, just as his heroes are believers in the future, and also an exponent of scientific rationalism; hence, a device that is reminiscent of the past, and specially of religious scriptures, would naturally not appeal to him. His experiments with style are consistent with his world-view. Rendering proletarian speech correctly in English is his aim, and his unconventional diction and radical experiments with vocabulary are all geared to this end.

One important difference between the styles of Raja Rao and Anand is that Anand's experiments are limited to the dialogue of his characters, while Raja Rao's special effects permeate his entire style. One notices a double level in Anand's style : passages of ornate conventional prose cluttered with adjectives and adverbs when the author speaks directly to the reader, and dialogues in racy peasant speech when the characters speak to each other. His experiments are thus part of a device of characterization. In this respect more Indo-Anglian writers are like Anand than they are like Raja Rao. Most of them, who do not normally attempt stylistic experiments, occasionally change the mode of English speech for the sake of characterization. For example, in B. Rajan's *Too Long in the West*, the speech of Satyamurthi is consistently marked by an absence of the definite article. Thus, "What is justification for unseemly disturbance ?" (p. 179), or "I am a man without possessions or testimonials. Yet owner of house has given me hospitality" (p. 179), or "Kindly cease anaemic blathering about blood. World knows you are unable to wring neck even of chicken" (p. 180). Similarly, in Santha Rama Rau's *Remember the House*, the Malayalee headmaster of a village school is created entirely in terms of the strange rhythm of his English speech : "You have inherited your esteemed mother's great talents ? You sing no doubt also ?" (p. 164), or "A chair, Mr. Krishnan, and a cup of coffee isn't it ? No trouble. We can get with ice, at once... In one minute the peon will bring" (p. 169). In these examples, two quite different issues are involved : first, rendering the English of an Indian speaker; second, rendering an Indian's speech in an Indian language into English. The first even a perceptive foreigner can do, and is especially easy when the intention is to provoke laughter.[8] The second is a far more subtle and difficult undertaking. And it is this second task that Indo-Anglian writers are tackling most of the time, because the English-speaking occasions of an Indian's life are limited in number.

In the case of Santha Rama Rau's headmaster, as a man from Kerala speaking to a Maharashtrian, he is most certainly shown to be speaking in English; in Rajan's case, one is not so sure. The misuse of the English definite article is a well-known source of much grief to Indians speaking in English. But in Rajan's novel, with the exception of an American, all the other characters are South Indians and presumably are not speaking to each other in English all the time. In that case it is difficult to see what purpose Satya-murthi's peculiarity of speech serves.

The more one reflects over the problems of the Indo-Anglian writer, the more complex seem the issues involved in the rendering of speech. S. Y. Krishnamurthy, author of an only novel, *Kalyani's Husband*, wrote a long preface to discuss his difficulties. According to him:

English novels of Indian life are poor stuff. To the Indian there is something unmistakably ridiculous in two Indians conversing with each other in the ornate and out of date English... or in phrases that read well in the original Tamil but are automatically burlesqued in the very translations.

Krishnamurthy is aware of the dangers of writing Indian fiction in English, yet proceeds to do so for two reasons : his lack of proficiency in Tamil, and his belief that a true account of South Indian life needs a bilingual narration because people speak in English as well as in Tamil; therefore whether one writes in Tamil or in English does not make any real difference.

Krishnamurthy's argument covers only a certain kind of novels dealing with urban settings. Not all Indo-Anglian novels attempt to describe bilingual situations. But in moving to a rural setting, the Indo-Anglian novelist faces another kind of difficulty—the problem of presenting local colour through dialect. Indo-Anglian novelists generally provide local colour by introducing descriptions of Indian landscapes or festivals or customs and manners. The only authentic dialect used noticeably in Indo-Anglian novels is not the dialect of a localised group, nor of a rural area, but the dialect of the Anglo-Indian community, which is spread all over India. Anglo-Indian speech most certainly has a special rhythm and a special diction and syntax different from the standard English taught in Indian schools, distinctive enough to merit separate linguistic analysis.[9] And because the Anglo-Indians are the only group that speak entirely in English, the Indo-Anglian novelist can use their speech to serve his purpose. Manohar Malgonkar uses Anglo-Indian speech effectively in *Combat of Shadows* where the hero, a *pucca* Englishman, a British public school product, gets involved with an Ango-Indian girl from a railway colony. The difference in their background and social status is enormous and the difference in their speech becomes a symbol of this essential incompatibility. Ruby Miranda speaks to Henry Winton about her boy friend :

> ...he was sweet on me—my, he was really jay ! ... "Eddie was always jay. He didn't like anyone even to speak to me." (p. 98)

Such expressions embarrass Henry Winton who wishes that Ruby wouldn't say things like 'ta muchly' or 'Give's a fag,' but he does not say anything to her about it, assuming that she might resent it. (p. 95) Ruby's development as a character is parallel to the improvement in the pattern of her speech, and later in the novel when a more refined, a vastly more self-assured Ruby Miranda is denied by Winton the realisation of the Anglo-Indian dream *par excellence* (namely, to be admitted into European society through marriage), she covers her humiliation under sarcasm :

> "Thanks," (said Ruby) "Thanks for everything." He (Winton) noticed that she was fully at home with the repetitive 'th' sound. It was astonishing how well she had overcome this almost insurmountable linguistic handicap of her race." (p. 149)

The difference between an English tea-planter and an Anglo-Indian call-girl proves insurmountable and Winton marries a girl of his own race and social class. Later he watches Ruby objectively, from a scientific, philological point of view :

> She hadn't said 'Oh My !' once, thought Henry, or things like 'ta muchly' or 'great !' and now she had to go and call Christmas 'exmas'. O pygmalion ! how difficult, how heart breaking it was to unlearn a way of speech ! So much more difficult than learning an altogether new language. (p. 187)

In *Combat of Shadows*, language becomes an important issue because the theme of the novel includes the social relations (or the lack of it) between the British in India and the Anglo-Indians. In delineating the nuances of class distinction, therefore, the rendering of the differences in speech is an effective device. But in another novel of Malgonkar, *The Princes*, where another Anglo-Indian girl appears, not much attention is paid to the pattern of her speech. In this novel, too, there is an enormous barrier between the hero Abhayraj and the Anglo-Indian girl Minnie Bradley, just as there was between Henry Winton and Ruby Miranda in the other novel. But here the difference is that between a prince and a commoner, a more fundamental class difference, and therefore external details of speech or dress or manners matter less. Besides, in the relationship between an Englishman and an Anglo-Indian, subtle differences in language assume an importance because the two of them are speaking two different dialects of a language that is native to both of them, while in the relationship between an Indian and an Anglo-Indian details of speech are not significant because the Indian is speaking a language that is not his own and therefore he is not too sensitive about it. We may conclude therefore that dialect is useful to the Indo-Anglian novelist only when he can employ it with discrimination to accentuate certain elements of the theme.

There are, however, some exceptions. Khushwant Singh's Anglo-Indian police sergeants do not serve any such thematic purpose, because they are minor characters. They conform to the stereotype with their 'old chaps' and 'mun' and 'bugger'. Not only in their speech but in their actions and attitudes they adhere to the somewhat exaggerated Anglo-Indian role, and are nearer caricatures than real portrayals. For example :

> "Great leader this chap, mun. You would not know looking at him would you ?" The other nodded his head slowly, scrutinizing Sher Singh from head to foot. "One never knows with these niggers."
> "One doesn't, does one !" (*I Shall not Hear the Nightingale*, p. 195)
> "You hear mister ? The Dee Cee wants to give you a chance to save your bloody neck from hanging because of your old Bap." (*ibid.*, p. 196)

Anglo-Indian speech is easy to caricature because it is in English, while the peculiarities of a Bengali or a Marathi speaker have to undergo a process of translation before they can be rendered in Indo-Anglian fiction, and in the process the rhythm of the original language is often lost.

In most of these novels changes in the normal syntax of English are made only in dialogues, and mainly for the purpose of characterization. Occasionally, as in G.V. Desani's *All About H. Hatterr,* the experimentation is sustained throughout, because the style in this novel is a device of characterization of Mr. Hatterr, the narrator. Hatterr is a clearly conceived character not to be confused with the author, and we are reminded more than once in the ten page foreword to the book that Hatterr is telling his own story in his own distinctive style. Hatterr is not a writer ; he is a half-educated Anglo-Malayan orphan who grew up in India, whose peculiar brand of English is justified thus in the foreword :

> As for the arbitrary choice of words and constructions... not

intended by me to invite analysis. They are there because I think they are natural to H. Hatterr... and jot this down too. I never was involved in the struggle for newer forms of expression. (p. 6)

Later Hatterr is made to defend himself :

... I write rigmarole English straining your goodly godly tongue, may be; but friend, I forsook my form, school and Head, while you stuck to yours : learning reading, 'riting and 'rithmetic. (p. 22)

After all this elaborate explanation, introduction and self-justifica-tion, the style that follows does not seem so very startling. It is characterised by a facetiousness, the use of heavy ponderous tech-nical sounding jargon to convey rather trivial information, as in this :

Medically speaking the feller was a doubtless melancholic psycho-sis case. In a panic and Agora-claustrophobia like that (a virtual manic-depressive mental state) a chap's subject to the hashish and mescaline poisoning type of paranoia, viz., a hell of a worry-ing disposition. (p. 174)

Another characteristic is sudden touches of would-be humorous eccentricities like writing 'fatigoo' for fatigue, or coining new words like 'Sinfant'. But if the purpose of the whole stylistic exercise was to create the distinctive character of Hatterr, it is not fulfilled because the style in the preface and the foreword is indistinguish-able from the style in the body of the novel.

Whatever the measure of his success, Desani's experiments are obviously intended as means of characterization. In this respect he is like Anand, Rama Rau, Malgonkar, and most other Indo-Anglian novelists. The only two exceptions—that is, writers whose experiments with style are not merely devices of characterization—are Raja Rao and R. K. Narayan. Other writers, most notable among whom is Anand, show an obvious dichotomy in their style. All innovations and experiments with language are limited to the dialogue of their fictitious characters, while a staid conventional

English prose is used when the author speaks in his own voice. In Raja Rao and R. K. Narayan we are not aware of this dichotomy. They are linked with their characters by a common vision and a common way of reacting to experience. Even when (as in the case of Narayan) the author conceives his characters in gentle irony, he is never superior to them. And this homogeneity is reflected in their style which is not a device for a certain end, but expressive of their total personality.

III

Experimenting with diction and syntax is usually a conscious process, but imagery reveals the author's natural mode of awareness. When an Indian writer records his real responses to life without echoing second-hand literary modes of perception, his writing is bound to have a quality which for want of a better term we may call 'Indian' imagery. This does not merely mean comparisons with the lotus or the elephant, but finding connections in experiences, events, and objects from real life. Since this is primarily an un-self-conscious process, it offers the literary critic a clue to the authenticity of a writer's vision. It should, however, be remembered that metaphors and similes are not the natural component of every writer's style. Some writers, for example, R. K. Narayan, write in a language almost devoid of imagery. Narayan's language is simple, almost deceptively so, his sentences are straight-forward in syntax and unobtrusive in diction. The authenticity of his style cannot be judged from the quality of his imagery, for the simple reason that imagery is not the vehicle of his perception. But in the case of other writers, whose writing is strewn with similes and metaphors, an examination of the texture of their style often reveals a great deal about their response to life. Take for example Venkataramani, whose two novels (written in 1927 and 1932) have been praised by commentators of Indo-Anglian literature.[10] Here are two representative sentences from Venkataramani's *Murugan the Tiller* :

The image of his mother stood in his storm-tossed soul as a wrecked ship in the sea would stand for its captain on the shore. (p. 9)

You are for me even as the sea is to the ship or the wind is to the sails. (p. 13)

Both novels are written almost wholly in this metaphor-laden language. It is undoubtedly a 'literary' style, i.e., its images are taken not from real life, but obtained at second hand from English literature. This dependence on English literature for his style is ironic in view of the aggressively nationalistic themes of Venkataramani's novels. His heroes Kandan and Ramu are both firm believers in traditional Indian values and they reject all that is western, therefore it is rather amusing that Venkataramani should make them speak in an ornate nineteenth century British idiom.[11]

Raja Rao's position is diametrically opposite. Images and metaphor are his natural mode of expression, and very little influence of English literature is discernible. His earlier work was full of fresh perception and a first-hand response to life. His language in the first two books is so richly strewn with similes that any passage quoted at random will serve to illustrate the elements of his style. Consider for example the following :

And as he lay down he saw before him a bare rocky hill and the moonlight poured over it like a milk and butter libation. (*The Cow of the Barricades*, p. 57)

... and when Moorthappa comes let the rice be fine as filigree and the mangoes yellow as gold, and we shall go out, horn and trumpet and gong before us and break coconuts at his feet. (*Kanthapura*, p. 156)

The imagery here happens to touch upon objects and experience that are distinctively Indian, yet one must distinguish them from mere attempts at appearing exotic before the non-Indian reader. Raja Rao does not always speak of mangoes and coconuts and the "sun rising behind the jack-fruit tree like a camphor censer alit," though he does so quite often. There is for example an early short story entitled "In Khandesh" in *The Cow of the Barricades* where the bleak menacing landscape of Eastern Maharashtra is evoked in a way that is almost frightening in its details :

In Khandesh the earth is black. Black and grey as the buffalo, and twisted like an endless line of loamy pythons, wriggling and stretching beneath the awful heat of the sun. (p. 146)

or

On the high palms two vultures sat, with their fleshy neck, bald as though they had eaten their own skin. (p. 146)

or

Somebody was walking down the twist of the ravine, an ass behind him. His shadow is black as congealed blood. (p. 157)

The imagery here cannot be regarded as exotic. For its evocation of atmosphere "In Khandesh" is one of the best pieces Raja Rao has written, and the effect depends mainly on the strength of observed details.

Raja Rao's style shows two distinct phases of development. In the earlier phase (in *Kanthapura*, 1938, and *The Cow of the Barricades*, 1945) there is a fond dwelling upon the concrete and the particular, be it the sky ("as blue as a marriage shawl," *Kanthapura*, p. 72) or women ("some beautiful as new-opened guavas and the others tender as April mangoes," *The Cow of the Barricades*, p. 55) or young boys ("bright as banana trunks," *Kanthapura*, p. 245), which is markedly absent in the two later books published after an interval of about fifteen years. In *The Serpent and the Rope* (1960) and *The Cat and Shakespeare* (1964) this concrete imagery is replaced by general reflections and abstract speculations. The reason for this change in style may be related to the increasingly metaphysical nature of his themes. But another possible reason cannot be ruled out altogether. At the time of writing *The Serpent and the Rope*, Raja Rao had already been an expatriate long enough to have lost touch with the vivid details of landscape and daily life in India that filled the pages of his early volumes. It is interesting to note that the details of French life and landscape never become as much a part of Raja Rao's imagery as those of a coastal village in South India did in his first novel.

Another Indo-Anglian novelist whose distinctive style and intensely individual imagery deserves mention is Anita Desai. She is a comparatively young writer who has written only three novels so far, but already her style shows a strong individuality. Her language is marked by three characteristics : sensuous richness, a high-strung sensitiveness, and a love for the sound of words. In her first novel the style had a curious compatibility with her theme, because the narrator of *Cry, the Peacock* is a hypersensitive young woman, tense and over-wrought. The manner of narration reveals elements of her personality. The narrator's slow advance towards insanity is the theme of the novel, and the main pattern is the contrast between this woman's response to the world through her senses, and her husband's response through his intellect. Gautama, the husband, is cerebral by nature while Maya, the narrator, lives by her senses of touch, smell, sight and taste. Here are some examples of her tremulous response to life around her :

> His [a baby's] lips were pink and tenuous, exposed and defenceless, like a moist peeled fruit. (p. 112)

> Bare feet on bare tiles, night cooled fur [of the cat] against bed warmed flesh [of the woman]. (p. 48)

> His [her husband's] hand as cool and dry as the bark of an old and shady tree. (p. 20)

At times such responses become overwhelming in their intensity and unbearable in their richness :

> The tremulous flower-tinted air is vibrant as a violin string set into motion by the fine tender legs of a brilliant grasshopper. High incessant sounds form out of the very sun and air on such a morning like crystals in syrup. (p. 32)

If the extravagance of sensuousness is somewhat oppressive here, it is not an inappropriate effect because this is the record of the perceptions of a woman on the brink of insanity. She is high-strung from the beginning, but before the final break-down comes, she is given some passages of startling imagery. The most striking passages are the description of summer, both during the day in its violence and at night under the moon. She describes the 'loo', the fierce North Indian hot wind thus :

Here was a carnival to enjoy, merry-go-rounds, and roller coasters, brass bands, fried food stalls, cavorting clowns... (p. 163)

And during a disturbed night under the sky :

the moon. . . when it rose out of the churn of my frenzy. . . it was not the gentle moon of love ballads and fairy revels. . . It was the mad demon of Kathakali ballets, masked, with heavy skirts swirling, feet stamping, eyes shooting beams of fire. . . (p. 24)

The conjecture that style in *Cry, the Peacock* is part of the device of characterization of the narrator seems plausible when we read Anita Desai's second novel, *Voices in the City*, which has some of the earlier intensity and richness, but lacks the extravagance of imagery found in the first. Also, the use of rare words is far less frequent now. In the second novel we no longer find words like 'oneirodynia', 'obmutescence', 'tenebrific', 'opsimaths', 'crepuscular', or 'sequaciousness', which were part of the general vocabulary of *Cry, the Peacock*. The second novel is not a first person narrative; it is divided into four unequal parts, telling the story of a brother, two sisters and their mother respectively, who live in separate worlds of their own but whose lives are indirectly woven together. In this case the style of narration cannot serve as a device of characterization. Only one section is an extract from a diary, hence written in the first person ; the rest is in the author's own voice. If any character in the novel is akin to the neurotic narrator of the earlier novel it is Monisha, a sensitive childless young woman imprisoned in a huge oppressive joint family household. Monisha's claustrophobia and exasperation culminate in suicide, and, appropriately enough, the style and imagery in the pages from Monisha's diary come closest to the language of the heroine of *Cry, the Peacock*, another desperate woman. One complaint that the reader could have against Anita Desai is that her writing is so tense and tightly strung throughout that it leaves him breathless. But this is at the same time her strength, because it is the natural mode of expression for her uniquely personal vision. In spite of the comparative smallness of her output to date, Anita Desai is a rare example of an Indo-Anglian writer who achieves that difficult task of bending the English language to her purpose without either a self-conscious attempt of sounding Indian or seeking the anonymous elegance of public school English.

Another author who succeeds in this delicate task is much better known and very different from Anita Desai. R. K. Narayan's style is most difficult to analyse or discuss, and he has a tendency to elude categories and classifications. He constantly underwrites, never emphasising, never caricaturing, and hardly ever passing moral or aesthetic judgments. His style is so unobtrusive and so devoid of purple patches that it is difficult to find quotable passages to illustrate his particular characteristics. On very rare occasions a casual description like the following startles the reader :

I loved this room because the sun came through a ventilator, bringing in a very bright beam of light and brilliant dust particles floated in it and the two boys who sat on the second bench looked all aflame. (*The English Teacher*, p. 10)

The real strength and the disarming quality of Narayan's style, however, lie not in these rare moments of beauty, but in his honest, straight-forward vision. Critics have commented upon Narayan's gentle irony and mild satire but quite often his irony is nothing but an honest recording of facts, without any colouring of conventional sentiment. This could be seen from Narayan's treatment (ironic treatment, one might say) of romantic love. Take for example the first encounter between Sriram and Bharati in *Waiting for the Mahatma* :

As he approached the market fountain a pretty girl came up and stopped him. 'Your contribution' she asked, shaking a sealed tin collection box. Sriram's throat went dry and no sound came. He had never been spoken to by any girl before ; she was slender and young, with eyes that sparkled with happiness. He wanted to ask 'How old are you ? What caste are you ? Where is your horoscope ? Are you free to marry me ?' (p. 19)

The last sentences of this passage could very well be regarded as an ironic comment on the Indian variety of romantic love, but they could also be seen simply as honest recording of the reactions of a small-town young man at the sight of an attractive girl. In *The Bachelor of Arts*, Chandran imagines that he has fallen in love with a girl, merely by seeing her from a distance on the beach. He contemplates going to see her again the next day :

> He was going to stare at her and take in a lot of details regarding her features. He had not made out yet whether she was fair or light brown; whether she had long hair or short, and whether her eyes were round or almond shaped, and he had also some doubts about her nose. (p. 68)

A great deal of Narayan's celebrated irony consists of an honest description of a state of mind without the conventional selection or rejection. Therefore, while certain passages can be clearly pointed out as ironic, in other passages a lingering doubt remains about the author's intention. In *The English Teacher*, where the usual Narayan traits of irony and humour are less in evidence, one is at a loss to know whether certain passages are to be taken seriously or not. For example the young English teacher and his creative efforts : are his nature poems to be taken as serious attempts of self-realisation, or as jejune exercises at verse-making, watery imitations of Wordsworth ? Here is a passage describing a moment of communion with nature :

> There are subtle invisible emanations in nature's surroundings : with them the deepest in us merges and harmonizes. I think it is the highest form of joy and peace we can ever comprehend. I decided to rush back to my table and write a poem on nature.

If there is a touch of irony in the last sentence it is an irony of recognition. As in the case of Sriram and Chandran in the two other passages quoted earlier, the experience of the English teacher recorded here is all too familiar to the Indian reader, and the irony depends on this element of recognition. Narayan never deliberately attempts to be Indian, but because he deals with convincing human beings in authentic situations, and records their responses honestly, and because these human beings happen to be Indians, he succeeds in achieving that difficult task : writing in a genuinely Indian way without being self-conscious about it. His writing is a perfect example of the fact that the matter and the style of a given piece of writing cannot be separated. He gives the reader no quotable quotation, but writes in an even tenor, without extravagant rhetoric or passages of drab prose.

At first this might seem no great achievement. The unobtrusiveness of his style makes it appear an easy task, but when we look at some of the other eminent Indo-Anglian writers we realise how Narayan's artlessness really conceals art. Apart from a few exceptions, the bulk of Indo-Anglian writing even now is marked by two characteristics, which are conspicuous in Narayan by their absence : a meretricious, ornate and adjective-ridden style, and a 1 excess of solemnity. Examples of the first characteristic can be taken from almost any writer, but here are two extracts from a single page of Rajan's novel, *Too Long in The West* :

> The clouds with their billowing purple belligerence rolled in procession over its adamant heights. . . (p. 2)
> It was a wry story the hill told, mingling both reverence and laughter in ways that seemed inconsistent but which fitted the illusions of the mountain, cloud and mist. Perhaps it also enabled those telling it to live with more startling realities, with a world that was violent, both in its uprooting and its benedictions, and which bloomed safely only in the oasis of miracles. (p. 2)

Rajan's style has a deliberate academic archness which weighs down even his passages of humour. To quote from the same novel :

> Kesavan, the great joiner, the dovetailer of hopes, and expert healer of schisms, who now sat in the sun of Mudalur's forthcoming adulation, the genuine sunlight being as usual absent. (p. 134)

or

> After four years of perseverance, he won the crossword puzzle
> of a famous periodical twice in succession, thereby becoming the
> first man to do it since the Emperor Ashoka, who did not do it
> either. (p. 8)

In both his novels Rajan writes consistently in this self-conscious
style. Even Mulk Raj Anand or Bhattacharya, when they are
not engaged in linguistic experiments, write in a wordy ornate
style. Thus Bhattacharya :

> But the end of one tale was the beginning of another. For like
> a quenchless heritage of hate, the bonfire of boats was prisoned
> and ever-alive in each fistful of ash. (*So Many Hungers*, p. 81)

The heavy alliteration in 'heritage of hate' and 'bonfire of boats'
indicates Bhattacharya's idea of desirable literary style. Anand
is aware of this general weakness of Indo-Anglian writers. In his
foreword to Venu Chitale's novel, *In Transit*, Anand said ". . .
and the narrative is sustained at an even pitch of writing without
the purple patch or the deliberate use of lovely words which mars
so many novels written in English by Indians who want to show
off their mastery of the alien tongue." But in spite of this awareness, Anand himself occasionally seems to write in a style that he
condemns in others. Not infrequently he punctuates his writing
with sentences that are heavy, complex and laden with excessive
imagery. Here is a fragment of a single sentence from Anand's
The Big Heart :

> A turbulent spirit and wanton in reaching out after life, he
> seemed now and then the poise of a furious calm in himself
> like that of a leaf suddenly come still in a storm, especially
> after he had been struggling like a tormented beast in the cage
> of his soul, in his recurrent dreams or in odd moments even in
> day light. . . (p. 13)

When we contrast such a style with the mild unpretentious manner
of Narayan's writing, we begin to realise the authenticity and

strength of Narayan's medium.   Style must always be an integral part of a man's vision and not an element that can be isolated from the content or theme of a novel.   The sincerity of Narayan's style is thus an inalienable part of his vision.   By the same analysis a pretentious style reflects the attitude of the writer towards his material.   This is not to suggest that only one kind of style is desirable in literature.   The prose styles of Henry James and of Hemingway are both equally valid because both are authentic and integral to their vision of life.   That is where the distinction between true style and false style comes in.   If style is something that can be added on to the material, like icing on a cake or embroidery on a sari, it is not integral to the author's point of view. No amount of experimentation with style, no amount of conscious innovation, will succeed in fiction unless it has an inevitability in the context of the particular theme the novel deals with. That is the reason why Anand's experiments succeed in some of his earlier novels where there is a compatibility between his theme and style, and fails in later works where he holds on to his devices without the corresponding urgency and sincerity that marked the earlier volumes. And in Raja Rao's novels, the important thing is not that he uses Indian imagery but that these images are part of his natural mode of perception. V. Y. Kantak has compared R. K. Narayan's style with a "one-stringed instrument (like that Ukelele-thing one sees farmers selling to city children)."[12]   It is true that the range of a one-string instrument is limited, and Professor Kantak in the same essay points out how at moments of intensity Narayan's instrument fails to satisfy the reader because of its lack of amplitude.   But no other instrument would have better suited the simple honesty of Narayan's vision.

An examination of the language of the Indo-Anglian novel need not therefore come to any conclusion about the 'Indianness' of a particular writer's style.   A more serious consideration is whether the style of a writer is genuine and individual rather than merely correct and competent.

NOTES

1. See F. Anstey's *Baboo Jabbarjee* (London, 1898), which is written in a style parodying 'Indian English'. Thus :
   "Had such shocking sentiments been aired by some of the other lady orators in this room, I must facetiously have recalled them to a certain fabular fox which criticised the unattainable grapes as too immature to merit mastication. But the particular speaker cannot justly be said to be on all fours with such an animal."

2. Incidentally, the phrase "crying over spilled milk" reminds one of this phrase used quite differently by Narayan in *Waiting for the Mahatma*. Jagadish, an underground revolutionary worker, is upset about a radio having gone out of order. He says,
   "I suppose I'd better take it back with me and repair it. As a soldier I will not cry over split milk."
   "Is it split milk ?" Sriram asked nervously.
   "Of course it is," asserted Jagadish. "When milk goes bad it splits into water and solid, you know. It's no use crying over split milk," he repeated. (p. 144)
   Venkataramani's conventional use of the staid phrase, and Narayan's playful use of it reveals the essential difference in their attitude towards the English language.

3. Memorizing a large number of idioms and phrases has traditionally been part of learning English, and the test paper in Compulsory English in the Union Public Service Commission examination (for entrance to government service) requires the examinee even today to 'make sentences of your own using the following idioms and phrases'.

4. Raja Rao also uses similar adjectives—as in "He gave her a very *warmful* bed" (*Kanthapura*, p. 21), or "Old Ramakrishnayya was sitting on the verandah, his hand upon his nose, deep *breathful* in meditation" (*ibid.*, p. 35).

5. *Writers Workshop Miscellany*, No. 8 (1961), 93.

6. "Raja Rao's aim is to create a style which will reflect the rhythms and sensibilities of the Indian psyche, and since it is in Sanskrit that the Indian mind has found its most consummate linguistic expression, he has tried to adapt his English style to the movement of a Sanskrit sentence." *Sewanee Review*, LXXII (1964), 516.

7. Compare a sentence uttered by Raju in Narayan's *The Guide* :
   "What can a crocodile do if your mind is clear and your conscience is untroubled. . ." (p. 41)

8. To take a random example, an Indian in Hilton Brown's *One Virginity* defends the garlanding of ministers by saying "I do not think any harm, you see, now the people are loving their leaders so much. They want to show" (p. 248). Indo-Anglians of course find it equally easy to parody the English of their countrymen; in G.V. Desani's *All About H. Hatterr*,

sadhu's disciple reports, "I am finding him soundly asleeping. I am awaking him up." (p. 226)

9.   See J. Spencer, "The Anglo-Indians and Their Speech : A Socio-Linguistic Study," *Lingua*, XVI, 57-70.

10.   K.R. Srinivasa Iyengar writes : ". . .Books like *Murugan* and *Kandan* are written out of one's heart's blood, and cannot be written to order : they are more than novels, and are really a poet's and a Vedantin's testament that bridges our traditional living past and the modern dynamic present and shows the way to a rich ambrosial future."—*Indian Writing in English*, p. 231.

11.   But so did the celebrated Indian exponents of Indian nationalism like Ranade and Gokhale and Surendranath Banerjea. They were not however attempting creative literature.

12.   "The Language of Indian Fiction in English," *Critical Essays on Indian Writing in English* (Dharwar, 1968), p. 149.

8

The Prospect

IT IS still too early to speak of trends or tendencies in Indo-Anglian fiction because although some two hundred titles have been published in the last forty years, hardly half a dozen writers have written consistently over a sufficiently long period of time and taken their craft seriously. There is however enough in bulk and variety to indicate at least a major shift in direction somewhere in the middle of our period of study. Sensibility does not change overnight, hence any date we choose to mark this shift is bound to be arbitrary. Yet broadly speaking one notices a certain difference between the concerns of the Indo-Anglian novelist in the pre-independence era, and his interests in the two decades since independence. Allowing for notable exceptions like R. K. Narayan or Mulk Raj Anand, whose visions have more or less remained consistent, most pre-independence fiction, it appears from our study, is concerned with large public issues and national or social problems, rather than with the many small and particular problems of the individual. In contrast to that, recent fiction has turned introspective and the individual's quest for a personal meaning in life has become a theme of urgent interest for the Indo-Anglian writer.

In Chapter 3 we saw how the struggle for independence became a major theme for the Indo-Anglian novelist. The struggle was not just a political struggle but a changed way of life for a whole generation, and not only the Indo-Anglian writer but also novelists in the regional languages were busy rendering this complex emotional

experience in terms of art.   Of the important Indo-Anglian novels
dealing with this theme, the majority were written during the storm
and stress of the movement, well before independence was achieved,
while some other novels took up this theme years later and recollected in relative tranquillity—or in the throes of some other struggle—
a movement that had been successfully concluded.   It is not
impossible to see the basic difference between the attitudes of these
two varieties of novels separated by the great historical divide
of 1947.   An early novel like *Kandan the Patriot* (1932), however
naive artistically, has a certain urgency that reveals the author's
personal involvement in his material. As a novel *Kandan* does not
satisfy the modern reader, but one has to agree with K. R. Srinivasa
Iyengar about the historical value of the book "for powerfully
evoking the tempo of the nation in 1930-31... excitement of a
modern Heroic age with Gandhiji making men out of clay and
heroes out of common humanity."[1]   The same involvement is
present in Raja Rao's *Kanthapura* (1938) where the author's ardour
for the movement he describes in a way gives the novel an additional
validity.   Mulk Raj Anand's *The Sword and the Sickle* (1942)
was written during the height of the independence movement, and
several conflicting political ideologies are shown in the novel to
pull the hero in different directions.   We have an impression of
being too near the event and the consequent blurring of focus is
felt in the crowding of the canvas with numerous political activities,
and yet the bewilderment of the central figure adds a certain
immediacy to the situation.

In novels written in the nineteen-fifties which deal with the same
theme, a noticeable distance between the author and the events or
the ideology has crept in, although this does not necessarily result
in a better artistic realisation of the theme. *Inquilab* (1955) or *A
Bend in the Ganges* (1964), both of which have been discussed in
some detail in Chapter 3, attempt a panoramic picture of a historical struggle where the emphasis is not so much on depth as on width
of coverage. And in *Waiting for the Mahatma* (1955) and *Chronicles
of Kedaram* (1961), the novelists are detached enough from the
course of history to treat Gandhi casually as a human being or an
idea rather than as an overwhelming symbol, and concentrate on
weaving stories of human relationships which only marginally

touch upon the political struggle.

If the national movement was the major public issue that interested the Indo-Anglian writer in the 'thirties and the 'forties, the social and economic problems of the people came second in order of importance. It has been indicated in Chapter 2 that "Progressive Realism" was an all-India movement in literature, that while Mulk Raj Anand and Khwaja Ahmed Abbas were dealing with the problems of untouchability, economic equality and social injustice in English, writers in Bengali, Hindi, Urdu, Marathi, Kannada and Malayalam were busy dealing with similar social evils in realistic fiction. Sarat Chandra Chatterjee in Bengali and Munshi Prem Chand in Hindi had already gained a large reading public both for their original works as well as in translation, by tackling the problems of a rigid rural society. Some writers in the regional languages continue even today to write in the tradition of "progressive" realism, but in the main the initial ardour and enthusiasm of the movement have been long over. Bengali and Marathi fiction, for example, have shown in recent years an intense preoccupation with the crises of individual man rather than of collective man.

Indo-Anglian fiction, in my view, is a part of truly Indian fiction and not a tenuous extension of English fiction. As discussed in Chapters 2 and 3, Indo-Anglian fiction reflects the same concerns as other Indian fiction of the period and has also undergone a considerable change in the last decade or two. Guarding against a too close adherence to the convenient line of demarcation of 1947, one might say that in spite of the fact that some Indo-Anglian novelists are still attempting to recapture a recent historical past, the majority of writers since 1950 have turned inwards to more private and personal concerns.

The six novels discussed in detail in Chapter 4 were all written in the late 'fifties and early 'sixties, and all these novels deal with the personal predicament of a particular individual. It so happens, however, that in each case the central character is an educated and sensitive individual who feels the drag of two cultures strongly and must closely analyse the elements of his personality to come to terms with himself. Even if this predicament is shared by a large number of persons today and is no more a rare instance, it still remains a personal issue, and the solution must be different for each individual. Unlike the social and political novels of the earlier decades, the resolution in these later novels cannot come from the outside.

The reason for the East-West obsession (see Chapter 4) is inherent in the historic situation of the Indo-Anglian writer himself. The educated Indian has for several decades been shaped by the immigrant influence of the West as well as by the native culture of the land and its traditions. This is not a unique situation for the writer of the 'fifties, because the process began from the day British culture entered Indian life. But until 1947 the independence movement provided a focus of life, a goal outside the individual self, that guided the purpose of more than one generation. After the formal achievement of independence, this external focus was lost and no adequate replacement was at hand. One Indian writer has confessed his predicament in terms that sum up the general intellectual situation : ". . . with independence, my generation in particular was unable to respond heroically to the moral confusion that was soon to prevail. We were ready to disintegrate because we were wholly unprepared for the shock of self-recognition. . . . We realised that we were living until then on an *ad hoc* basis, taking what we could from the petty cash boxes of two different cultures, and were suddenly confronted with bankruptcy."[2] Hence the turning inward; hence the introspective sorting out of the elements of two cultures that got inextricably woven together, to discover the root of the malady.

This turning inward is evident in other Indian literatures as well, though the shift of emphasis has naturally not been simultaneous nor the same in extent in every language. S. H. Vatsayan, in a survey of modern Hindi literature has characterised the modern age by its concern for the individual :

In a tradition where the age had always been more important than the artist, literature had inevitably been concerned more with the creation of types rather than of individuals, and poetry tended to be the poetry of motifs and conceits rather than the expression of individual sensibility. As the Hindi writer discovered himself as an individual, he became aware that as a creator he was concerned with persons. The realisation was as powerful as the discovery had been awkward and embarrassing.[3]

In dealing with this newly discovered individual, Indo-Anglian fiction for a while continued to cast the stock character in a stock situation of conflict : namely, an Indian educated abroad is confronted with the problem of adjustment to India on his return home. The Indian values were often embodied in one person (usually a woman) and the central character had to choose between her and another person symbolising the West. This was the most superficial statement of the dilemma. Often the resolution was not untinged with nostalgia or sentimentality for values from which the author in real life had become alienated (see Chapter 4). Even as late as in 1971 a restatement of the same theme can be seen in *Tiger's Daughter*, a first novel by Bharati Mukherjee published in New York. But there are a few novels where a deeper probe is attempted into the individual psyche, and such novels give us reason to hope that the Indo-Anglian novelist can move away from the more obvious problems and predictable solutions. Nirode, the hero of Anita Desai's novel *Voices in the City* (1965) is a complex character whose predicament cannot be explained away by any glib discussion of the conflict of cultures. It is tempting to relate this hero to the heroes of Camus, or to detect the impact of existentialism here, but a more relevant observation—an observation that once again establishes the close connection between Indo-Anglian fiction and contemporary fiction in other Indian languages—is that Nirode is a counterpart of the new protagonists of Bengali fiction (who in their turn are also influenced by French Existentialism) as seen in the novels of Shirshendu Mukhopadhya and Shymal Gangopadhyay. Nirode loathed the world that could offer him no "crusade, no pilgrimage, and he loathed himself for not having the true unwavering spirit of either within him. There was only this endless waiting, hollowed out by an intrinsic knowledge that there was nothing to wait for." (p. 196) And in spite of this vague despair and inexplicable perplexity of the misfit hero, the novel is very much rooted in temporal and local reality, to the terrifying meaninglessness of the city of Calcutta to a man who runs away from success. In her third novel *Bye Bye Blackbird* (1971) Anita Desai widens the canvas to deal with a group of Indian immigrants in London, and in her sensitive manner traces their complex emotional relationship with the two countries of their birth and adoption. With their fate is involved that of Sarah Sen, an Englishwoman married to an Indian. Like the central characters in Anita Desai's earlier novels Sarah is a woman of acutely developed sensuous responses and an introspective nature. She feels she is playing two roles in a charade—of being an Englishwoman at work and an Indian at home and "when she was not playing them she was nobody. Her face was only a mask, her body a costume." It seems at first that her husband's decision to return home might resolve her dilemma, but the novel also suggests that no solution is ever final, and that communication between human beings can at best be only partial. The same refusal of simple solutions is found in Arun Joshi's *The Foreigner*, a novel published in 1968, about a young man twice removed from his country of birth, who is an alien everywhere physically as well as metaphorically. Like Hemingway's American hero fighting an Italian battle in *A Farewell to Arms*, Sindi Oberoi in *The Foreigner*, an Indian Kenyan who returns to India after years in the West, lacks involvement in the life he leads. At the end his wish to achieve tranquillity through non-attachment turns out to be a self-delusion.

Arun Joshi's second novel *The Strange Case Of Billy Biswas* (1971) presents an unusual character who suffers from a sense of unreality about the world around him, and decides to opt out of civilisation to go and live with a primitive tribe in Madhya Pradesh. It is a compelling novel about a strange quest, drawing upon myth and folk-lore to reiterate its elemental concerns. While the writer does not disregard circumstantial reality—Billy Biswas' expensive schooling, education abroad, holidays in Simla, all contribute to the making of his character—on another level the novel transcends the axes of time and space, probing into a fundamental metaphysical question. In both the novels of Arun Joshi renunciation is a dominant theme and he has the power to make the reader disturbingly aware of the many levels of reality.

I

The novel as a modern and western genre of literature is rooted in the concept of history, the concept that man is shaped by the changing forces around him. Behind most of the novels discussed in this study we find an awareness of historical time—a recognition of inexorable change from the traditional values of an agrarian society to those of the agro-industrial modern age. Mulk Raj Anand's trilogy intends to present a comprehensive picture of the disintegration of the old order. In the first volume, *The Village*, the hero began life as a farmer's son; in spite of his rebellious spirit, he was made to accept the strict social hierarchy of the village based on caste and money. But in the second volume when he returns after his years abroad with the British army, the pattern has changed. The break-down of the social structure is indicated in such details as a cart driver's son driving a motor-bus, a farmer's son working in a factory, and finally in the fact that the hero could marry the landlord's widowed daughter. In a later work, *The Big Heart*, Anand dealt with a particular aspect of this change in greater detail.

Though not as consciously or as extensively as Anand, many other novelists have also dealt with this theme of change in one way or another. *In Transit, Wounds of Spring, Athawar House, Sunlight on a Broken Column,* all deal with social change which either transmutes or disintegrates a large joint family. Menon Marath (*Wounds of Spring*) described the change in a large matriarchal Nair *tharawad* in Kerala, Venu Chitale (*In Transit*) wrote of an orthodox Brahmin household in Poona, Attia Hosain (*Sunlight on a Broken Column*) depicted a traditional Muslim family in Lucknow with its strict rules of purdah. Whatever the geographical location or social and cultural milieu, the transformation works in a similar way in each case. The same change is seen on a broader scale in the context of a whole village or a town, at different levels of artistic success, in novels like *Kanthapura, Chronicles of Kedaram, A Goddess Named Gold, Nectar in a Sieve*. Even in the highly poetic and imaginative novels of Sudhin Ghose one notices a sense of changing times through the tetralogy. The pastoral childhood world of the first volume gives way to the agrarian realities of the second volume; in the third and fourth volumes, the scene shifts from the rural Penhari Parganas to the impersonal urban locale of Calcutta. There is the sense of an impending calamity as the tetralogy comes to a close. At the end of the four volumes, the hero, unable to adjust himself to the crooked values of the metropolis, renounces the world "to seek other forms of wisdom." The values to which he had so far adhered are seen to be useless in the new *kalpa* that is emerging, and he has no solution but to abandon the material world.

Thus the attitude towards change differs considerably in novelists as different as Anand and Ghose, Bhattacharya and Nagarajan, Hosain and Markandaya; some accept it with despair and resignation, others with hope and promise of a better future. But hardly anyone has totally denied the existence of these forces of change.

There is however one notable exception. While Kedaram and Kanthapura, Sona Mitti and Nandpur, change with the changing times, there is one little town in Indo-Anglian fiction that remains immutable. Life goes on in its own familiar way on the streets and market-places of Malgudi, shops ply their customary trade, lawyers keep adjourning their cases, and crooks attend to their shady deals with no forces of transition threatening to change their identity. Narayan's attitude to the tremors of dislocation has been analysed at some length in Chapter 5 where it is seen that almost all of Narayan's novels are constructed round a pattern that can be formulated as "Order—Dislocation of order—Reintegration of order." In a way which is almost *puranic*, Narayan sees change not as a fact of history but merely as an illusion, a bubble that must sooner or later burst with the normal order of life reasserting itself.

II

Many of the themes that have attracted the Indo-Anglian novelist so far are of a pan-Indian nature. The national movement was the first of such "all-India" experiences, but later the social novels also touched upon problems which were valid all over the sub-continent. The disintegration of the joint family system, the changing rural scene, even the theme of East-West encounter, all have a common background of interest all over

India. The ideals of renunciation and self-sacrifice that crop up intermittently in Indo-Anglian fiction are again rooted in a Sanskrit-based Hindu tradition which provides a common emotional hinterland to most Indians. The use of myths (discussed in Chapter 6) by Indo-Anglian novelists is yet another national frame of reference which the Indian novelist can draw upon.

As a contrast, themes of local interest are conspicuous by their absence in Indo-Anglian fiction. Thakazhi Sivasankara Pillai's *Chemmeen* with its highly localised theme of fisherfolk in Malabar, (localised geographically as well as emotionally), was originally written in Malayalam; Rajendra Singh Bedi's prize-winning Punjabi novelette—translated into English as *I Take This Woman*— also deals with a peculiarly localised social situation. Neither of these two works loses its regional flavour in English translation, yet the Indian writer has generally been unable to do the same thing when he writes in English. The fact that Indo-Anglian fiction has usually steered clear of such situations reveals at once a certain self-consciousness as well as a weakness of this branch of writing. The motivation behind the choosing of a theme that will be "Indian" rather than merely real, may be attributed to the Indo-Anglian novelist's uncertainty about his audience. Very often, in his desire to find a theme that will have trans-Indian interest, he has to spurn situations and characters around him that are more vivid and alive. The partition of Bengal, for example, which has provided material to the Bengali novelist for two decades has not yet been tackled head on by any Bengali novelist writing in English. At the other end of the country, Khushwant Singh has attempted a rendering of the cleavage of the Punjab in one novel. But it amounts to no more than a study of the moment, of the surface brutality and violence, rather than a gauging of the vast human tragedy inherent therein. The longer lasting psychological effects of partition have not yet been seriously explored in Indo-Anglian writing. Similarly, except for Anita Desai's novel mentioned earlier in this chapter, nowhere else in Indo-Anglian fiction do we get the feel of a metropolis like Calcutta or Bombay, where life has a rhythm and tempo so vastly different from the flow of life in the small towns and villages all over India. Delhi, on the other hand, appears quite frequently as the locale of an Indo-Anglian novel because it has a synthetic 'all-India' character which makes it ideally suitable for Indo-Anglian fiction.

It must be admitted that Indian villages, in spite of the differences in language and the subtleties of social structure, provide a more common basic pattern recognisable all over India than do the few cities each with its own individual character. The most illustrative case of this all-India appeal of the rural novel is the tremendous popularity of Bengal's Sarat Chandra Chatterjee. Years after he has been relegated to the background in Bengali literature, he continues to be read and enjoyed in translation in the remotest corners of India. Tagore's novels, almost contemporary with Sarat Chandra's, never had an audience anywhere comparable to Sarat Chandra's, which indicates the possibility that Tagore's fiction, more 'modern' in themes (they deal with crises of the inner being) and more sophisticated in techniques, did not have the emotional universality in terms of all-India readership which Sarat Chandra's homespun tales of rural India possessed.

It is therefore often in the rural context that the regional reality and the *Indian* reality more or less merge. Kanthapura is very recognisably a Karnataka village; the caste divisions, occupations of the people, wedding customs, festivals, even conversation, testify to its regional reality. Yet Indians from all regions (in spite of other differences) have had no difficulty in recognising it as the prototype of the village that they all know. Small towns like Malgudi or Kedaram also have something universal about them so that no Indian has any serious difficulty in indentifying them in his experience.

Here is the paradox that characterises Indo-Anglian fiction as a genre. The few novels which have succeeded are usually the ones firmly rooted in time and place; yet most Indo-Anglian novelists are constantly aiming at an Indianness bereft of temporal and spatial values. The question is not merely of geographic location but of regional characteristics and localised responses as well. When a critic talks of Narayan's "South Indian realism and irony," he uses the epithet in an effort to distinguish a particular regional quality from a similar product emanating from elsewhere in the country. If a novelist's attitude towards his material has a special quality belonging to his region, it is only to be expected that characterization and situation in his novels will not remain unaffected by that attitude. The future of Indo-Anglian fiction seems to lie in the direction of further authenticity through exploiting the particular, local and regional reality—without, of course, calculated 'documentation' or 'explanation'—rather than through the effort of finding more 'all-India' themes. In other words, a conscious awareness of audience—whether at home or abroad—definitely limits the scope of the Indo-Anglian novelist, confining him to a handful of unmistakably Indian themes. If the Indo-Anglian novel is to develop vigorously along with the novel in Indian languages, it must outgrow its general concerns and grapple with the particular, the concrete and the immediate.

It may be expected that this effort to grapple with an immediate reality will have a perceptible effect on the language of the novelist. No matter what the purists advocate, the pure and modern idiom of England may not always be suitable for expressing the sensibility and responses of an Indian writer. The Indo-Anglian writers' various experiments in giving English a distinctively Indian tone and colouring without doing violence to its basic linguistic structure have been discussed at length in Chapter 7. From the discussion it emerges that in each case it is basically an attempt to find an individual style rather than an 'Indian' style and in this sense the Indo-Anglian novelist's experiments are no different from the experiments of creative writers anywhere in the world. The creation of an "Indian English" is by no means the primary duty of the Indo-Anglian novelist, and only if the style is a natural and inalienable part of the author's vision, will it be artistically valid.

A cautionary note may not be out of place here about the attempt made by an Indian specialist in linguistics like Dr. Braj Kachru to postulate an "Indian English" based on examples drawn from Indo-Anglian writers.[4] Dr. Kachru seems to mislead himself by regarding the Indo-Anglian novelist's departures from norms of the English language, specially as represented in the speech of Indian characters, as some kind of 'standard' Indian English. The Indo-Anglian writer should be allowed the freedom to experiment with the language for his own artistic needs rather than be herded into a system of linguistics in search of that elusive medium—a standard Indian English.

The question of whether there is or should be an Indian English is not really relevant to a critical discussion of contemporary Indo-Anglian fiction. As for the question of *should* Indians write novels in English, this cannot have a bearing on the novels which have already been written. Even the debatable future of the English language in India need not inhibit an examination of the work which is already in existence. Whatever linguists theorise or politicians decide, the rate of publication of Indian novels in English has not yet shown any marked decline. The older writers are still active : R. K. Narayan's latest, *The Vendor of Sweets,* came out at the end of 1967 while Mulk Raj Anand's largest novel so far, *Morning Face* (1969), is apparently the second novel of a projected seven-volume series. Bhabani Bhattacharya's *Shadows from Ladakh* received a Sahitya Akademi Award for 1967. Raja Rao's much publicised work on the Ganga and her sisters must be nearing completion. Bodley Head have recently reprinted G.V. Desani's *All about H. Hatterr* and Anand's *The Private Life of an Indian Prince.* Writers like Amir Ali and Ahmed Ali, who have been silent for a long time, have both come out with their second novels, *Via Geneva* and *Ocean of Night* respectively. Of the following generation, Nayantara Sahgal continues to write of political high life in *Storm in Chandigarh* (1969) and adds to it the theme of the survival of a sensitive individual in a ruthlessly materialistic society in her fourth novel *The Day in Shadow* (1971), while Kamala Markandaya has covered new grounds in her *A Handful of Rice* (1967), *The Coffer Dams* (1970) and *The Nowhere Man* (1973). Newer names like Anita Desai and Arun Joshi are beginning to gain recognition, neglected names like Sudhin Ghose and K. Nagarajan are being aired again. Not only are more novels being written but new themes are being explored, preoccupations are revealing themselves. That as long as novelists continue to write, critics will continue to assess the work, is as much a truism as saying that as long as there are mountains, mountaineers will climb them. Indo-Anglian fiction, which has served for so long as a file of documents of sociology or anthropology or educational theory, must now be regarded as literature and evaluated as such. That is the service it requires from critics, and this study is a modest essay in that direction.

NOTES

1. In "The Indo-Anglian Novelist as a Story-teller," an unpublished paper taken as read at the seminar on Indian Writing in English at the University of Mysore in January 1968.
2. Victor Anant, "The Hypnotised People," *Partisan Review* (1960), quoted by V. Y. Kantak in a paper "The Achievement of R. K. Narayan" read at the seminar referred to above.
3. "Hindi Literature," *Contemporary Indian Literature, A Symposium* (New Delhi, 1937), p. 84.
4. See his "The *Indianness* in Indian English," *Word*, XXI (December 1965), 391-410; and "Indian English : A Study in Contextualization," in C. E. Bazell et al (eds) *In Memory of J.R. Firth* (London : Longman, 1966), pp. 255-287.

Note on Indian Novels in English Translation

IT WOULD have been most convenient for the purpose of this study if a fairly representative selection of major works of fiction in Indian languages were available in English translation. This would have permitted greater depth of comparative discussion than has been possible in Chapter 2 and elsewhere in the context of viewing Indo-Anglian fiction in the larger perspective of Indian fiction in general.

A number of Indian novels have been translated into English, but such material cannot generally be used in serious critical discussion because of two reasons. Firstly, most of the available translations are indifferently, even very badly, done by translators to whom English is a second language. Secondly, the existing material neither adequately represents the major achievements of Indian fiction in various languages nor does it satisfactorily represent the best novels of any one language. Further, some novelists—like Rabindranath Tagore in Bengali or Munshi Prem Chand in Hindi/Urdu—have been translated more often than their contemporaries who deserve to be translated no less. More recent writers, of course, have to wait until posterity confers status upon them before they are translated. The total result is an unbalanced and incomplete picture.

Most of the questionable observations about Indian fiction made by foreign commentators like Dorothy M. Spencer or M. A. Derrett can be attributed to the fact that neither could read Indian fiction in the original and had to depend upon English renderings available in print. It will never be possible to discuss in English the subject of Indian fiction with any validity—as we can, for example, discuss French or German or Russian fiction—until we have good translations in English of major works and a large enough number of them from various languages.

Select Bibliography

I. *Indo-Anglian Novels*

(Date within brackets after a title indicates first publication; full publication details have been mentioned for the edition actually used.)

ABBAS, KHWAJA AHMED. *Inquilab*. Bombay : Jaico Publications, 1955.

ALI, AAMIR. *Conflict*. Bombay : National Information and Publications, 1947.

——*Via Geneva*. Bombay : Pearl Publications, 1967.

ALI, AHMED. *Ocean of Night*. London : Peter Owen, 1964.

——*Twilight in Delhi*. (1940). Bombay : Oxford University Press, 1966.

ANAND, MULK RAJ. *Across the Black Waters*. (1940). Bombay : Kutub-Popular, 1955.

——*The Big Heart*. (1945). Bombay : Kutub-Popular, n.d.[1]

——*Coolie*. (1933). Bombay : Kutub-Popular, n.d.

——*Morning Face*. Bombay : Kutub-Popular, 1968.

——*The Old Woman and the Cow*. Bombay : Kutub-Popular, 1960.

——*The Private Life of an Indian Prince*. London : Hutchinson, 1953.

——*The Road*. Bombay : Kutub-Popular, 1961.

——*The Sword and the Sickle*. (1942). Bombay : Kutub-Popular, 1955.

——*Two Leaves and a Bud*. (1937). Bombay : Kutub-Popular, 1966.

ANAND, MULK RAJ. *Untouchable*. (Preface E. M. Forster, 1935), Bombay : Kutub-Popular, n.d.

——*The Village*. (1939). Bombay : Kutub-Popular, 1954.

ANANT, VICTOR. *The Revolving Man*. London : Macgibbon and Kee, 1959.

ANANTANARAYAN, M. *The Silver Pilgrimage*. New York : Criterion Books, 1961.

ATHOGIAS, SALLY, *Gold in the Dust*. Bombay : Jaico Publications, 1960.

BASU, ARINDAM. *Picoro or Me*. Calcutta : Writers Workshop, 1972.

BHARUCHA, PERIN. *The Fireworshippers*. Bombay : Strand Book Stall, 1968.

BHASKARA RAO, *Candle against the Wind*. Bangalore : Bhaskara Rao, 1963.

BHATTACHARJEE, JYOTSNA. *Shadows in the Sunshine*. Calcutta : Alpha-Beta Publications, n.d.

BHATTACHARYA, BHABANI. *A Goddess Named Gold*. New York : Crown Publishers, 1960.

——*He Who Rides a Tiger*. Bombay : Jaico Publications, 1954.

——*Music for Mohini*. New York : Crown Publishers, 1952.

——*Shadow from Ladakh*. London : W.H. Allen, 1966.[2]

——*So Many Hungers*. Bombay : Hind Kitabs, 1947.

BOND, RUSKIN. *The Room on the Roof*. Bombay : Wilco Books, 1958.

BRATA, SASTHI. *Confessions of an Indian Woman Eater*. London : Hutchinson, 1971.

CHINNA DURAI, J. *Sugirtha : An Indian Novel*. London : Hulbert Publishing, 1929.

CHINTAMANI, V. V. *Vedantam : The Clash of Traditions*. London : Heath Cranton, 1928.

CHITALE, VENU. *In Transit*. Bombay : Hind Kitabs, 1950.

DALAL, NERGIS. *The Sisters*. Delhi : Hind Pocket Books, 1973.

DANIELS, MICHAEL CHACKO. *Anything Out of Place is Dirt*. Calcutta : Writers Workshop, 1971.

—— *That Damn Romantic Fool*. Calcutta : Writers Workshop, 1972.

DESAI, ANITA. *Cry, the Peacock*. London : Peter Owen, 1963.

—— *Voices in the City*. London : Peter Owen, 1965.

——*Bye Bye Blackbird*. Delhi : Hindi Pocket Books, 1971.

DESANI, G. V. *All about H. Hatterr*. London : Francis Aldor, 1948.

FUTEHALLY, ZEENUTH. *Zohra*. Bombay : Hind Kitabs, 1951.

GANGULLY, J. M. *When East and West Meet*, 1960.
GHOSE, SUDHIN N. *And Gazelles Leaping*. London : Michael Joseph, 1949.
——*Cradle of the Clouds*. London : Michael Joseph, 1951.
——*The Flame of the Forest*. London : Michael Joseph, 1955.
——*The Vermilion Boat*. London : Michael Joseph, 1953.
GHOSH, SARATH KUMAR. *The Prince of Destiny*. London : Rebman, 1909.
——*Verdict of the Gods*. London : Heinemann, 1906.

HIRO, DILIP. *A Triangular View*. London : Dobson, 1969.
HOME, D. C. *Flood along the Ganges*. Bombay : Peoples' Publishing House, 1953.
——*Poison and Passion*. Bombay : Kanak Publishers, 1955.
—— *So Many, So Gallant*. Bombay : Current Book House, 1951.
HOSAIN, ATTIA. *Sunlight on a Broken Column*. London : Chatto and Windus, 1961.
HUSSAIN, IQBALUNNISA. *Purdah and Polygamy*. Bangalore : D. N. Hosali, 1944.

ISVANI, G. *The Brocaded Sari*. London : John Day, 1946.
—— *Girl in Bombay*. London : Pilot Press, 1947.

JOSHI, ARUN. *The Foreigner*. Bombay : Asia Publishing House, 1968.
——*The Strange Case of Billy Biswas*. Bombay : Asia Publishing House, 1971.
——*The Apprentice*. Bombay : Asia Publishing House, 1974.

KABIR, HUMAYUN. *Men and Rivers*. Bombay : Hind Kitabs, 1945.
KAPUR, VIMLA. *Life Goes On*. Lahore : Associated Publications, 1946.
KARAKA, D.F. *Just Flesh*. Bombay : Thacker and Co., 1941.
—— *There Lay the City*. Bombay : Thacker and Co., 1942.
—— *We Never Die*. Bombay : Thacker and Co., 1944.

KAUL, NARENDRANATH. *The Heart's Way.* New Delhi : Hamsa Publications, 1957.

KAVERI BAI, H. *Meenakshi's Memoirs.* Madras : G.A. Natesan, 1937.

KHOSLA, G. D. *The Price of a Wife.* Bombay : Jaico Publications, 1958.

KRISHNASWAMY, S. Y. *Kalyani's Husband.* Madras : S. Y. Krishnaswamy, n.d.

KULKARNI, G. V. *Heritage of Murder.* Bombay : Kutub-Popular, 1963.

LALL, ANAND. *The House at Adampur.* Bombay : Pearl Publications, 1958.

—— *Seasons of Jupiter.* London : Jonathan Cape, 1958.

LAXMAN, R. K. *Sorry, No Room.* Bombay : Pearl Publications, 1968.

MALGONKAR, MANOHAR. *A Bend in the Ganges.* London : Hamish Hamilton, 1964.

—— *Combat of Shadows.* London : Hamish Hamilton, 1963.

—— *Distant Drum.* Bombay : Asia Publishing House, 1960.

—— *The Princes.* London : Hamish Hamilton, 1963.

MARATH, S. MENON. *Wounds of Spring.* London : Denis Dobson, 1961.

—— *The Sale of an Island.* London : Dobson, 1968.

MARKANDAYA, KAMALA. *A Handful of Rice.* Delhi : Hind Pocket Books, 1967.

—— *Nectar in a Sieve.* London : Putnam, 1954.

—— *The Nowhere Man.* London : Allen Lane, 1974.

·—— *Possession.* London : Putnam, 1963.

—— *A Silence of Desire.* London : Putnam, 1960.

—— *Some Inner Fury.* London : Putnam, 1955.

MARKANDAYA, KAMALA. *The Coffer Dams.* London : John Day, 1969.

MITRA, S. M. *Hindupur.* London : Luzac, 1909.

MUKHERJEE, ANIL KUMAR. *My Mother.* Ranchi : Education Press, 1959.

NAGARAJAN, K. *Athawar House.* Madras : Higginbotham's, 1939.

—— *Chronicles of Kedaram.* Bombay : Asia Publishing House, 1961.

NARAIN, RAM. *The Tigress of the Harem.* New York : Macaulay, 1930.

NARASIMHAN, RAJI. *The Herrt of Standing is You Cannot Fly.* Calcutta : Writers Workshop, 1972.

NARAYAN, R. K. *The Bachelor of Arts.* (Introd. Graham Greene, 1937). New York : Pocket Books Inc., 1951.

—— *The Dark Room.* Bombay : Pearl Publications, 1960.

—— *The English Teacher.* (1945). Mysore : Indian Thought Publications, 1955.[3]

—— *The Financial Expert.* (Introd. Graham Greene, 1952). Mysore : Indian Thought Publications, 1958.

—— *The Guide.* Mysore : Indian Thought Publications, 1963.[4]

—— *The Maneater of Malgudi.* (1961). London : New English Library (Four Square Books), 1965.

—— *Mr. Sampath.* (1949). Mysore : Indian Thought Publications, 1956.[5]

—— *The Vendor of Sweets.* Mysore : Indian Thought Publications, 1967.

—— *Waiting for the Mahatma.* East Lansing : Michigan State University Press, 1955.

NIMBKAR, JAI. *Temporary Answers.* New Delhi : Orient Longman, 1974.

NITYANANDAN, P. M. *The Long, Long Days.* Bombay : Asia Publishing House, 1960.

NOON, FEROZE KHAN. *Scented Dust.* Lahore : Gulab Singh, 1942.

NORONHA, LESLIE DE. *The Mango and the Tamarind Tree.* Calcutta : Writers Workshop, 1970.

PAINTAL, VEENA. *Serenity in Storm.* Bombay : Allied Publishers, 1966.

RAINA, VIMALA. *Ambapali.* Bombay : Asia Publishing House, 1962.

RAJA RAO. *The Cat and Shakespeare.* New York : Macmillan, 1965.

—— *Kanthapura.* (1938). Bombay : Oxford University Press, 1947.

—— *The Serpent and the Rope.* London : John Murray, 1960.

RAJAN, BALCHANDRA. *The Dark Dancer.* London : Heinemann, 1959.

—— *Too Long in the West.* Bombay : Jaico Publications, 1961.

RAMA RAU, SANTHA. *Remember the House.* London : Victor Gollancz, 1956.

—— *The Adventurers.* London : Michael Joseph, 1971.

RAMA SARMA, M. V. *The Stream.* Masulipatam : Triveni Publishers, 1946.

ROY, DILIP KUMAR. *The Upward Spiral.* (1946). Bombay : Jaico Publications, 1946.

SAHGAL, NAYANTARA, *This Time of Morning.* London : Victor Gollancz, 1965.

——*A Time to be Happy.* (1952). Bombay : Jaico Publications, 1963.

—— *Storm in Chandigarh.* Delhi : Hind Pocket Books, 1969.

—— *The Day in Shadow.* Delhi : Vikas Publications, 1971.

SARABHAI, MRINALINI. *This Alone is True.* London : Meridian Books, 1952.

SEN GUPTA, PADMINI. *Red Hibiscus.* Bombay : Asia Publishing House, 1962.

SHRINAGESH, SHAKUNTALA. *The Little Black Box.* London : Secker and Warburg, 1955.

SINGH, HUTHI. *Maura.* (Introd. E. M. Forster). London : Constable, 1951.

SINGH, KHUSHWANT. *I Shall Not Hear the Nightingale.* London : John Calder, 1959.

—— *Train to Pakistan.* London : Chatto and Windus, 1956.[6]

SINHA, KRISHNA NANDAN. *Wait Without Hope.* Calcutta : Writers Workshop, 1967.

VENKATRAMANI, K. S. *Kandan the Patriot.* Madras : Svetraya Ashrama, 1934.

—— *Murugan the Tiller.* London : Simpkin, Marshall, Hamilton, Kent, 1927.

II. *Discussion of Indo-Anglian Fiction in books*

BAKHTIYAR, IQBAL (ed.) *The Novel in Modern India.* Bombay : The P. E. N. All-India Centre, 1964.

BELIAPPA, MEENA. *The Fiction of Anita Desai.* Calcutta : Writers Workshop, 1971.

BHATTACHARYA, BHABANI. "Indo-Anglian," in *The Novel in Modern India,* pub. P.E.N. (Bombay, 1964), pp. 41-48.

BHUSHAN, V. N. (ed.) *The Moving Finger.* Bombay : Padma Publications, 1945.

BRUNTON, T. D. "India in Fiction—The Heritage of Indianness," in *Critical Essays on Indian Writing in English*, ed. Naik *et al.* (Dharwar, 1968), pp. 51-61.

COWASJI, SAROS. (ed.) *Author to Critic : The Letters of Mulk Raj Anand.* Calcutta : Writers Workshop, 1972.

CHANDRASEKHARAN, K. R. "East and West in the Novels of Kamala Markandaya," in *Critical Essays etc.,* ed. Naik *et al.* (Dharwar, 1968), pp. 62-85.

DERRETT, M. E. *The Modern Indian Novels in English : A Comparative Approach.* Brussels : Editions de l' Institut de Sociologie, Universite Libre de Bruxelles, 1966.

EZEKIEL, NISSIM (ed.). *Indian Writers in Conference : The Sixth P.E.N. All-India Writers Conference—Mysore, 1962.* Bombay : The P.E.N. All-India Centre, 1964.

GOKAK, V. K. (ed.) *Modern Indian Languages.* New Delhi : Publications Division, Ministry of Information and Broadcasting, 1957.

GOKAK, V. K. *English in India : Its Present and Future.* Bombay : Asia Publishing House, 1964.

HARREX, S. C. *The Modern Indian Novel in English.* Calcutta : Writers Workshop, 1971.

HEMENWAY, STEPHEN : *The Novel of India :* Vols. I & II. Calcutta : Writers Workshop, 1973.

HOLMSTROM, LAKSHMI. *The Fiction of R. K. Narayan.* Calcutta, : Writers Workshop, 1973.

IYENGAR, K. R. S. "A General Survey," in *The Novel in Modern India*, ed. Bakhtiyar (Bombay, 1964), pp. 1-24.

—— *Indian Writing in English*. Bombay : Asia Publishing House, 1962.

KANTAK, V. Y. "The Language of Indian Fiction in English," in *Critical Essays etc.*, ed. Naik *et al.* (Dharwar, 1968), pp. 147-159.

KUMAR, SHIV K. "Some Indian Writers of English Fiction," in *Modern Indian Languages*, ed. Gokak (New Delhi, 1957), pp. 282-286.

McCUTCHION, DAVID. *Indian Writing in English : Critical Essays*. Calcutta : Writers Workshop, 1969.

MEHTA, P. P. *Indo-Anglian Fiction : An Assessment*. Bareilly : Prakash Book Depot, 1968.

MORAES, DOM. *Gone Away*. London : Heinemann, 1960. See pp. 22-24, 44-50, 68-69.

MUKHERJEE, MEENAKSHI. "Beyond the Village : An Aspect of Mulk Raj Anand," in *Critical Essays etc.*, ed. Naik *et al.* (Dharwar, 1968) pp. 192-201.

NAIK, M. K., S. K. DESAI and G. S. AMUR (eds). *Critical Essays on Indian Writing in English*. Dharwar : Karnatak University, 1968.

NAIK, M. K. " *The Serpent and the Rope*—The Indo-Anglian Novel as Epic Legend," in *Critical Essays etc.*, ed. Naik *et al* (Dharwar, 1968), pp. 214-248.

NAIPAUL, V. S. *An Area of Darkness*. London : Andre Deutsch 1964. See pp. 66-71.

NARASIMHAIAH, C. D. (ed.) *Fiction and the Reading Public in India* Mysore : University of Mysore, 1967.

—— (ed.) *Indian Literature of the Past Fifty Years, 1917-1967*. Mysore : University of Mysore, 1970.

—— *The Swan and the Eagle*. Simla : Indian Institute of Advanced Study, 1969.

PRESS, JOHN (ed.) *Commonwealth Literature : Unity and Diversity in a Common Culture*. London : Heinemann Educational Books, 1965.

RAJAN, B. "Identity and Nationality," in *Commonwealth Literature*, ed. Press (London, 1965), pp. 106-109.

[SAHITYA AKADEMI], *Contemporary Indian Literature : A Symposium*. New Delhi : Sahitya Akademi, 1957; 2nd ed. revised and enlarged, 1959.

SINGH, BHUPAL. *A Survey of Anglo-Indian Fiction*. London : Oxford University Press, 1934.

SPENCER, DOROTHY, M. *Indian Fiction in English*. Philadelphia : University of Pennsylvania Press, 1960.

TARANATH, RAJEEV. "The Average as the Positive," in *Critical Essays etc.*, ed. Naik *et al.* (Dharwar, 1968), pp. 362-374.

VERGHESE, C. PAUL. *Problems of the Indian Creative Writer in English*. Bombay : Somaiya Publications, 1971.

WADIA, A. R. *The Future of English in India*. Bombay : Asia Publishing House, n.d.

WALSH, WILLIAM. *A Human Idiom : Literature and Humanity*. London : Chatto and Windus, 1964.

WILLIAMS, HAYDN MOORE. *Studies in Modern Indian Fiction in English* : 2 vols. Calcutta : Writers Workshop, 1973.

III.   *Articles on Indo-Anglian Fiction in periodicals*

[ANONYMOUS], "India's Search for Self-expression," *The Times Literary Supplement*, August 10, 1962.

ALPHONSO, J. B. "Indo-English Fiction, 1857-1947," *Indian Book Reporter*, III : 6 (1957), 1-7.

ALPHONSO, J. B. "Indo-English Fiction," *Literature East and West*, VIII : 1 (Winter 1964), 6-14.

ALPHONSO-KARKALA, J. B. "Symbolism in *The Financial Expert*," *Indian Writing Today*, 11 (1970), 14-18.

AMUR, G. S. "Raja Rao : The Kannada Phase," *Journal of the Karnatak University*, X (1966), 40-52.

ANNIAH GOWDAH, H. H. 'Rajan : The Serious and the Comic," *The Literary Half-Yearly*, V : 1 (1964), 45-46.

ANNIAH GOWDAH, H. H. "Raja Rao's *The Serpent and the Rope*," [A.I.R. Bangalore talk,] *The Literary Half-Yearly*, IV : 2 (1963), 36-40.

BUTTER, PETER. "Some Indian Periodicals," *Review of English Literature*, IV : 2 (1963), 35-44.

BRANDER, LAURENCE. "Two Novels by Ahmed Ali," *Journal of Commonwealth Literature*, 3 (1967), 76-86.

COWASJEE, S. "Mulk Raj Anand and His Critics," *Banasthali Patrika*, 12 (1969), 57-63.

CHALAPATI RAO, M. "The Indo-Anglian," *The Illustrated Weekly of India*, May 26, 1963.

CLIFFORD, WILLIAM. [Review of Raja Rao's *Kanthapura*], *Saturday Review*, January 11, 1964, p. 62.

EZEKIEL, NISSIM. [Review of Kamala Markandaya's *Possession*], *Imprint*, February 1964, pp. 188-193.

FISKE, ADELE M. "Karma in Five Indian Novels," *Literature East and West*, X : 1-2 (1966), 98-111.

GEMMILL, JANET POWERS, "Rhythm in *The Cat and Shakespeare*," *Literature East and West*, XIII : 1-2 (1969), 27-42.

GEROW, EDWIN. "The Quintessential Narayan," *Literature East and West,* X : 1-2 (1966), 1-18.

HARREX, S. C. "R. K. Narayan's *The Printer of Malgudi*," *Literature East and West*, XIII : 1-2 (1969), 68-82.

HARTLEY, LOIS. "In 'Malgudi' with R. K. Narayan," *Literature East and West*, IX : 2 (1965), 87-90.

KRISHNAMURTHI, M. G. "Indian Writing in English," *Humanist Review*, I : 4 (1969), 35-45.

KRISHNAMURTHI, M. G. "The Chronicles of Kedaram : A Question of Form," *Indian Writing Today*, 11 (1970), 27-31.

LAL, P. "English and English Writing in India," *Conspectus*, II : 2, 37-47.

—— "Literary Traditions—6 : Indian Writing in English," *The Illustrated Weekly of India*, October 25, 1964.

—— "Indian Writing in English," *Harvard Educational Review*, XXXIV : 2 (1964), 316-319.

McCUTCHION, DAVID. "The Novel as Sastra," [review of Raja Rao's *The Serpent and the Rope*], *Writers Workshop Miscellany*, 8 (1961), 91-99.

——"Le Style C'est L'homme," [review of B. Rajan's *The Dark Dancer*], *Writers Workshop Miscellany,* 6 (1961), 21-24.

MEHTA, VED. "The Train Had Just Arrived at Malgudi Station," *The New Yorker,* September 15, 1962, p. 57.

MUKHERJEE, MEENAKSHI. "Awareness of Audience in Indo-Anglian Fiction," *Quest,* 52 (1967), 37-40.

—— "Style in Indo-Anglian Fiction," *Indian Writing Today,* 11 (1970), 6-13.

—— "Raja Rao's Shorter Fiction," *Indian Literature,* X : 3 (1967), 66-76.

—— "The Tractor and the Plough : The Contrasted Visions of Sudhin Ghose and Mulk Raj Anand," *Indian Literature,* XIII : 1 (1970), 88-101.

MUKHERJEE, NIRMAL. "Some Aspects of the Literary Development of R. K. Narayan," *Banasthali Patrika,* 13 (1969), 76-87.

MUKHERJEE, SUJIT. "The Indo-Anglian Novelist as Best-seller," *Literature East and West,* XIII : 1-2 (1969), 83-93; also in *Quest,* 65 (1970), 34-43.

NAGARAJAN, S. "An Indian Novel," [review of Raja Rao's *The Serpent and the Rope*], *Sewanee Review,* LXXII : 3 (1964), 512-517.

NAIK, M. K. "*Kanthapura* : The Indo-Anglian Novel as Legendary History," *Journal of the Karnatak University,* X (1966), 26-39.

NANDAKUMAR, PREMA. "Achievement of the Indo-Anglian Novelist," *The Literary Criterion,* V : 1 (Winter 1961).

—— "Indian Writing in 1964 : English," *Indian Literature,* VIII : 2 (1965), 51-59.

—— "English : A Piquant Effect," *Indian Literature,* IX : 4 (1966), 25-33.

NARASIMHAIAH, C. D. "Raja Rao's *Kanthapura* : An Analysis," *The Literary Criterion,* VII : 2 (1966), 54-77.

—— "Raja Rao : *The Serpent and the Rope*—A Study," *The Literary Criterion,* V : 4 (1963), 62-89.

—— "R. K. Narayan's *The Guide* with a Note on the Sahitya Akademi Award to the Novel," *The Literary Criterion,* IV : 2 (1961), 63-92.

NARAYAN, R. K. A. I. R. Interview, *Writers Workshop Miscellany*, 8 (1961), 50.

—— "English in India," *The Times of India*, December 2, 1964.

—— "To an Inquirer," *The Illustrated Weekly of India*, May 26, 1963.

PAYNE, ROBERT. [Review of Kamala Markandaya's *Possession*], *Saturday Review*, May 25, 1963, p. 34.

RAJA RAO. "The Writer and the Word," *The Literary Criterion*, VII : 1 (1965); reprinted in *Fiction and the Reading Public in India*, ed. Narasimhaiah (Mysore 1967), pp. 229-231.

RAJAN, B. "Remarks on Identity and Nationality," *Literature East and West*, IX : 2 (1965), 91-94.

—— "The Indian Virtue" *Journal of Commonwealth Literature*, 1 (1963), 79-85.

—— "Writing in English," *The Illustrated Weekly of India*, May 26, 1963.

RAJIVA, STANLEY F. "Contemporary Indian Writing in English," *Quest*, 60 (January-March 1969), 72-75.

[RAMAN] A. S. R. "Chiaroscuro : A Meeting with Raja Rao Recalled," *The Illustrated Weekly of India*, September 25, 1966.

RANCHAN, S. P. and RAZDAN, B. M. "The Serpent and the Rope," *The Illustrated Weekly of India*, March 13, April 3 and 10, 1966.

RIEMENSCHNEIDER, D. "An Ideal of Man in Mulk Raj Anand's Novels," *Indian Literature*, X (1967), 29-51.

SHARPE, PATRICIA L. "The Challenge to the Indian Writer Today," *Quest*, 59 (1968), 31-39.

TYRNER, A. G. "Indo-Anglian Literature and the Indian Elite," *Cornell Journal of Social Relations*, I : 1 (1966), 25-32.

VERGHESE, C. PAUL, "Man in Indo-Anglian Fiction," *Indian Literature*, XIII : 1 (1970), 6-25.

—— "The Problem of the Indian Novelist in English, *Banasthali Patrika*, 13 (1969), 83-97.

—— "Raja Rao, Mulk Raj, Narayan and Others," *Indian Writing Today*, 7 (1969), 31-38.

WALSH, WILLIAM. "Indian Novelists," *The Times of India*, October 1 and 2, 1964.

WENDT, ALLAN. "Indian Fiction for Indians : A Study of Short Fiction in *The Illustrated Weekly of India*," *Literature East and West*, X : 1-2 (1966), 42-50.

WHITE, ROBIN. "Fiction in India," *Current Events*, X : 8 (1964), 41-45.

NOTES

1. No date of publication is mentioned in this edition, but the date 1944 appears at the end of the text.
2. Awarded Sahitya Akademi prize for 1967.
3. Printed in U.S.A. as *Grateful to Life and Death* (1963).
4. Awarded Sahitya Akademi prize for 1961.
5. Printed in U.S.A. as *The Printer of Malgudi* (1957).
6. Printed in U.S.A. as *Mano Majra* (1956).

Index

Abbas, K. A., 30, 36, 37, 55, 56, 58, 61, 94, 200
  Inquilab, 36, 37, 55, 58, 61
Achebe, Chinua, 86, 87, 95
Across the Black Waters, 45, 74, 171
Advaita Vedanta, 199
Agyeya, 22
Albert, Ethel, 73, 95
Ali, Ahmed, 209
Ali, Amir, 209
All About H. Hatterr, 105-108, 127n, 184-85, 196, 209
Amur, G. S., 14
Anand, Mulk Raj, 13, 22, 26, 30, 36, 37, 43, 44, 45, 54, 61, 73, 74, 75, 76, 77, 107, 108, 126, 133, 158, 159, 161, 167, 169, 171, 172, 173, 175, 176, 180, 185, 194, 195, 198, 199, 200, 204, 205, 209
  Across the Black Waters, 45, 74, 171
  Apology for Heroism, 73, 76
  The Big Heart, 74, 76, 172, 191, 204
  Coolie, 75, 108
  Morning Face, The, 209
  Old Woman and the Cow, The, 74, 75, 76, 132, 158, 159, 175
  Private Life of an Indian Prince, The, 169
  Road, The, 108, 172, 173
  Sword and the Sickle, The, 26, 37, 43, 44, 45, 61, 171, 175, 199
  Untouchable, 74, 76, 108
  Village, The, 45
Anandamath, 102, 166
Anant, Victor, 210
Anguriya Binimoy, 19

Annals of the Parish, 11
Anstey, F., 196
Apte, Hari Narayan, 20
Arakshaniya, 21
An Area of Darkness, 13
Athawar House, 107, 204
Aurobindo, Sri, 127n
Ayyub, Abu Sayeed, 16n

Baboo Jabberjee, 196
Bachelor of Arts, The, 11, 104, 154, 198
Bahadur, Umrao, 20
Bakhtiyar, Iqbal, 127n
Baladitya, 20
Bandopadhyaya, Manik, 127n
Bandopadhyaya, Tarashankar, 127n
Banerjee, Surendra Nath, 197
Bazell, C. E., 210
Bedi, Rajendra Singh, 206
Bellow, Saul, 85
Bend in the Ganges, A, 36, 58, 59, 60, 68
Bewley, Marius, 23
Bhagwad Gita, The, 96, 99
Bhattacharya, Bhabani, 29, 102, 103, 112, 114, 119, 126, 167, 172, 176, 177, 179, 180, 194, 205, 209
  Goddess Named Gold, A, 103, 172, 174, 204
  He Who Rides a Tiger, 102, 114-119, 126, 174
  Music for Mohini, 172, 173, 174, 179
  So Many Hungers, 174, 179, 194
Bhule Bisre Chitra, 21

Bhusan, V. N., 9
Booth, Wayne C., 45, 62n
Bose, Buddhadev, 22
Blackmur, R. P., 31
Brown, Hilton, 11, 196
Bye Bye Blackbird, 203

Camus, 202
Captive Ladie, The, 166
Cat and Shakespeare, The, 96, 97,
    126, 178, 188
Catcher in the Rye, 85, 168
Centaur, The, 162n
Chaitanya, Krishna, 162n
Chander, Krishen, 30
Chandrakanta, 20
Char Adhyaya, 21
Chatterjee, Bankim Chandra, 20,
    33n, 102, 159, 166
Chatterjee, Sarat Chandra, 21, 30,
    63, 200, 207
Chemmeen, 206
Chintamani, V. V., 65
Chitale, Venu, 37, 194, 204
Chronicles of Kedaram, The, 37, 46,
    47, 48, 49, 61, 173, 199,
    204
Coffer Dams, The, 209
Combat of Shadows, 68, 96, 170,
    182, 183
Commonwealth Literature, 63, 95
Contemporary Indian Literature, 33n,
    95, 210
Coolie, 75, 108
Cousins, James, 16n
Cow of the Barricades, The, 42, 139,
    177, 187, 188
Cradle of the Clouds, The, 132, 133,
    135, 151-156, 162n
Cranford, 11
*Critical Essays on Indian Writing in
    English*, 14, 197
Cry, the Peacock, 100, 189, 190

Dark Dancer, The, 58, 77, 81, 82,
    84, 86-88, 96, 132, 133, 156-
    158, 164n
Dark Room, The, 133, 150
Das Gupta, Surendranath, 127n
Derrett, M. E., 12
Desai, Anita, 100, 188, 189, 190
    191, 202, 203, 209
    Bye Bye Blackbird, 203
    Cry, the Peacock, 100, 189, 190
    Voices in the City, 190, 202
Desai, S. K., 14
Desani, G. V., 11, 30, 106, 126,
    127n, 184, 196, 209
Destiny of Mind, The, 163n
Devdas, 63
Diary of a Writer, The, 95n
Distant Drum, 58, 68
Dive for Death, The, 33n
Don Mane, 21
Du Bois, Cora, 72, 74, 95
Dubte Mastool, 23
Dutta, Amlan, 16n
Dutt Family Album, 17
Dutt, Michael Madhusudan, 166
Dutt, Romesh Chander, 17, 20, 166
    Lake of Palms, The, 166
    Maharashtra Jeevan Prabhat, 17
    Slave Girl of Agra, The, 166
Dutt, Toru, 17, 33n

*The East and West Must Meet ; A
    Symposium*, 95n
Eccentric Design, The, 33n
Eliade, Mircea, 143
Eliot, T. S., 70, 128, 130
Elliot, Brian, 54
Ellison, Ralph, 85
English in India, 16n
English Teacher, The, 191, 192
Esmond in India, 63
Ezekiel, Nissim, 95

*Fables of Identity : Studies in Poetic
    Mythology*, 162n

Financial Expert, The, 149

Flame of the Forest, The, 104-106, 126, 135, 136-139

Foreigner, The, 203

Forster, E. M., 27, 84

Frazer, 130, 153

Frye, Northrop, 26-27, 130, 163*n*

Futehally, Zeenat, 54

Future of English in India, The, 14

Galagnath, 20

Gandhi, M. K., 41, 60, 61, 62, 166, 199

Gangopadhyay, Shyamal, 202

Ganguly, J. M., 64

Garh Ala Pan Simha Gela, 20

Gerow, Edwin, 162, 163*n*, 164*n*

Ghar, 23

Ghose, Sarath Kumar, 20, 33*n*, 64

Ghose, Sudhin N., 103, 104, 132, 133, 134-139, 151, 163, 204, 209

   Cradle of the Clouds, The, 132, 133, 136, 155, 156, 162*n*

   Flame of the Forest, The, 104-106, 126, 136-139

Ghosh, Aurobindo, 17

Ghosh, Manmohan, 17, 33*n*

Goddess Named Gold, A, 103, 172, 174, 204

Gogol, 70

Gokak, V. K., 14

Gokhale, Gopal Krishna, 166, 197

Golden Bough, The, 153, 163*n*

Gone Away, 13

Greene, Graham, 11

Guide, The, 102, 112, 119-126, 133, 150, 152, 196

Haas, William, 162*n*

Hamlet, 129

Handful of Rice, A, 209

Hemingway, Ernest, 195

Herzog, 89

He Who Rides a Tiger, 102, 112, 114-119, 126, 174

Hindupur, 20, 33*n*

History of Indian Philosophy, A, 127*n*

Hirwa Chapha, 21

Hosain, Attia, 26, 38, 50, 55, 81, 202

   Sunlight on a Broken Column, 26, 37, 38, 50-52, 71, 77, 79-82, 204

House for Mr Biswas, A, 168

Huckleberry Finn, 168

Human Idiom, The, 12

Hussain, Iqbalunnisa, 11

Indian Contribution to English Literature, 9

Indian Fiction in English, 11, 163*n*

Indian Writers in Conference, 95

Indian Writing in English, 9, 197

Indo-Anglian Literature, 9

Inquilab, 36, 37, 55, 58, 61, 199

In Transit, 37, 194, 204

In Memory of F. R. Firth, 210

Invisible Man, 85

I Shall Not Hear the Nightingale, 172, 184

I Take This Woman, 206

James, Henry, 27, 31, 37, 70, 161, 195

J. B., 162*n*

Jhabvala, Ruth Prawer, 16*n*, 63

Joshi, Arun, 203, 209

Joshi, Ila Chandra, 23

Joyce, James, 32, 128, 130

Jung, 132, 133

Just Flesh, 67

Kachru, Braj, 208

Kallol, 22, 33*n*, 130

Kalyani's Husband, 181

Kamala, A Story of Hindu Life, 33n
Kanchan Mruga, 21
Kandan, the Patriot, 22, 37, 197, 199
Kanetkar, Vasant, 23
Kantak, V. Y., 195, 210
Kanthapura, 36, 37, 38, 39, 43, 48,
    54, 60, 96, 97, 133, 134, 140-
    142, 145, 156, 169, 172, 173,
    176, 187, 188, 199, 204, 207
Karaka, D. F., 57, 66, 67, 69
Karmabhumi, 21
Karve, Irawati, 160
Khandekar, 21
    Kanchan Mruga, 21
    Hirwa Chapha, 21
    Don Mane, 21
Khatri, Devaki Nandan, 20
Kipling, Rudyard, 9
Kirevsky, 70
Kluckohn, Clyde, 72, 95
Kluckohn, Florence, 95
Krishna, Bal, 33n
Krishnamurthy, S. Y., 181, 182

Labangalata, 20
Lake of Palms, The, 166
Lal, Anand, 112, 114
    Seasons of Jupiter, 112-114
Lal, P., 127n
Lawrence, D. H., 159
Letters of Henry James, The, 95
Love of Kusuma, The, 33n

MacLeish, Archibald, 162n
Mahabharata, The, 39, 129, 132,
    133, 156, 157, 160, 161, 162n
Main Street, 11
Malgonkar, Manohar, 13, 36, 58,
    59, 67, 68, 69, 95, 170, 182, 183,
    185
    Bend in the Ganges, A, 36, 58, 59,
        60, 68
    Combat of Shadows, 68, 95, 170,
        182, 183
    Distant Drum, 58, 68, 77

Princes, The, 13, 68, 183
Maneater of Malgudi, The, 132,
    146-150, 156
Mandy, Shaun, 127n
Marath, Menon, 26, 204
Mardhekar, 23
Markandaya, Kamala, 10, 50, 54,
    80, 84, 103, 106, 108, 109, 170,
    205, 209
    Coffer Dams, The, 209
    Handful of Rice, A, 209
    Nectar in a Sieve, 204
    Nowhere Man, The, 209
    Possession, 103, 106, 126
    Silence of Desire, A, 103, 108,
        109-112, 126
    Some Inner Fury, 50-54, 71,
        77, 80-84
Martanda Varma, 20
McCutchion, David, 13, 16n, 93,
    162n, 178
Mehta, Naresh, 23
Melville, Herman, 70
Mitra, S. K., 20
Modern Indian Novel in English, The,
    12
Moraes, Dom, 13
Morning Face, The, 209
Morris, Charles, 73, 95
Mourning Becomes Electra, 128
Moving Finger, The, 9
Mukherjee, Bhudeb Chandra, 19
Mukhopadhyay, Shirshennu, 208
Murray, Gilbert, 129
Murugan, the Tiller, 22, 32, 65, 173,
    186, 197
Music for Mohini, 172, 173, 174, 179
Mysore Cha Wagh, 20

Nagarajan, K., 11, 46, 61, 67, 107,
    126, 173,
    Athawar House, 107, 204
    Chronicles of Kedaram, The, 37,
        46, 47, 48, 49, 61, 173, 199,
        204

Nagarajan, S., 13, 95, 163*n*, 178
Nagarjun, 30
Nahal, C. L., 16*n*
Naik, M. K., 14
Naipaul, V. S., 13, 16*n*
Nandkumar, Prema, 62
Narasimhaiah, C. D., 13
Narasimhan, Chakrabarti V., 163*n*
Narayan, R. K., 10, 11, 12, 13, 25,
    28, 30, 36, 38, 43, 61, 67, 69,
    80, 101, 102, 112, 119, 126,
    127, 133, 150, 152, 169, 185,
    186, 191, 196, 205, 207,
    209
    Bachelor of Arts, The, 11, 101,
        149, 192
    Dark Room, The, 133, 149
    English Teacher, The, 191, 192
    Financial Expert, The, 149
    Guide, The, 10, 102, 112, 119-
        126, 133, 150, 152, 196
    Maneater of Malgudi, The, 132,
        146-150, 156
    Vendor of Sweets, The, 209
    Waiting for the Mahatma, 38,
        40-43, 44, 61, 101, 196
Native Son, 31
Nectar in a Sieve, 204
New Day, The, 168
No Longer at Ease 86, 95
Novel in Modern India, The, 126*n*

Oaten, Edward Farley, 9
Ocean of Night, 209
O'Hara, John, 25
Old Woman and the Cow, The, 74,
    75, 76, 126, 158, 159, 175
O'Neill, Eugene, 128
One Virginity, 196

Pallisamaj, 21
Panchapakesa Ayyar, 20
Panchatantra, The, 18, 133
Parsons, T., 95
Payne, Robert, 16*n*

Passage to India, A, 27, 84
Pather Dabi, 21
Peacock Flute, The, 9
Phadke, N. S., 21
Pillai, Raman, 20
Pillai, Thakazhi Sivasankara, 206
*Portrait of the Artist as a Young
    Man*, 84
Possession, 103, 106, 126
Prem Chand, 21, 30, 159, 200
Prince of Destiny, The, 20, 33*n*, 64
Princes, The, 13, 68, 183
Private Life of an Indian Prince, 169,
    209
Purdah and Polygamy, 16*n*
Putul Nacher Itikatha, 127*n*

Quest for Myth, 162*n*

Rajan, B., 13, 31, 58, 65, 71, 77, 78,
    84, 86, 95, 133, 157, 164*n*, 181,
    193, 194
    Dark Dancer, The, 58, 77, 81,
        82, 84, 86, 87, 88, 96, 132, 133,
        156-158, 164*n*
    Too Long in the West, 78, 157,
        180, 193
Rajadhyaksha, M. V., 33*n*
Rajmohun's Wife, 33*n*, 166
Raj Singha, 20
Rao, Chalapati, 16*n*
Rao, Raja, 13, 36, 38, 39, 42, 43,
    60, 71, 89-94, 97, 106, 127*n*,
    132-135, 139, 141, 163*n*, 167,
    169, 172, 174, 176-178, 180,
    187, 188, 195, 196*n*, 199, 209
    Cat and Shakespeare, The, 98,
        99, 100, 126, 187, 188
    Cow of the Barricades, The, 42,
        139, 177, 178, 188
    Kanthapura, 36-39, 43, 48, 54,
        60, 96, 97, 133, 134, 140-142,
        145, 156, 169, 172, 173, 176,
        187, 188, 199, 204, 207

Serpent and the Rope, The, 42, 71, 77, 89-94, 98, 133, 135, 147-155, 177, 178, 188

Rama Rau, Santha, 71, 79, 80, 81, 85, 99, 170, 181, 186

Ramakrishnan, T., 33*n*

Ramayana, The, 39, 129, 131, 133, 160, 161, 162*n*

Ranade, 197

Ranchan, S. P., 13, 95

Ratri Cha Divas, 23

Razdan, B. M., 13, 95

Reddy, C. R., 11

Reid, Vic, 168

Remember the House, 71, 77, 79, 81, 82, 88, 99, 170, 181

Road, The, 108, 172, 173

Roy, Annanda Shankar, 76

Roy, Rammohun, 166

Sahgal, Nayantara, 38, 46, 48, 81, 101, 209

  Time to be Happy, A, 37, 38, 46, 48, 49, 50, 53, 77, 81, 82, 88, 101, 133

  Storm in Chandigarh, 209

Salinger, J. D., 85

Sampson, George, 33*n*

Sarabhai, Bharati, 27

Sathianandan, Krupabai, 33*n*

Schorer, Mark, 37

Seasons of Jupiter, 112-114

Serpent and the Rope, The, 42, 71, 77, 89-94, 98, 133, 135, 145-155, 177, 178, 188

Sevasadan, 21

Shadow from Ladakh, 209

Shils, Edward, 95

Silence of Desire, A, 103, 108, 109-112, 126

Singh, Bhupal, 9

Singh, Khushwant, 57, 172, 184, 206

Singh, Natwar, 162*n*

Sketch of Anglo-Indian Literature, A, 9

Slave Girl of Agra, The, 166

So Many Hungers, 174, 174, 179, 194

Some Inner Fury, 50, 51-54, 71, 77, 80-84, 88, 133

Spencer, Dorothy, 11, 159

Spencer, J., 197

Srinivasa Iyenger, K. R., 9, 10, 11, 14, 16*n*, 102, 197, 199

Steele, Flora Annie, 9

Steiner, George, 70, 95

Strange Case of Billy Biswas, The, 209, 210

Studies in Classical American Literature, 159

Sunlight on a Broken Column, 26, 37, 38, 50-52, 71, 77, 79-82, 204

Survey of Anglo-Indian Literature, A, 9

Sword and the Sickle, The, 26, 37, 43, 44, 45, 61, 171, 175, 199

Tagore, Rabindranath, 14, 21, 207

Taylor, Meadows, 9, 20

There Lay the City, 67

Things Fall Apart, 95*n*

Tilak, Balgangadhar, 166

Time to be Happy, A, 37, 38, 46, 48, 49, 50, 53, 77, 81, 82, 88, 101, 133

Tippoo Sultan, 20

Tolstoy, Leo, 70

Too Long in the West, 78, 157, 180, 193

Towards a General Theory of Action, 95

Train to Pakistan, 57

Tribute to E. M. Forster, 163*n*

Turgenev, 70

Ulysses, 128

Untouchable, 74, 76, 108

Unveiled Court, The, 20

Updike, John, 25, 162*n*

Vatsayan, S. H., 65, 201
Vedantam, the Clash of Traditions, 65
Vendor of Sweets, The, 209
Venkataramani, K. S., 22, 31, 65, 173, 174, 186, 187, 196
Verma, Bhagavati Charan, 21
Via Geneva, 209
Village, The, 45, 204
Vishnu Purana, 133
Voices in the City, 190, 202

Wadia, A. R., 14
Waiting for the Mahatma, 38, 40-43, 44, 61, 101, 196
Walcott, Derek, 168

Walsh, William, 12, 16n
Waste Land, The, 128
We Never Die, 58, 67
When East and West Meet, 64
Wounds of Spring, 26, 204
Wright, Richard, 31
Wundt, Wilhelm, 129

Yashpal, 30
Yeats, W. B., 130
Yoga Vasistha, 96
Yuganta, 164n

Zohra, 54, 55

Four Important Series on Indian Literature

ARNOLD HEINEMANN PUBLISHERS
(INDIA) PRIVATE LIMITED
AB/9 Safadargang Enclave, New Delhi-16

INDIAN WRITERS SERIES

General Editor : C. D. Narasimhaiah

This is a series of critical monographs in which leading scholars attempt analysis and evaluation of the representative works of Indian writers of English with a view to winning attention of such aspects of their work as the organisation of the material, the range and depth of experience that have gone into the organisation, the resources of language, especially the adequacy, for the purposes on hand, of English for the Indian writer, and the writer's awareness of his own tradition—individual, racial or national—which has shaped his work.

Twenty-eight volumes have been commissioned in the series and *the first eight volumes published are :*

1. MULK RAJ ANAND
   By M.K. Naik   Rs. 16.50

2. NIRAD C. CHAUDHURI
   By C. Paul Verghese   Rs. 10.00

3. MANOHAR MALGONKAR
   By G.S. Amur   Rs. 13.50

4. RAJA RAO
   By C.D. Narasimhaiah   Rs. 16.50

5. SUDHIN N. GHOSE
   By Shyamala A. Narayan   Rs. 13.50

6, R.K. NARAYAN
   by P.S. Sundaram   Rs. 13.50

7. BHABANI BHATTACHARYA
   By K.R. Chandrasekharan   Rs. 16.50

8. ANANDA K. COOMARASWAMI
   By P.S. Sastri   Rs. 16.50

   In preparation :

9. NISSIM EZEKIEL
   By Chetan Karnani

10. NAYANTARA SAHGAL
    By A.V. Krishna Rao

INDIAN NOVELS SERIES

General Editor : Ka Naa Subramanyam

Though Indian fiction in the various languages of India has had an innings of over a hundred years and has come of age, readers of India have not yet been exposed to it. An attempt is made in this series to present to readers both the work of the pioneers as well as the work of writers with definite modernistic trends, thus creating an image of Indian fiction that will be valid as a tradition.

The first two titles published in the series are :

1. ZERO
   By C. Radhakrishnan
   Translated from Malayalam

This book fully portrays how things physical in India tend to become metaphysical. Told with great art and intensity it is Indian fictional art at its best. Symbolic and serious, this novel will mould the image of Indian fiction in the right perspective.   Rs. 18.00

2. ONION PEEL
   By K.M. Trishanku

Written in English the novel portrays an existentialist situation with charm, vigour and completeness. A mature novelist who deals with the exciting theme of a man's impending loss of virility and the pre D-Day g.ut of girls making the fulness of a living.

Rs. 20.00

Forthcoming volumes in the series are :

3. TRICKY GROND
   By Indra Parthasarthy
   Translated from Tamil

4. THE VIRGIN FISH OF BABU GHAT
   By Lokenath Bhattacharya
   Translated from Bengali
   By Meenakshi Mukherjee

5. SHUL AMITH
   By Meera Mahadevan
   Translated from Hindi

6. AROGYANIKETAN
   By Tara Sarkar Banerjee
   Translated from Bengali
   By Enakshi Chatterjee

INDIAN STORIES SERIES

The short story is held to be the form most effectively practised by Indian writers. Beautiful, emotional themes, superb craftsmanship, rich sentiments inform the world of the short stories written in English and the Indian languages. This world of the Indian short story will be made available to the reader in English for the first time systematically.

The first two volumes published in the series are :

1. DEATH OF A SONG
   By Kartar Singh Duggal

A new collection of short stories by one of the most outstanding writers in modern Punjabi literature. Besides his mastery and control of the form, his range of subjects is remarkable. The stories have been translated with great care to preserve the local colour in which they are so rich and make immensely rewarding reading.   Rs. 16.50

2. THE HOUSE IN THE HILLS
   By Sujatha Bala Subramanian

Sujatha's stories range from tales of simple village folk to the highly contemporary scene in the stream of consciousness style. For the last fifteen years, her stories have appeared in many English periodicals and journals in India and England including Argosy. She has twice won the Roscoe Award for the best short story in the U.K. and the commonwealth.   Rs. 12.00

The third volume to be published in the series is :

3. MODERN INDIAN SHORT STORIES
   Edited by Suresh Kohli

A collection of twenty remarkable stories from the best known Indian writers writing in various languages including English with an introduction to each story.   Rs. 25.00

INDIAN POETRY SERIES

In this series will appear the most distinguished of India's contemporary and non-contemporary poets, some writing in English, others translated from the Indian languages.

The first two volumes published in the series are :

1. **ARANGETRAL**
   By S. Santhi

The poems in this selection are both profoundly Indian and wholly modern. The range of vocabulary, rhythm and imagery is impressive, and so are the tone and texture. C. Day Lewis and Stephen Spender have spoken highly of Mr. Santhi's poetic talent.

Rs. 20.00

2. **MODERN INDIAN POETRY**
   Edited by Pritish Nandy

Here for the first time is an outstanding anthology of modern Indian Poetry that attempts to capture the challenging complexity of the contemporary literary scene in India. Sixty poets, representing all the major languages, are here.

Rs. 35.00

SYMBOL OF BEST BUY IN

INDIAN LITERATURE

ARNOLD HEINEMANN PUBLISHERS
(INDIA) PRIVATE LIMITED